HOREMHEB

HOREMHEB

THE FORGOTTEN PHARAOH

CHARLOTTE BOOTH

AMBERLEY

First published 2009
Reprinted 2010

Amberley Publishing plc
Cirencester Road, Chalford,
Stroud, Gloucestershire, GL6 8PE

www.amberley-books.com

© Charlotte Booth 2009

The right of Charlotte Booth to be identified as the Author of this work has been asserted in accordance with the Copyrights, Designs and Patents Act 1988.

All rights reserved. No part of this book may be reprinted or reproduced or utilised in any form or by any electronic, mechanical or other means, now known or hereafter invented, including photocopying and recording, or in any information storage or retrieval system, without the permission in writing from the Publishers.

British Library Cataloguing in Publication Data.
A catalogue record for this book is available from the British Library.

ISBN 978-1-84868-687-8

Typesetting and Origination by Diagraf (www.diagraf.net)
Printed in Great Britain

CONTENTS

Acknowledgements		6
Chronology		7
Horemheb's timeline		9
Illustrations		10
Introduction		15
Chapter 1	Setting the Scene	19
Chapter 2	A King is Born	32
Chapter 3	Horemheb's Early Career	45
Chapter 4	Ascension to the Throne	63
Chapter 5	Horemheb – Lord of the Two Lands	85
Chapter 6	Restoring the Golden Era	95
Chapter 7	The End of an Era	124
Chapter 8	Aftermath	139
Notes		148
Further Reading		155
Index		159

ACKNOWLEDGMENTS

I have been writing this book on and off for many years, and therefore there are a number of people who have encouraged me in the past not to give up on *Horemheb*. In the production of the book I would like to thank Richard Lunn and Peter Billington for their comments on the manuscript which were gratefully received, and John Poulter for his initial advice on publication. Thomas Vivian and the team at Amberley have been very encouraging and they have done a great job with the finished product. Some images and illustrations were kindly provided by Robert Partridge, Peter Robinson, Clare Banks, and the Petrie Museum but I would like to give special thanks to Brian Billington for his help with sourcing illustrations and photographs, as well as being generally supportive and understanding. There are many other people who have offered advice and information, and they have not been forgotten, but are too plentiful to list here. I hope *Horemheb* was worth the wait.

CHRONOLOGY

PREDYNASTIC PERIOD

The Badarian period – 4400-4000 BCE
Maadian period – 4000-3300 BCE
The Amratian period – 4000-3500 BCE
The Gerzean period – 3500-3200 BCE
The Negada III period – 3200-3050 BCE

EARLY DYNASTIC PERIOD

Dynasty 0 – 3150-3050 BCE
Dynasty 1 – 3050-2890 BCE
Dynasty 2 – 2890-2686 BCE

OLD KINGDOM

Dynasty 3 – 2686-2613 BCE
Dynasty 4 – 2613-2500 BCE
Dynasty 5 – 2498-2345 BCE
Dynasty 6 – 2345-2333 BCE

FIRST INTERMEDIATE PERIOD

Dynasties 7 & 8 – 2180-2160 BCE
Dynasties 9 & 10 – 2160-2040 BCE

MIDDLE KINGDOM

Dynasty 11 – 2134-1991 BCE
Dynasty 12 – 1991-1782 BCE

SECOND INTERMEDIATE PERIOD

Dynasty 13 – 1782-1650 BCE
Dynasty 14 – ?
Dynasty 15 – 1663-1555 BCE

Dynasty 16 – 1663-1555 BCE
Dynasty 17 – 1663-1570 BCE

NEW KINGDOM

Dynasty 18 – 1570-1293 BCE
   Ahmose 1570-1546
   Amenhotep I 1551-1524
   Thutmosis I 1524-1518
   Thutmosis II 1518-1504
   Thutmosis III 1504-1450
   Hatshepsut 1498-1483
   Amenhotep II 1453-1419
   Thutmosis IV 1419-1386
   Amenhotep III 1386-1349
   Amenhotep IV/Akhenaten 1350-1334
   Smenkhkare 1336-1333
   Tutankhamun 1333-1324
   Ay 1324-1321
   Horemheb 1323-1308

Dynasty 19 – 1308-1185 BCE
   Ramses I 1308-1306

Dynasty 20 – 1185 – 1070 BCE

THIRD INTERMEDIATE PERIOD

High Priests (Thebes) – 1080-945 BCE
Dynasty 21 (Tanis) – 1069-945 BCE
Dynasty 22 (Tanis) – 945-715 BCE
Dynasty 23 (Leontopolis) – 818-715 BCE
Dynasty 24 (Sais) – 727-715 BCE
Dynasty 25 (Nubians) – 747-656 BCE
Dynasty 26 (Sais) – 664-525 BCE

LATE PERIOD

Dynasty 27 (Persian) – 525-404 BCE
Dynasty 28 – 404-399 BCE
Dynasty 29 – 399-380 BCE
Dynasty 30 – 380-343 BCE
Dynasty 31 – 343-332 BCE

GRAECO-ROMAN PERIOD

Macedonian Kings – 332-305 BCE
Ptolemaic Period – 305-30 BCE

HOREMHEB'S TIMELINE

In the absence of accurate dates for all events only dates have been stated for those which are known or are likely.

1362 BCE	Horemheb is born
	Horemheb starts school
	Horemheb starts military training
1350 BCE	Akhenaten becomes *King*
1345 BCE	Gebel el Silsileh expedition (year 5)
	Horemheb and Amenia marry
	Hittite problems in the Near East
1347 BCE	Death of Akhenaten
	Smenkhkare comes to the throne
1333 BCE	Tutankhamun becomes *King*
	Rise in career to *Royal Scribe* and *General*
	Battles of Tutankhamun
	Tutankhamun names Horemheb as *Deputy King*
1324 BCE	Tutankhamun dies
1324 BCE	Ay comes to the throne
	Horemheb is named as heir
	Amenia dies
	Horemheb marries Mutnodjmet
1321 BCE	Horemheb is crowned *King*
1321 BCE	Celebrates the Festival of Ptah at Karnak (year 1)
	Begins the Restoration Programme
	Horemheb travels the length of Egypt hearing complaints
	Mutnodjmet dies in childbirth
	Horemheb names Prameses as heir
	Horemheb built temple at Abahuda
	Horemheb starts building at Qantir
1306 BCE	Horemheb dies (year 15)
1306 BCE	Ramses I becomes *King*
	Horemheb is worshipped as a god

ILLUSTRATIONS

FIGURES

1. Map of Egypt and the Near East. *Produced courtesy of Peter Robinson*
2. Statue of Amenhotep III (Luxor Museum). *Photograph by the author*
3. Colossi of Memnon of Amenhotep III. *Photograph by the author*
4. Statue of Akhenaten (Louvre Museum). *Photograph by the author*
5. Boundary Stela at Amarna. *Photograph by the author*
6. Tomb of Paatenemheb at Amarna. *Drawing by the author after Davies 1908, pl XIII*
7. Horemheb receiving shebyu collars, Saqqara. *Drawing by the author after Martin 1991*
8. Weapons and model shields (Luxor Museum). *Photograph by the author*
9. Amenhotep II practicing with a copper target and chariot (Luxor Museum). *Photograph by the author*
10. Ostacon showing military training (Luxor Museum). *Photograph by the author*
11. Amenia and Horemheb detail from Saqqara (British Museum). *Photograph courtesy of Brian Billington*
12. Dyad of Horemheb and Amenia. Saqqara (Luxor Museum). *Photograph by the author*
13. Sementawy from Saqqara. *Drawing by he author after Martin 1991*
14. Royal Body Guard from an Amarna tomb. *Photograph by the author*
15. North Riverside Palace of Amarna and the military area. *Drawing by Brian Billington*
16. Horemheb making offerings to Thoth from Gebel el Silsileh. *Drawing by the author*
17. Interpretation scene from Saqqara. *Drawing by the author after Martin 1991*
18. Chariot battle of Tutankhamun, from a reused block at the mortuary temple of Horemheb. *Drawing by the author after Johnson 1992, fig 15*
19. An Egyptian soldier tying up a Libyan captive. Reused blocks from the mortuary temple of Horemheb. *Drawing by the author after Johnson 1992, fig 11*
20. Victory parade of Tutankhamun after the Asiatic battle. *Drawing by the author after Johnson 1992*
21. River parade of Tutankhamun. *Drawing by the author after Johnson 1992 figure 22*
22. Feasting from the Memphite tomb of Horemheb. *Drawing by the author after Martin 1991*
23. Memphite tomb of Horemheb. *Drawing by Brian Billington after Martin 1993*
24. Internal structure (upper level) of the Memphite tomb of Horemheb. *Drawing by Brian Billington after Martin 1978*
25. Internal structure (lower level) of the Memphite tomb of Horemheb. *Drawing by Brian Billington after Martin 1978*

26 Amun Min and Horemheb (British Museum). *Photograph courtesy of Brian Billington*
27 Ay and Tiy; Ay's tomb Amarna. *Photograph by the author*
28 Tutankhamun's death mask. *Photograph by Clare V. Banks*
29 Horemheb protected by Amun (Luxor Museum). *Photograph by the author*
30 Foreign delegation at the coronation of Ay from Saqqara (Louvre Museum). *Photograph by the author*
31 Cartouches of Ay
32 The mortuary temple of Ay, Medinet Habu. *Drawing by Brian Billington after Hölscher 1939*
33 Dancers at the Opet Festival of Tutankhamun usurped by Horemheb, Luxor Temple. *Photograph by the author*
34 Soldiers at the Opet Festival of Tutankhamun usurped by Horemheb, Luxor Temple. *Photograph by the author*
35 Scene from tomb of Ptahemhat-Ty (Berlin Museum). *Drawing by the author*
36 Breaking the Red-Pots, Saqqara. *Drawing by the author after Martin 1991*
37 Mutnodjmet and her nieces. *Drawing by the author after Tyldesley 2005*
38 Mutnodjmet shabti figure (British Museum). *Photograph courtesy of Brian Billington*
39 Mutnodjmet as a sphinx from the coronation statue in Turin. *Drawing by the author*
40 Horemheb and Amun, detail (Luxor Museum). *Photograph by the author*
41 Cartouches of Horemheb
42 Horemheb and Atum (Luxor Museum). *Photograph by the author*
43 Second Pylon at Karnak. *Photograph by Brian Billington*
44 Hypostyle Hall of Horemheb, Ramses I, Sety I and Ramses II, Karnak. *Photograph by the author*
45 Back of the tenth Pylon at Karnak. *Photograph by the author*
46 Ninth Pylon at Karnak. *Photograph by Brian Billington*
47 Talatat blocks within the body of the ninth pylon at Karnak. *Photograph by the author*
48 Reconstruction of talatat blocks (Luxor Museum). *Photograph by the author*
49 Festival Hall of Amenhotep II between pylon nine and ten at Karnak. *Photograph by the author*
50 Horemheb making offerings to a god from Gebel el Silsileh. *Drawing by the author*
51 Opet Festival of Tutankhamun usurped by Horemheb. Luxor Temple. *Photograph by the author*
52 Temple of Thutmosis III at Deir el Bahri (left of Hatshepsut's temple). *Photograph by the author*
53 The mortuary temple of Tutankhamun, Ay, and Horemheb at Medinet Habu. *Photograph by the author*
54 Horemheb as Atum (?) (National Museum Alexandria). *Photograph by the author*
55 Horemheb as Hapy (British Museum). *Photograph by the author*
56 Speos Temple at Gebel el Silsileh. *Drawn by Brian Billington after Hari 1964*
57 Horemheb suckling from Taweret at Gebel el Silsileh. *Drawing by the author*
58 The temple of Abahuda. *Drawing by Brian Billington after Sirdo 2006*
59 Coronation of Horemheb from Abahuda. *Drawing by the author*
60 Bows and arrows form the tomb of Tutankhamun (Luxor Museum). *Photograph by the author*
61 Kushite campaign from Gebel el Silsileh. *Drawing by the author*

62 Acacia plaque from KV57. *Drawing by the author after Davies 2001*
63 Amphora jar of Horemheb (Petrie Museum UC19160). *Photograph courtesy of the Friends of the Petrie Museum*
64 Door Jamb from the Memphite tomb of Horemheb (British Museum). *Photograph courtesy of Clare V. Banks*
65 Valley of the King's tomb of Horemheb (KV57). *Drawing by Brian Billington after Reeves & Wilkinson 1996*
66 Fragment of embalming table (British Museum). *Photograph courtesy of Brian Billington*
67 Wooden deity statues. Valley of the Kings (British Museum). *Photograph courtesy of Brian Billington*
68 Turtle-Headed Diety. KV57 Valley of the Kings. *Photograph courtesy of Brian Billington*
69 The mortuary temple of Horemheb. *Drawing by Brian Billington after Hölscher 1939*
70 Priestly Ramesside family worshipping the deified Horemheb, Saqqara. *Drawing by the author after Martin 1991*
71 Ramses I as a *General* receiving shebyu collars, Saqqara. *Drawing by the author after Martin 1991*
72 Cartouches of Ramses I
73 Valley of the King's tomb of Ramses 1 (KV16). *Drawing by Brian Billington after Reeves & Wilkinson 1996*
74 Mummy of Ramses I (?) (Luxor Museum). *Photograph by the author*
75 Scene from the tomb of Roy. *Drawing by the author*

Illustrations

COLOUR PLATES

1. Akhenaten (Luxor Museum). *Photograph by the author*
2. Nefertiti worshipping the Aten (Ashmolean Museum). *Photograph by the author*
3. Dyad of Amenia and Horemheb from Saqqara (British Museum). *Photograph courtesy of Brian Billington*
4. Door jamb from the Memphite tomb of Horemheb (British Museum). *Photograph courtesy of Clare V. Banks*
5. Horemheb as a scribe. *Photograph courtesy of Robert Partridge, Egypt Picture Library*
6. Tomb of Tutankhamun showing the opening of mouth ceremony, and his wife Ankhesenamun making offerings of water to him. *Photograph by the author*
7. Medinet Habu with the mortuary temples of Horemheb, Ay and Tutankhamun outside of the enclosure wall. *Photograph by the author*
8. Mourners at the funeral of Horemheb from Saqqara (Louvre Museum). *Photograph by the author*
9. Canopic jar of Mutnodjmet. Saqqara (British Museum). *Photograph courtesy of Brian Billington*
10. Coronation Statue of Horemheb. *Photograph courtesy of Robert Partridge, Egypt Picture Library*
11. Detail of Horemheb (KV57). *Photograph courtesy of Robert Partridge, Egypt Picture Library*
12. Tutankhamun/Horemheb as Amun. Luxor Temple. *Photograph by the author*
13. Ankhesenamun/Mutnodjmet as Amunet. Luxor Temple. *Photograph by the author*
14. Rear of Pylon Ten at Karnak. *Photograph courtesy of Brian Billington*
15. Opet Festival of Tutankhamun usurped by Horemheb. Luxor Temple. *Photograph by the author*
16. Horemheb as Hapy (detail) from the British Museum. *Photograph by the author*
17. Sarcophagus of Horemheb in KV57 with the Book of Gates in the background. *Photograph courtesy of Robert Partridge, Egypt Picture Library*
18. Horemheb making offerings to Hathor (KV57). *Photograph courtesy of Robert Partridge, Egypt Picture Library*
19. Horemheb making offerings to Osiris (KV57). *Photograph courtesy of Robert Partridge, Egypt Picture Library*
20. Canopic Jar lid of Horemheb (KV57). *Photograph courtesy of Robert Partridge, Egypt Picture Library*
21. Coffin of Horemheb/Ramses I? (Cairo Museum). *Photograph courtesy of the Robert Partridge, Egypt Picture Library*
22. Osiris bed lid bearing the face of Horemheb (KV57). *Photograph courtesy of Robert Partridge, Egypt Picture Library*
23. Tutankhamun/Horemheb statue from the the mortuary temple at Thebes. *Photograph courtesy of Robert Partridge, Egypt Picture Library*
24. Funerary Statue of Ramses I, Valley of the Kings. *Photograph courtesy of Brian Billington*
25. Abydos King List. *Photograph by the author*

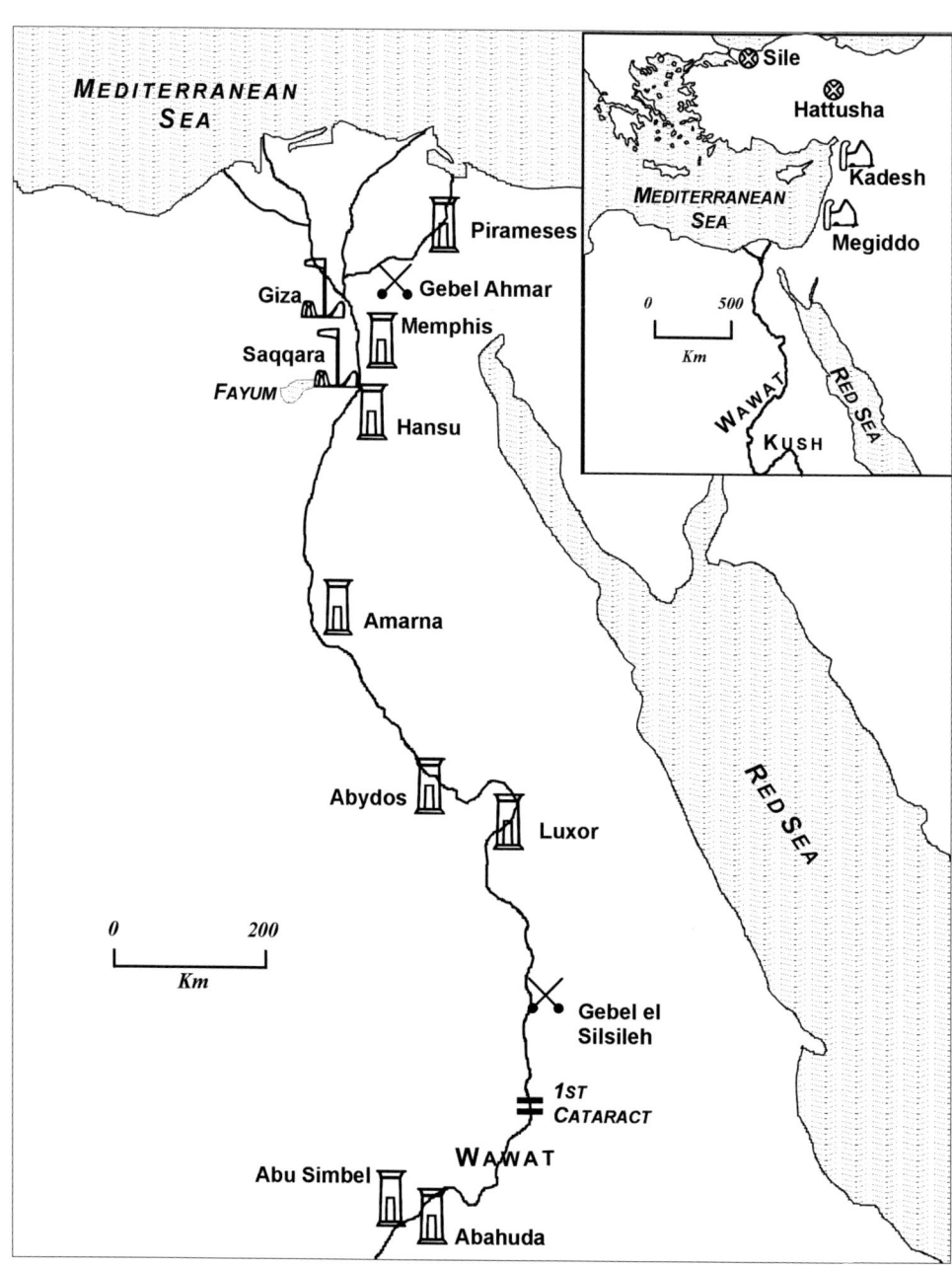

1 Map of Egypt and the Near East. *Produced courtesy of Peter Robinson*

INTRODUCTION

Throughout the history of any nation there are always a few individuals who stand out from the crowd; whether they are known for a heroic or criminal deed or because of an early demise, the reason varies. Egypt is no different. Many people have heard of Tutankhamun and his wonderful tomb discovered in 1922 by Howard Carter and Lord Carnarvon; one of the most important archaeological finds of the twentieth century. The tomb produced thousands of objects, many of gold, catching the attention of not only archaeologists but lay people alike, and was one of the first sites to be excavated in a truly scientific manner. Carter insisted all objects were photographed and recorded *in situ* and then when removed, photographed and drawn again, producing detailed records of all the tomb contents. These elaborate records are currently at the Griffith Institute, Oxford[1] and show the dedication of Carter to the project. Although the tomb contents, especially the golden mask are world famous, most people know very little about the *King* himself and his life as an individual. This led me to write *The Boy Behind the Mask*,[2] a biography of the *King*'s life and his reign rather than focusing on his death and burial. I wanted to make Tutankhamun become a personality; someone we could relate to, enabling us to understand him and his world better.

Many people have also heard of Tutankhamun's predecessor, Akhenaten and his wife Nefertiti, with numerous groups adopting one or both figures as their own to fulfil or reinforce their own political agendas. The bust of Nefertiti in Berlin, for example, has been adopted by Afrocentrists as proof of black involvement in world history, even though the family background of Nefertiti is unknown and any black ancestry is unproven. Some Christians and Jews see Akhenaten as the first monotheist in history. However this idea is based on the misunderstanding of Akhenaten and his religious revolution. He did not actually *disbelieve* in the pantheon of Egyptian gods, he simply chose to revere the Aten above all others. In addition only he and the royal family were allowed to worship the Aten. Everyone else worshiped Akhenaten and Nefertiti who were considered divine and part of a triad with the Aten. This meant there were *three* gods worshipped at the time, not one. Akhenaten has also been adopted by Marfan's Syndrome charities as a potential sufferer of the disease; based purely on the highly stylised artistic representations of the period. Without the body of Akhenaten there is no evidence that he suffered from any disease, and the artistic representations are not enough to base such diagnosis on (*colour plate 1*).

Many books, articles, and television programmes have been produced about these two popular figures, Tutankhamun and Akhenaten, often from different angles; presenting Akhenaten as a megalomaniac, a spiritual man, or a poet, and Tutankhamun always as a pawn in the game of older officials, who was murdered as soon as he came of age, potentially at a time when he was making his own decisions in conflict to those of his advisors. It was only in 2005 that the evidence for the murder of Tutankhamun was proved to be greatly exaggerated, and in fact evidence suggests he died of an accident. Although the theories vary, one thing is almost certain;

one figure who although key, only plays a small part, if included at all is Horemheb. Although a prominent figure in the story of both Akhenaten and Tutankhamun, Horemheb is a little known character. He is represented in popular commentaries on the Amarna period in one of three ways; he is either overlooked altogether, portrayed as the murderer of Tutankhamun and therefore an ambitious man, or he is used as a means of rounding off the story of the Amarna period into a tidy conclusion. In fiction he is also portrayed thus, although this is always as a contrasting figure to the main protagonists, Akhenaten or Tutankhamun. In Paul Doherty's trilogy about Akhenaten, he focuses on the military aspect of Horemheb and describes him as *'the great warrior, with his thickset body, square stolid face and the eyes of a ferocious panther'*,[3] a mountain of a man, of impressive appearance:

> He proved himself to be a born fighter, a skilled archer, excellent with hand weapons. By now he had filled out, and sported strong muscular shoulders and arms, a slim waist, powerful thighs and legs. Nothing seemed to trouble him, neither the heat of the midday sun nor the biting cold of desert nights. He was a man born with the breath of Montu in him.[4]

He is also presented in this trilogy as a cold, unfeeling and ambitious man, a person one would want as an ally rather than an enemy. Naguib Mahfouz, the Egyptian novelist, in *Dweller in Truth*[5] presents Horemheb as a maintainer of order over chaos. A modern representation of President Mubarak, and Akhenaten as President Sadat. Agatha Christie adds her own take to the story with Horemheb as a stereotypical British General boring people with the tales of fighting old 'fuzzy wuzzy' using improvised props.[6] Although each author has a distinct way of presenting this enigmatic character, the relationship between him and Akhenaten or Tutankhamun is always considered of more importance than the character himself. It is always clear when reading about Horemheb to ascertain whether the author likes or dislikes him which is often based on stereotypes and assumptions. Each fictionalisation is as diverse as the academic characterisation of Horemheb; but which is closest to the truth? This is what this volume will hope to answer.

It has become apparent that Horemheb deserves more attention than he is traditionally given. It is easy to forget when writing or reading about people so far in the past, in this case over 3000 years, that they were all complex characters with motivations, emotions and personal histories and therefore cannot be categorised as either one thing or another. People today cannot be classified as one thing (whether it be vengeful, ambitious, or diplomatic) and neither should those in the past. The reason people of the past are treated in this way, is because the evidence available means there are often large gaps in many aspects of their lives, meaning conjecture needs to be employed. This does not indicate that such biographies are not worth the effort. On the contrary, they can be interesting, diverse and lively, helping to bring the characters to life and add another piece to the jigsaw that is Egyptian history.

No individual, especially one as diverse and important as Horemheb, should be treated as little more than a literary tool in the life of 'so-called' more important characters. He has a story to tell of his own, although it cannot be told in isolation of the lives of Akhenaten, Smenkhkare, Tutankhamun, Ay and even the later Ramses II as their lives are closely intertwined.

Horemheb's representation as the final *King* of the eighteenth dynasty and a tidy end to the upheaval of the Amarna period is a relatively modern construction based on the writings of Greek historian Manetho, (third century BCE), and not a role the ancient Egyptians bestowed upon him. Manetho introduced the dynasty system as we know it, and he melded the eighteenth and nineteenth dynasties together, which have only later been separated into two. Africanus (also writing in the third century BCE) attributed sixteen *Kings* to the eighteenth dynasty (which he termed the Kings of Diospolis) with Horemheb as the fourteenth followed by Ramses I and Merenptah.[7] He has omitted Ramses II, presumably because he did not have information about him, showing these sources are at best greatly flawed.

Horemheb was seen by the ancients as the start of the new empire, and the Ramesside period, after the chaotic era of the Amarna kings. However in modern works it is easier to start the Ramesside period with Ramses I totally obliterating Horemheb from the beginning of the historical high point which is the nineteenth dynasty. Ramses I would have remained a *General* in the army until his death, to be followed in this career by his son and grandson, if Horemheb had not named him as the heir to the throne in the absence of children of his own. Rather than being the end of the Amarna period Horemheb paved the way for the Ramesside dynasty choosing his *General* as heir, because he already had a son, Sety, and a grandson who was later to become Ramses II. This guaranteed the new dynasty would continue. Horemheb believed Ramses and his family would bring his dream of a traditional Egypt, with the reinstated religion, firm politics and safe environment, to fruition, and that he would continue the work he started and stabilised during his 15-year reign. Had he lived he would not have been disappointed with his choice. If he had not chosen Ramses as his heir, the throne would have been left open to usurpation from any power-hungry individual; something Horemheb wanted to avoid. How different Egyptian history would have been if Ramses II had simply been a *General* in the army rather than *King*.

The young Ramses II may have met the elderly king Horemheb before his grandfather took over the throne, even though he was very young at the time. It is also likely that Ramses II was regaled throughout his childhood with tales of this king and the boon bestowed on the Ramesside family. Once Ramses II was on the throne, Horemheb was deified, and numerous offerings and dedications to his deified form were made, showing the importance of Horemheb to his family and the gratitude they felt to him.

This strong connection between Horemheb and the nineteenth dynasty is either played down or ignored entirely in most publications. It is for this reason that I have written this book. Horemheb, to me, was an astute career man and diplomat who worked his way up from an average middle-class up-bringing, through the military ranks, to the most important position in Egypt; that of king. I have always been intrigued as to how he managed to secure this position from such humble origins and he was either blessed with luck or achieved it through diplomacy, skill and dedication. The representation of him as an ambitious cad, who turned to murder to secure his place on the throne, never really rang true with the available evidence about his rise to power. Horemheb survived and continued to rise in influence and wealth during four very different reigns; that of Akhenaten, Smenkhkare, Tutankhamun and Ay, whilst remaining loyal to each of them, gaining their trust and maintaining and improving his position of power. This either shows a genuine individual who was charismatic and trustworthy or a duplicitous man who was clever and deceitful, convincing each king of his loyalty whilst being loyal only to himself. Perhaps he was a combination of the two. Whichever characteristics are correct it shows there is clearly more to Horemheb than presented in the popular publications and historical fiction about the Amarna period, showing he does indeed warrant a volume dedicated only to him rather than a paragraph or at most a chapter. Therefore my purpose in researching and writing about his life is to unravel the mystery surrounding him, and to flesh out the complicated layers of this intriguing individual. Through the exploration of official texts, excavation of his tombs, monuments, statues and general archaeological and textual evidence of the Amarna period I am able to put together a full biography of Horemheb, as well as place him appropriately within the historical context of Egypt.

Not only will this biography give the reader a fuller understanding of the royal court of Amarna, and of Tutankhamun and how it differed from that of Horemheb, but will also investigate how this influenced the reign of the first two Ramses' and the Ramesside period on the whole. In short, I will be giving Horemheb the recognition he deserves as the founder of the nineteenth dynasty, raising his profile and making his name live forever.

CHAPTER 1
SETTING THE SCENE

Horemheb ruled Egypt for perhaps 15 years (1323-1308 BCE), at the end of the eighteenth dynasty, one of the most successful dynasties of Egyptian history. This dynasty was also one of noteworthy rulers such as Ahmose, Hatshepsut, and Thutmosis III before the heretic king Akhenaten and the Amarna period. The history of the eighteenth dynasty is one of tradition and expansion and this is the Egypt Horemheb re-created after the changes imposed by the Amarna kings. The progression of the eighteenth dynasty is a circular one starting with the Hyksos rule at the end of the seventeenth dynasty and their expulsion by Ahmose, the first king of the New Kingdom and the eighteenth dynasty, followed by the empire building of Thutmosis III and complex international relations of Amenhotep III. The latter years of Amenhotep III saw a decline in these international relationships which were further abandoned during the reign of his son, Akhenaten. Egypt gradually started to fall into further decline at the death of this king, which may have proved disastrous had Horemheb not grasped the nettle, bringing the dynasty around full circle by following Ahmose in bringing Egypt back from chaos to an era of tradition and power.

The reign of Horemheb is important for his restoration of Egyptian values and not just as a tidy ending to the Amarna period. Therefore in order to understand the extent of the changes made by Akhenaten and therefore what Horemheb needed to do to correct it, it is essential to understand what Egypt was like before he came to the throne. This will enable us to identify the extent to which Horemheb achieved a traditional rule, a traditional Egypt and a traditional religion before he died.

Horemheb was raised with the traditional religion, and the pantheon of gods, with the solar deity Amun-Ra as the supreme deity. The pantheon comprised hundreds of gods, some specific to certain areas, or associated with particular traits or characteristics. There was a deity to appeal to everyone, from the king down to the lowliest illiterate farmer. Horemheb and all other young boys were no doubt raised on stories of great kings gone by and it was the achievements of these kings that provide the key to the motivations behind the acts and policies of Horemheb both as diplomat and as king.

The founder of the eighteenth dynasty and the New Kingdom was Ahmose I, the son of Seqenenre Tao II of the seventeenth dynasty (c.1574 BCE), who was ruler of Thebes whilst the Hyksos rulers dominated the north. They had ruled Egypt for over a century, rising to power from the Asiatic community that were settled in the Delta region. As the power of the Hyksos gradually moved southwards, Seqenenre Tao II began a campaign to expel them. After his own death at the hands of the Hyksos, the campaign was continued and completed by Seqenenre's sons Kamose and Ahmose I. The Hyksos campaign is recorded on the Kamose stela which was originally set up at Karnak temple. Kamose pushed the Hyksos king, Apophis and his army northwards back towards Avaris, their capital in the Delta, resulting in a siege outside the fortified city. Kamose stood outside the reinforced walls of Avaris taunting Apophis who was barricaded inside. Apophis refused to fight, so Kamose returned to Thebes claiming a triumph. Although Kamose did not capture Avaris his campaign was considered a success. At the death of Kamose, his brother Ahmose continued with the campaign, against the new Hyksos king Khamudy. In Ahmose's campaign he first took Sile on the Egypt-Sinai border, cutting contact between the Hyksos and Canaan, as precaution against reinforcements arriving from this region. Then he besieged and captured Avaris. In the tomb of Ahmose, son of Ebana at El Kab it describes how the king drove the Hyksos out of Avaris and chased them until they reached Sharuhen. There is also evidence that all the towns on the way to Sharuhen were sacked by the Egyptians. After a three year siege, Ahmose finally defeated the Hyksos and returned to Egypt. Ahmose recorded his victory over the Hyksos at his temple at Abydos. Due to his heroic deeds in the fight against the Hyksos Ahmose was revered by later Egyptians for freeing Egypt from the chaos of foreign rulers, and restoring Egypt to its former glory by founding a new dynasty and era.

The eighteenth dynasty continued to grow and expand, reaching a pinnacle during the reign of Thutmosis III, the son of Thutmosis II and a secondary wife called Isis. His father died when Thutmosis III was still an infant, and therefore unable to rule independently. A marriage was arranged between his father's widow, his stepmother and aunt, Hatshepsut. For over 20 years Hatshepsut and Thutmosis III ruled as co-regents although for the majority of this period Hatshepsut ruled Egypt as king, pushing the young Thutmosis III aside. Although Hatshepsut went against tradition by shunning her natural role as queen for the more powerful role of king, she was a successful king and would have been revered had she been male. During this time Thutmosis III spent his childhood and teenage years training in the army, until the death of Hatshepsut in year 22 (1476 BCE) of their reign. At this time he took over the throne as a fully-grown adult and military leader and continued to rule Egypt for over 20 years as sole ruler. Thutmosis III spent his adult life fighting and claiming land in the name of Egypt, leaving elaborate military records telling of his exploits in Syria; the most noteworthy being the battle of Megiddo, in the first year of his sole rule. The king of Kadesh in Palestine was gathering an army with which to attack Egypt, and was occupying the fortified town of Megiddo, strategically placed for trade and protection. Thutmosis III and the Egyptian army travelled to Megiddo, attacking the Syrian army. The Syrians fled to within the walls of the fortifications, leaving the Egyptians outside. They lay siege to the fortified town for seven months before it fell to the Egyptians. The Egyptian army then swept across the region capturing a further 119 towns[1] adding to the expanding Empire of the Thutmoside line. Twenty years later he achieved his final victory, capturing Tunip and Kadesh on the Orontes, completing the Egyptian domination of Syria which lasted from the reign of Thutmosis III to that of Ramses III. These kings were of military background and training and all royal sons were trained in these skills.[2]

Continuing down the Thutmoside line of kings was the grandfather of Tutankhamun, Amenhotep III (1386-1349 BCE) (2), the son of Thutmosis IV and a secondary wife Mutemwia. Amenhotep III and his Chief Royal Wife, Tiye, had at least six children; four daughters and two sons. The princes were raised at the palace at Memphis, the home of the sun-god Ra and were educated in typical royal pursuits such as hunting, charioteering and archery. Being raised at Memphis exposed them to a prominent solar cult, as near Memphis lay Heliopolis, the site of one of the creation myths, where the primeval mound rose from the primeval waters, producing the first dawn. At Heliopolis the solar deities Atum, Ra, Khepri and Horakhty were worshipped and the young princes would have become well acquainted with the cult practices and rituals.

Although the Aten is associated primarily with the reign of Akhenaten it is during the reign of Amenhotep III that the Aten was increasingly mentioned mainly in

Setting the Scene 21

2 Statue of Amenhotep III (Luxor Museum). *Photograph by the author*

connection to the royal solar bark, the palace and royal names; more than any other deity, in order to try to limit some of the power held by the prominent priesthood of Amun at Karnak. The cult of Amun, especially in the Theban area, was the wealthiest and most powerful in Egypt. The power of the priesthood of Amun had increased so much they played an active role in the choice of heir to the throne, and in fact Amenhotep III's father Thutmosis IV took away this privilege, by claiming himself heir[3] at the command of the solar god, Horemkhu-Kheper-Ra-Atum, of the Sphinx at Giza. The power of the Amun priesthood was further limited during the reign of Amenhotep III, with the gradual rise of the Aten cult.

Amenhotep's main achievement however during his 38-year reign was his foreign policy. When he became king he did not get much opportunity to show his prowess on the battlefield, as foreigners wanted to be his friend rather than his enemy due to the strength of the Egyptian empire.[4] Through a number of diplomatic marriages, Amenhotep III cemented political alliances, documented in the 'Amarna Letters', a collection of over 380 tablets written in the international diplomatic language of the time, cuneiform, consisting of correspondence of foreign kings to Amenhotep III, Akhenaten and perhaps even one to Tutankhamun. These letters are written by the rulers of Babylon, Mitanni (Syria), and Arzawa (South Western Anatolia), and primarily are writing to the Egyptian king as a superior ruler of an economically stronger country. They all request gold which 'is like the sand in Egypt, you simply gather it up.'[5] In exchange for these golden diplomatic gifts, the foreign kings sent their daughters and sisters to the Egyptian king for marriage, along with expensive 'wedding gifts'. Amenhotep had two Mitannian wives, at least one Anatolian, and two Babylonian wives, although there may have been more, as his harem is thought to have contained over 1000 women. It is clear from these letters that the Egyptians were the superior nation but the Babylonian king Kadashman-Edil I tried to push the boundaries in regard to their relationship by requesting an Egyptian bride be sent to him. He was told in no uncertain terms that Egyptian brides were never sent abroad. Kadashman-Edil also complains that Amenhotep III constantly kept his messengers waiting, on one occasion for over six years. As the superior negotiator in these relationships, the Egyptian king felt he was within his rights in keeping the messengers waiting.

The economy of Egypt was strong during the reign of Amenhotep III, due to these strong international alliances, as well as gold mining in the Wadi Hammamat and Kush. There was no warfare during his reign, meaning Amenhotep concentrated primarily on building projects in Egypt, including his palace at Malkata, and this was a particularly large project although all that is left are mud-brick foundations and painted plaster fragments. His mortuary temple on the west bank of the Nile at Thebes on the other hand was reputed to have been the biggest and most beautiful in Egypt, although this has also disappeared over the years with the two colossi of Amenhotep which originally stood at the pylon gateway, known now as the Colossi of Memnon, being the only two standing elements left (3). They stand alone in an all but empty field, and for many years due to damage caused by an earthquake in 27 BC, they moaned at dawn as the rock expanded in the heat. Greek travellers gave them the name 'Colossi of Memnon' in reference to the mythological Memnon crying for his mother Eos, the goddess of the dawn. Current excavations at the site, however have uncovered architectural remains, and further statues which were situated within this temple. Amenhotep III also built and decorated a large part of Luxor temple, completed by Tutankhamun, as well as constructing the third pylon, and the complex of Mut at Karnak which stands just outside of the current enclosure walls, and includes an unusual horse-shoe shaped sacred lake, and a sanctuary filled with over 700 life-size statues of the goddess Sekhmet, the goddess of epidemics. These were thought to have been commissioned near the end of his reign, whilst suffering from illness. What this illness was remains unspecified.

Between year 16 and 27 of Amenhotep III's reign (1370-1359 BCE), his oldest son and heir, Thutmosis, died, leaving the youngest son Amenhotep (Akhenaten) as heir to the throne. It is often stated that he was a sickly youth, although in reality there is no information about his health, and this assumption is based primarily on the epithet he chose to use later in later life, 'Great in his Duration' meaning 'The Long Lived' which may have been an expression of hope, as due to ill health he expected to die young.

The reign of Amenhotep IV/Akhenaten has been discussed in great depth in numerous other publications, so will only be outlined in brief here (4). There are numerous controversies surrounding his reign which includes his ascension to the throne. Some believe he came to the throne upon the death of his father Amenhotep III, whereas others believe there was a co-regency which may have lasted for up to 12 years. However the evidence in support of the co-regency is not conclusive. One such piece of evidence is a scene on the third pylon at Karnak, showing Amenhotep III presenting Amenhotep IV to Amun, perhaps illustrating the time the co-regency between them was announced. The inscription under the image of Amenhotep IV states:

I rule by his agreement, I join with his strength, I take possession of his power.[6]

It was customary for any king coming to the throne whether as king or co-regent, to address the oracle of Amun, in order to gain his support. The oracle was very popular during the New Kingdom and approached by all, although non-royal people needed to use an intermediary to converse with the god. This pylon scene could represent the divine support for the joint rule of Amenhotep III and IV. However alternative evidence in the form of the Amarna letters, between Tushratta and Tiye imply Akhenaten came to the throne after the death of his father. A later letter between the Hittite king Suppiluliumas to Amenhotep IV further asserts that he started his rule on the death of his father, and has led some scholars to believe the co-regency was an illusion.[7]

From the beginning of Amenhotep IV's reign, whether as a co-regent or sole ruler, he showed an extraordinary interest in the god newly revered by his father, the Aten or sun disc. In year two, he announced there was to be a *sed* festival to mark his third anniversary. The *sed* festival was carried out by the king to show his continuing ability and strength to rule Egypt, and necessitated the king racing around markers representative of the boundaries of Egypt. Normally this festival was carried out after thirty years of rule and has led some scholars to think it corresponded with year 30 of Amenhotep III. Amenhotep IV used this monumental festival to commemorate his devotion to his new god and new temples dedicated to the Aten were soon built at Karnak. The following year he reinvented a number of traditional rituals to exclude the traditional gods and by the end of year five all pretence had been dropped, and Aten was the Supreme Deity.[8] This was shortly followed by the change of name from Amenhotep IV (*Amun is Satisfied*) to Akhenaten (*Spirit of the Aten*) to show his total devotion to his new god. The worship of the Aten was very different to that of the traditional pantheon. The temples to the traditional gods were dark, enclosed places with the focus of the cult being the sanctuary at the back of the temple, which housed the statue of the deity. The Aten cult by contrast did not have statues, as the sun disc itself could always be seen. For this end the temples were open to the sky so the god could be felt in all areas. The temples were not dominated by statues but rather offering tables set up throughout the monument. At the Aten temple at Karnak the foundations of over three thousand tables have been discovered,[9] which were piled high with food offerings spiritually nourishing the Aten. Many of the Karnak offering tables are inscribed with the name of Nefertiti, giving her a prominent role

3 Colossi of Memnon of Amenhotep III. *Photograph by the author*

4 Statue of Akhenaten (Louvre Museum). *Photograph by the author*

in the worship of the Aten (*colour plate 2*), unprecedented by any other queen giving some indication to the uniqueness of this reign. In order to prevent everyone from worshipping the forever visible deity it was stipulated that only the *High Priest* (Akhenaten) could make offerings directly to the god.[10]

The change in the state religion coincided with the capital city moving from Memphis and Thebes to Tell el Amarna (Akhetaten) in Middle Egypt. It is thought perhaps Akhenaten received threats or open hostility in Thebes due to his religious changes forcing him to move somewhere safer. One of the boundary stelae surrounding the city of Akhetaten, hints at this problem in Thebes although it does not list specifics but stated he no longer wanted to hear the 'evil words'. One of the boundary stela (*5*) at Amarna is thought to be an actual record of one of Akhenaten's speeches:

> It was worse than those things I heard in regnal year four,
> It was worse than those things I heard in regnal year three,
> It was worse than those things I heard in regnal year two,
> It was worse than those things I heard in regnal year one,
> It was worse than those things Nebmaatre (*Amenhotep III*) heard,
> It was worse than those things which ... heard,
> It was worse than those things Menkheperure (*Thutmosis III*),
> And it was worse than those things I heard by any kings who had ever assumed the White Crown (*rule of the south*).[11]

5 Boundary Stela at Amarna. *Photograph by the author*

The nature of these 'things' are unknown, but Nicholas Reeves suggests it may have been an assassination attempt by the Amun priesthood or the followers of the Amun cult. Whatever the problem was, it led Akhenaten to middle Egypt to the site of Tell el Amarna (Akhetaten) taking the entire royal court and religious community with him.

The site for the new city was chosen by Akhenaten, based on a dip in the cliffs through which the Aten rose on specific days. Amarna had never before been used for a settlement or place of worship for any deity and seemed to Akhenaten an ideal place for his city. To everyone else it must have seemed a barren place with little going for it. Akhenaten however in only a few years created a city out of this bleak landscape. The construction of this town in such a short space of time took its toll on the workmen who were working here and recent excavations of the Amarna's cemetery shows many of them were subjected to carrying heavy loads from a young age causing marked compression of the spine. Coupled with poor living conditions, comprising small dirty homes, riddled with fleas, bedbugs and rats the cemetery has also shown that 36 per cent of the skeletons examined suffered from anaemia due to having a diet poor in iron.[12] Another inevitable side effect of building on such a large scale in such a small space of time is that the building-work was of a low standard.

Once complete, 20,000-50,000 people lived at Amarna, ten per cent of whom were the 'elite'. Although the city was not fortified, it was closed to any who did not have a function within it and this was monitored by a strong military presence. As the city was located on the open valley of the El Amarna plain, it was easily patrolled.[13] The city was initially planned as a single project, centred on official buildings such as palaces, temples and military barracks. Shops, taverns or schools, as we know them, do not appear to have existed, although it is unlikely a large city could survive without them. The lack of buildings with these specific functions suggests these activities either took place in the open or in non-specialised buildings. Boys may have been educated in the houses of scribes, or in public areas, leaving little evidence, and the market place was anywhere someone wanted to trade, with no need for an official structure. However, factories and workshops discovered at Amarna were closely associated with private houses, and Amarna is particularly famous for glass and faience production. A number of 'factories' continued producing faience until halfway through the reign of Tutankhamun, when the majority of the town was abandoned.

The chariot was the general mode of transport at Amarna, rather than used purely as a military or hunting vehicle and many of the houses had doorways large enough to accommodate a chariot and two horses. The royal family also favoured it as a method of transport and introduced a daily royal procession down the 'King's Road', the central street in the city, enabling their favoured officials to view their divine splendour. The procession started at the North Riverside Palace continuing south towards the Great Palace and the King's House, probably stopping at the Great Aten Temple and the Small Aten Temple on the way, leaving offerings for the god. This ensured they were viewed by most people in the city. These processions replaced the religious processions which were the foundation of the traditional religion; suggesting Akhenaten was setting himself and Nefertiti up as replacements for the gods normally carried in these traditional processions.

For the next four years the Aten cult however was practised alongside other more traditional cults throughout Egypt, and it was not until year nine that Akhenaten started his campaign against them. This began by gradually closing the temples, diverting their revenue to Amarna. Particular attention was paid to the cult of Amun and Karnak. By year 12, Akhenaten sent his men to destroy every image of Amun and every occurrence of his name, including the name of his father (Amenhotep), his own name prior to the change to Akhenaten in year five, and any rendering of the plural word for gods. This destruction can still be seen at Karnak, and in the tombs in the Valley of the Nobles. The iconoclasts were thorough and it is clear they were able to read hieroglyphs as the offending words were carefully removed leaving those surrounding them unharmed.

In year 13 another protagonist was introduced, and one that has caused untold controversy; Smenkhkare. The collapse of the so-called monotheist's dream was a slow gradual decline, although from an archaeological view it is vague and mostly unrecorded, so we can only make suggestions as to the actual sequence of events and how they affected the politics of the time. From year 13, Akhenaten (1337 BCE) was beset with a number of personal tragedies, which would no doubt have had a detrimental effect on his emotions and potentially his reasoning. At this time his wife Nefertiti disappeared from the official records and is replaced as Akhenaten's 'Great Royal Wife' by their daughter Meritaten, and inscriptions at the Sunshade Temple at Amarna show Nefertiti's name was erased. This has led some scholars to comment that there was a religious disagreement between Nefertiti and Akhenaten resulting in her banishment to the Northern Palace.

However, as not all images and instances of Nefertiti's name were destroyed, some scholars believe there was no hate campaign against Nefertiti and her name was replaced as her role had changed, although scholars are unable to agree what this change was. Some believe she died, and others that she adopted the new name of Smenkhkare taking the role of co-regent with Akhenaten. Professor Harris in the 1970s was the first to suggest this and only now is this gaining more acceptance. Smenkhkare, whoever he or she was, was the co-ruler of Akhenaten in the later years of his reign, and then ruled alone for a short period after Akhenaten's death.[14] The evidence however, is inconclusive.

A major part of the argument that Nefertiti assumed the role of co-ruler and then king, is her conduct as queen consort, when she adopted kingly attributes such as wearing kingly crowns, accompanying Akhenaten in religious ceremonies, being depicted at a relative height to the king, being shown standing with her left foot forward in the manner of a king, and riding her own chariot, full of kingly equipment. However although she adopted many aspects of kingship she did not adopt the royal titulary although her name was often enclosed within cartouches, and was written unusually with the god's name written backwards to face the image of the queen.

The discovery of the body in KV55 and the identification of the younger lady from KV35 as Nefertiti have added further dimensions to this debate. The identification of the body in KV55, as Smenkhkare, was based on the fact that it appears to be a male, and aged about 20 years old. Due to cranium shape and sharing the same blood group as Tutankhamun and the mother of Queen Tiye, Thuya (A2 and MN) it was considered likely he was a brother to Tutankhamun. This is not however conclusive evidence he is Smenkhkare. He was 'laid out as a woman with the trappings of royalty'[15] and the names on the coffin were removed, meaning the body cannot be identified as Smenkhkare, but as he was the only male that 'fit', the identification has stuck. In the 1920s it was initially believed to be Akhenaten, but Dr Derry who studied the body, doubted this identification because through studying the teeth he could tell the body was younger than 25 years old at death. Harrison who x-rayed the body, came to the same conclusion. Joyce Filer, a British anthropologist, examined the KV55 bones in 1999 and also concluded it was a younger male 'it points to somebody perhaps no more than mid-twenties; certainly, by the teeth I would go even younger than that,'[16] eliminating Akhenaten but not conclusively identifying the body as Smenkhkare. In 2010 DNA testing was carried out on a number of Egyptian mummies including the KV55 mummy, KV35 Younger Lady and Tutankhamun, with the results that rather than being simply the brother of Tutankhamun, the KV55 mummy is in fact his sibling-father. However, this does not bring us much closer in identifying whether the KV55 mummy was Akhenaten or Smenkhkare.

The identification of the younger lady as Nefertiti is also shrouded in controversy as she was found with no coffin and nothing identifying her as the queen. She was discovered in a side room of the tomb of Amenhotep II (KV35) in the Valley of the Kings alongside the Elder Lady and an unidentified young boy. Initially the younger lady was identified as M. Loret as a young man, based on the shaved head but the discovery of a wig nearby has been used to identify the mummy as that of a young woman from the Amarna period based on the style. Through examination of the body it has been suggested that the mummification process used, places her at the end of the eighteenth dynasty and the cranium shape is perceived to be similar to that of Tutankhamun.

Other observations used as proof were the shaved head, which some scholars claim was necessary to wear the blue crown worn by Nefertiti. This is doubtful, as with oil hair can be sleeked back to enable a tight fitting wig, skullcap or headdress to be worn with ease and comfort and this tall crown could hide a great deal of hair underneath. It was pointed out by one scholar, that Elizabeth Taylor in the film *Cleopatra* famously wore such a crown and did not shave her head.[17] From the remaining ear on the younger lady it was observed that it had two piercings and this is used as further proof it was Nefertiti, as these were 'observed in more than one of Nefertiti's *probable* portraits.'[18] This word 'probable' indicates the images being compared to the mummy may not be Nefertiti at all, and therefore are not proof of identity. The two holes appear to have been planned on the Berlin bust of Nefertiti although never drilled and this is added as support for the argument, as well as a comparison between the profile of the mummy and the bust. However the bust itself has no identifying inscriptions and is only *assumed* to be Nefertiti based on the crown alone; so although scholars are quite certain it represents the queen there is no proof. There is also no proof that the bust is a realistic portrait of the queen and may simply be a stylistic rendering of her. A study carried out in 2009 by German scholar Alexander Huppertz, involved a CT scan of the bust of Nefertiti, which discovered that beneath the stucco was a stone core which bore a different face to that with which we are familiar. These differences included a bump on the ridge of the nose, creases around the mouth and a different angle to the eyelids.[19] If this was indeed a portrait of Nefertiti, which one was the true likeness?

The age of the younger lady is also under scrutiny; with Grafton Elliott Smith in 1912 claiming she was less than 25 years old, James Harris in the 1970s concluding after x-rays she was about 20 years old, and Joanne Fletcher in 2000 claiming she was aged between 19-30 with Zahi Hawass adding she looks younger, perhaps only 16 years old. It would therefore appear that she is at the younger end of the 19-30 scale, rather than as Fletcher claims nearer to 30.[20] This would make the younger woman too young to be the queen,[21] who bore at least six daughters, and lived through the entire Amarna reign and possibly ruling on her own after Akhenaten's death. It is estimated that she had her first child at 14 and disappeared from the records when she was approximately 28 years old.[22] A DNA sample taken from the Younger Lady in 2005 threw up a surprising result to be added to the argument. The Younger Lady is not female but male[23] and therefore cannot be Nefertiti. However in 2010 further DNA tests were done on KV35 Younger Lady only to reidentify her as female, and the mother of Tutankhamun. However as the mother of Tutankhamun is generally thought to be a secondary wife Kiya, we are no closer to identifying whether this mummy is Nefertiti or not, and in a circular way whether she was the same person as Smenkhkare.

So if Smenkhkare was not Nefertiti who was he? This is a question which poses many problems, as little is known about him other than his name, and his position as co-ruler and then king. Many assumed, as he was chosen as co-ruler by Akhenaten, then he must have been a relative; either a son or brother. It is widely accepted that he was a brother to Tutankhamun and a son of Akhenaten, although probably not a son of Nefertiti as she is recorded as only ever bearing daughters.

Tutankhamun is believed to be the son of a secondary wife Kiya and it is widely believed Smenkhkare was also the son of a secondary wife, although whether this is Kiya is uncertain. An image from the restored plaster fragments of the North Palace at Akhetaten shows an effeminate figure in a chariot, believed to be Smenkhkare, followed by a smaller chariot ridden by Tutankhamun, showing they took part[24] in the daily chariot processions through the city. This indicates they were members of the royal family and probably children of Akhenaten as he was always accompanied on this procession by his wife and his six daughters showing it was very much a family affair.

The Paser Stela, showing two royal personages seated together, is often interpreted by some as representing Akhenaten and a son, with the affectionate embrace reminiscent of his relationship with his daughters in traditional Amarna art. Although it is clear the figures represent kings according to their regalia, they are both presented in a slightly feminine, even androgynous fashion which has led some to consider that one of the figures is a woman. It must be considered that the artistic style of the time was to present the royal family in this androgynous way, as a means of displaying their divine nature; that of possessing both male and female characteristics. Many people make the mistake of believing Amarna human representation is realistic whereas it should be treated as another form of stylised artwork, albeit stylised in a new and unique way. Without a name identifying the figures in the Paser Stela their identities will remain ambiguous and the subject of much debate, as will the question of whether Smenkhkare was a woman. However the nature of Smenkhkare is also questioned and graffiti in the Theban tomb of Pere (TT139), a Wab Priest and Overseer of the Peasants of Amun during the reign of Amenhotep III, has led to the suggestion that Smenkhkare ruled from Thebes whilst Akhenaten ruled from Amarna with Meritaten taking Nefertiti's place as his 'Chief Royal Wife'. The inscription states:

> Year 3, third month of inundation, day 10. The King of Upper and Lower Egypt, Lord of the Two Lands, Ankhkheperure (*Smenkhkare*), Beloved of Neferkheperure, Son of Ra Neferneferuaten Beloved of Waenra giving praise to Min, prostration before Onnophris, by the wab priest, scribe of the divine offerings of Amun in the house of Ankhkheperure in Thebes, Pawah, born of Iotesfsoneb

This text indicates Ankheperure (Smenkhkare) had a temple in Thebes, dedicated to Amun, and it is clear the cult of Amun was re-established during the early years of his reign:

> My heart desires to see you. My heart rejoices O Amun, you champion of the poor man. You are the father of the motherless and husband to the widow. Agreeable it is the pronunciation of your name. It is like the taste of life. It is like the taste of bread to the child, a loincloth to the naked. You are like the taste of wood in the season of heat, ... the breath of freedom to a man who has been in prison ... You were here before anything had come into existence[25]

It has been suggested this rule divide between Thebes and Amarna may have been because of a change in religious policy where rather than keeping the Aten cult contained in Amarna, Akhenaten wanted it spread throughout Egypt. By sending his co-regent Smenkhkare to the religious centre of the south he was able to remain in his city whilst still spreading the word. Perhaps Ankhkheperure was the first evangelical missionary. However, the graffiti in Pere's tomb, shows that whatever led Smenkhkare to Thebes, he followed the traditional religion of Egypt, rather than the religion of the Aten. It is thought he began to reinstate the cult of Amun so reviled by Akhenaten or at the least, to lapse in the enforcement of the Aten cult in Thebes.

The delegation of responsibilities to a co-ruler may be the result of the tragedies befalling Akhenaten and his family. Following the disappearance of Nefertiti in year thirteen, he suffered a number of family deaths. In year fourteen (1336 BCE), his daughter Meketaten died and was buried in the royal tomb at Amarna. The mourning scene in the tomb depicts a nurse maid with a baby hurrying away from the death bed. Some believe it is Kiya on the funerary bier and that the child is Tutankhamun, suggesting she died in childbirth. However, it is suggested that rather than childbirth, Meketaten died from the plague epidemic sweeping through Amarna. This plague may have claimed the lives of many members of the royal family further leading to the downfall of the Amarna period, as this would be viewed by the general populous as punishment of the gods for their neglect during Akhenaten's reign. This plague, known as the 'Asiatic Illness', is described on the Hearst Medical Papyrus as 'When the body is blackened with black spots' and elaborated on in the London Medical Papyrus as:

> When the body is coal black with charcoal (spots) in addition to the water (urine) as red liquid (i.e. bloody).[26]

This was a particularly unpleasant death, which did not discriminate between the poor and the wealthy.

Evidence suggests Meritaten was the next member of the royal family to die, followed by Akhenaten in year 17. The mass destruction of the pantheon of gods was the final recorded act of Akhenaten who died shortly after the grape harvest of year 17 of his reign; approximately July 1334 BCE when he was in his 30s, another victim of the 'Asiatic Illness' or the plague. A recent study of fossilised insect remains at Amarna carried out by Eva Panagiotakopulu[27] a paleoentomologist from Sheffield University, UK, indicates the Nile Rat may have carried the flea responsible for the bubonic plague which then came into contact with the Black Rat (both present in Egypt at this time) spreading this infection worldwide. This Amarnan plague or epidemic is also recorded by the Hittites as spreading from Egypt to Hattusha (the Hittite capital) upon the capture of Egyptian prisoners. This plague was highly contagious, and did not only affect the royal family but many others at Amarna. However as many of the bodies were not buried here but shipped to other villages in Egypt for traditional burials the extent of the epidemic cannot truly be quantified.

In 2006, a cemetery of poor burials was uncovered at Amarna showing hundreds of people died and were buried here. However early studies have not yet identified the cause of death, although it appears from the skeletal remains they led short and difficult lives conducive with a plague-ridden city, rather than the glorious utopia Akhenaten was hoping to create. The spread of this epidemic was primarily due to squalid living conditions, again something totally unexpected in this new and economically strong city, but it was clearly contagious enough to spread to the royal family who were the richest and cleanest in the city. At the death of Akhenaten, there was no known male heir. Nefertiti and Kiya, his two main wives, had only borne him daughters, although Tutankhamun may have been the son of Kiya. It would appear for all intents and purposes the Amarna dream of a paradise overlooked by the Aten was coming to a close. Smenkhkare ruled alone for a matter of a few months before succumbing to death himself. Add these deaths to those in the earlier years of the reign of Akhenaten of his parents (assuming there was a co-regency), Tiye in year 14

(1336 BCE) and Amenhotep III in year 12 (1338 BCE) as well as his youngest daughters Setepenre and Neferneferura who disappear from the records and Kiya in year 12 and possibly Nefertiti in year 13, and it tells a tragic family history. This plague spelt the beginning of the end for the Aten cult, as traditionally in this situation the king and the population appealed to the deities of disease, namely Sekhmet, Selket or Hathor. With these avenues of redemption closed, coupled with the fear that this was caused because of the neglect of the gods, the people were more than willing to return to the 'old ways' in order to save themselves. Therefore re-gaining the pleasure of the gods was one of the first things which needed to be carried out by the next king at the collapse of the Amarna regime.

The disintegration of the Aten cult was inevitable once the main protagonists were dead, leaving only Tutankhaten, a young boy of about eight or nine, as the only male member of the family left, and even his parentage is shrouded with doubt. This young boy was surrounded by advisors, most of whom were officials to the king prior to the move to Amarna, and prior to the rise of the Aten, which helped the re-establishment of the traditional religion. The first act of defiance against the Aten cult was the change of his name from Tutankhaten to Tutankhamun in honour of the god Amun, and then to move the capital city from Amarna back to Thebes and Memphis. Once Amarna was neglected by the king and the royal court, everyone else gradually followed leaving the city all but abandoned. There were only a few faience factories still in production in the city during Tutankhamun's reign but all importance, wealth and power had left. The city was totally abandoned during the reign of Horemheb and it provided a good scapegoat for everything that was wrong with Egypt.[28]

Tutankhamun was very young, born and raised at Amarna, and did not know anything other than the Aten cult and the Amarna lifestyle. He was therefore very carefully influenced by his officials in his policies and innovations, until he came of age, when he could exert his own power. Whether this was welcome or not is unknown. He died at eighteen years old, before he could make his mark on the history of Egypt, although with a bizarre twist of fate he is the best-known Egyptian king in the world.

Between the discovery of the tomb in 1922 and the CT scan in 2005, it was thought Tutankhamun was murdered due to a power struggle for the throne. The x-rays by Harrison in 1968 seemed to support this when they uncovered a fragment of bone in his skull, leading to the assumption that he may have been murdered by a blow to the head. The CT scan of Tutankhamun's body exposed a number of fractures and breaks both pre- and post-mortem which led to the conclusion he died of an accident. The 2010 DNA studies also suggest that Tutankhamun was a carrier of malaria, and should he have been suffering from malaria at the time of or just after the accident his immune system would have been too weak to cope and would have contributed to a seedier demise. The loose bone in his skull appears to have been caused by Carter's archaeological team, finally putting the murder theory to rest.

At Tutankhamun's death, after ten years on the throne he left no heirs and therefore his uncle Ay succeeded him. He was an elderly man and only ruled for four years leaving the throne clear for Horemheb who he named as his heir. So who was Horemheb? Where did he come from and how does he fit into this arena of religious intrigue and political struggle?

CHAPTER 2
A KING IS BORN

It is very difficult to place Horemheb's birth and early years into the colourful chronology of Egyptian history as there is little written evidence referring to his early years. The earliest absolute identification of Horemheb comes from his tomb at Saqqara, built at the beginning of the reign of Tutankhamun. At this stage in his career he was already an army *General* and a *Royal Scribe*, at the peak of his career indicating almost certainly that he was an adult at this time. From this assumption we are able to work backwards to piece together the details of his early career.

Based on the length of time between the beginning of Tutankhamun's reign, and the end of his own reign, Horemheb lived for at least 30 years (10 years of Tutankhamun, four years of Ay, and up to 15 of his own). However, at the beginning of the reign of Tutankhamun, he was already advanced in his military and scribal career, indicating he was at least twenty years old at this time, if not thirty.[1] Using this as a starting point we can estimate when he was born. Assuming he was thirty at the start of the reign of Tutankhamun, at the start of Akhenaten's reign, seventeen years earlier (1350 BCE) he was twelve years old. Regardless of whether the co-regency happened between Amenhotep III and Akhenaten it is likely he was born during the reign of Amehotep III. If the twelve-year co-regency occurred then Horemheb was born in year 14 of Amenhotep III's reign (1362 BCE), but if the co-regency did not happen then he was born in year 26 (1362 BCE) of the reign of Amenhotep III. Although the exact year cannot be known without further information, it is likely he was born during his reign, and at a time when Egypt was at a cultural, political and economic high point; and was one that Horemheb tried to emulate throughout his own reign.

Some scholars believe Horemheb was named Paatenemeb at birth, meaning 'Aten is in Festival' but changed it at the end of the reign of Akhenaten to Horemheb, 'Horus is in Festival', reflecting the Aten's fall from grace with the death of Akhenaten. This is based on the discovery of an unfinished tomb at Amarna (TA24),[2] belonging to Paatenemheb, who held similar titles to Horemheb. The tomb itself is incomplete and had been carved no further than the entrance, and the approach to the tomb was by rough cut steps (6). Initially when it was excavated the base of jambs were inscribed in black ink, advising of the name and titles of the owner. He was the *General of the Lord of the Two Lands, Overseer of Works in Amarna, Royal Steward,* and *Overseer of Porters at Amarna* and is thought by some to be the same person. There are many scholars who are not convinced that Paatenemheb was Horemheb, and do not believe the argument is a strong one. The main argument against these two men being the same is the difference in names, and it is thought that should Paatenemheb have changed his name it would be to Pa–*Hor*-emheb, although there has never been an example of Pa preceding Horus in a name, whereas it precedes Ra and Aten on many occasions.[3] One scholar also believes they could not be the same individual as there is no evidence that Horemheb had ever converted to Atenism.[4] However there is equally no evidence to suggest he did not, or at least convert as a form of lip-service to the new king and his god. However it is equally possible, he was named Horemheb

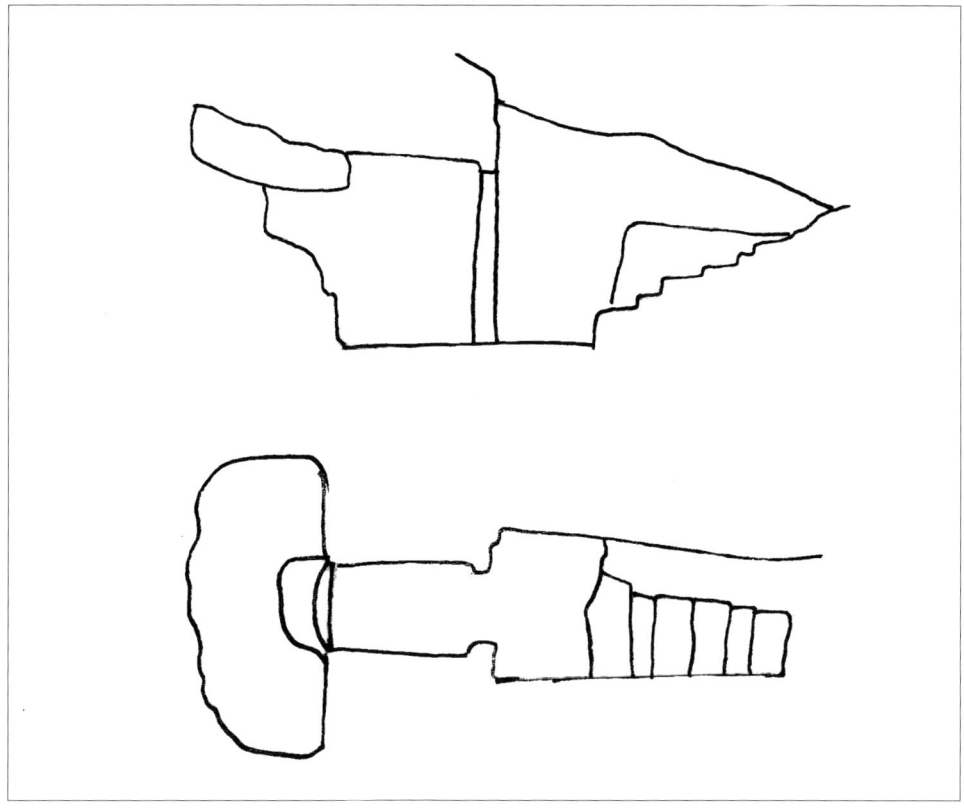

6 Tomb of Paatenemheb at Amarna. *Drawing by the author after Davies 1908, pl XIII*

at birth, and when it was clear at the end of the reign of Amenhotep III that the god Aten was rising in royal favour, it may have been considered essential for his career to change his name showing allegiance to the Aten. This ensured Horemheb and his family held a place in the new city of the Aten at Amarna. In year five of Akhenaten's reign, Horemheb was 17 years old, had completed his military training and was working his way up the scribal and military ladder and needed to be in the capital city to succeed.

The rock-cut tomb, although unfinished reflects the wealth at Paatenemheb's disposal, and should it be the first tomb of Horemheb it enables us to see his power began during the reign of Akhenaten. Its unfinished state indicates it was abandoned at the collapse of the Amarna regime, and was perhaps started in the last five years of Akhenaten's reign, when Horemheb was in his mid-twenties.

Horemheb was not of royal blood, and as he started his career as a simple soldier, he was probably born to a middle-class family. Horemheb initially held scribal titles, indicating he was literate, and was educated as a child. Only middle-class and elite families could generally afford to educate their children. Whether Horemheb's father was a military scribe too is unknown, but as most sons followed in their father's career it is quite possible.

In later years Horemheb favoured the small town of Hansu (Herakleopolis or modern Ihnasya el-Medina), close to the Faiyum, and worshipped the local god, to such an extent he claimed Horus of Hansu chose him at birth to be king, and protected him, until the time was right and he could take his place on the throne.

Despite this affiliation with Hansu, no monuments dedicated by Horemheb have been discovered in the area, although he has dedicated monuments elsewhere to the local god, rather than embracing whole-heartedly the state god Amun. Nevertheless, Horemheb continued, once king, to worship this deity suggesting he had close ties with the area. Herakleopolis was an important town with a long history, and was the capital during the ninth and tenth dynasties (2160-2040 BCE) when a local family took over the throne, and may even have ruled the whole of Egypt at one point, although with the frequent change in rulers no one king was able to leave his mark.[5] The earliest remains at this town date to the twelfth dynasty (1991-1782 BCE), and the temple here dedicated to the ram-headed god Herishef (He who is upon his lake) was enlarged during the New Kingdom, primarily by Ramses II. There is no clear evidence of any work carried out here by Horemheb although the enlargements of the temple started in the eighteenth dynasty and may have been added to by him.

The details of Horemheb's childhood and training have sadly not survived although there is a great deal of information regarding schooling and apprenticeships during the New Kingdom giving a relatively clear idea of what experiences Horemheb may have had whilst growing up. The Faiyum was a holiday destination of the New Kingdom elite, with many people travelling to the area for hunting, and fishing, as well as housing the royal harem, which was later to be the home, albeit briefly, for Ankhesenamun, Tutankhamun's wife. Although not living in the Faiyum itself, Horemheb and his family may have taken advantage of the close proximity and taken in the sites, perhaps meeting important people in the area. Perhaps through such a meeting Horemheb was given a break, enabling him to rise quickly through the military ranks. If however this was not the case, the more traditional training route started at approximately five years old involving lots of hard work.

If a boy was to get an education, he started learning to read and write hieratic from five years old, and evidence indicates this could be administered in a number of ways. There were a number of official scribal schools during the New Kingdom; situated at the Mut complex and the Amun temple at Karnak, the Ramesseum, the region of Deir el Medina, Memphis and Sais. These official schools were primarily for the children of the upper elite, although the Middle Kingdom *Instruction of Khety for his son Pepi* (also known as the *Satire of the Trades*) tells of their journey from Sile in the Delta to:

> the school for scribes, among the children of the Magistrates, with the elite of the Residence[6]

This suggests children of non-elite families could be admitted. This particular Theban school appears to have been for those expecting a future career in central government, whereas other schools specialised in the priesthood, medical profession, or the army. In the New Kingdom literary text *The Story of Truth and Falsehood* a boy was:

> sent to school and learnt to write well and practised the arts of war, surpassing his older companions who were at school with him.

Due to Horemheb's swift rise through the ranks of military scribedom, to the role of *Royal Scribe* and *General* when he was in his twenties, it can be assumed he was lucky enough to attend one of these schools, enabling his skills to be acknowledged and nurtured. For boys not lucky enough to go to these elite educational institutions, there were local alternatives; although these may not have led to such high profile positions as Horemheb held. Some children were educated by their fathers, or were 'adopted' by a local scribe who taught his craft, in order for the young lad to inherit his position. Although the young students were given the title 'son' or 'staff of old age' they were adopted as an apprentice rather than as a biological son. It is thought that once adopted, even in this work relationship the child might even have resided at the house of their adopted father in order to fully absorb the career path they had chosen.

Whichever branch of education was open to him, Horemheb would have experienced the same teaching methods. His training started in 1357 BCE when he was five years old, and was harsh and difficult. Should he not excel at his studies it was considered acceptable to beat him. An Egyptian proverb even states:

A boy's ear is on his back; he hears when he is beaten[7]

This idea is reiterated in the *Miscellanies* (a collective book of teaching materials) where a pupil praises his teacher:

You smote my back and so your teaching entered my ear[8]

This indicates beatings were part of the daily teaching routine; a lot was expected of such small children. They were taught the three 'R's, reading, writing and arithmetic, enabling them to enter into a number of professions. The ancient Egyptians were taught hieratic first and if they excelled at this they could progress onto the hieroglyphs used primarily in religious contexts.

Children initially were taught hieratic phrases and sentences though dictation which they copied onto gesso-coated wooden or stone tablets. These could be wiped clean after use and examples have been found where the earlier texts are visible beneath. They also learnt by reciting out-loud famous Middle Kingdom texts. This was in an archaic version of the language which would have been alien to these New Kingdom children. Once the student could recite the texts by heart they wrote them down, initially through copying a standardised version of the text, and then as they became more advanced students, from memory. Many surviving school texts and practice pieces, show numerous aural errors corrected by the tutor. Once the student was able to master the hieratic script in this manner, he progressed to learning the hieroglyphic script; no mean feat for anyone, let alone a child of five or six considering there are several hundred signs to master.

This primary education lasted for four years, before the child now aged nine was required to make a decision as to their future. If talented scribes, they would consider whether they wanted to pursue a career in the temple, central government or the militia. This would be a daunting choice to make at any point in one's life, but at nine years old it would be almost impossible, and most boys followed their father's career. Once the decision was made the child entered into an apprenticeship, to train on the job, in preparation for taking over the role at the death of their father or mentor. This apprenticeship lasted for approximately ten or twelve years depending on the complexity of the role they were training for and the ability of the individual.

Although careers were dictated by the skills of the individual child, it did not prevent 'the sales pitch' for other options. A number of texts praising the life of the scribe over that of the soldier have been discovered and one wonders if these were used as teaching aids for the impressionable young Horemheb, influencing his choice of a career. Papyrus Lansing, for example, appealed to the weaker, non-sporty boys, who were considering joining the army, encouraging them to enter the less glamorous scribal career:

Be a scribe! Your body will be sleek, your hand will be soft. You will not flicker like a flame, like those whose body is feeble. For there is no bone of a man in you. You are tall and thin. If you lifted a load to carry it, you would stagger. Your feet would drag terribly, you are lacking in strength. You are weak in all of your limbs, poor in body. Set your sights on being a scribe, a fine profession that suits you[9]

The *Satire of the Trades* describes the life of the scribe in glowing terms, as a means to encourage able-bodied young boys to enter the scribal profession rather than the army or other more exciting trades by describing each profession in less than flattering terms. Scribedom on the other hand is:

... the greatest of all callings, there's none like it in the land. Barely grown, still a child, he is greeted, sent on errands, hardly returned he wears a gown. I never saw a sculptor as envoy, nor is the goldsmith ever sent[10]

This description makes it clear even a young scribal apprentice, receives wealth and respect and is sent on errands that those in other professions would not be trusted with. Horemheb was familiar with many of these texts and they may even have been instrumental in his decision to be a military scribe. The role of a military scribe was not a sedate one, as they followed the army into battle recording the campaigns and manoeuvres, putting themselves at great risk. Perhaps he wanted to be involved with the army and be part of a life which promised glory, foreign trips and potential acknowledgment by the king, whereas the scribal profession offered knowledge, wealth and respect. Between the ages of nine and 20 years old he was in training for his chosen career and was probably housed at one of the army barracks, training alongside other military scribes. However it would seem that during this apprenticeship, Horemheb changed the focus of his training to include military manoeuvres showing a great deal of prowess; earning the title of soldier alongside that of scribe. This military training however, was far more rigorous than the scribal training with harsher punishments than he suffered at the hands of his scribal tutor. Papyrus Anastasi III, written during the reign of Sety II, although copied from an earlier text, by a scribe describing the hardships of the army to a potential recruit, Inena:

What is it that you say they relate, that the soldier's is more pleasant than the scribe's profession? Come let me tell you the condition of the soldier; that much exerted one. He is brought while a child to be confined in the camp. A searing beating is given to his body, a wound inflicted on his eye and a splitting blow to his brow. He is laid down and beaten like papyrus. He is struck with torments.

Come, let me relate to you his journey to Khor (*a general term for Palestine and Syria*) and his marching upon the hills. His rations and water are upon his shoulder like the load of an ass. His neck has become calloused, like that of an ass. The vertebrae of his back are broken. He drinks foul water and halts to stand guard. When he reaches the enemy he is like a pinioned bird, with no strength in his limbs. If he succeeds in returning to Egypt, he is like a stick which the woodworm has devoured. He is sick, prostration overtakes him. He is brought back upon an ass, his clothes taken away by theft, his henchmen fled. ... turn back from the saying that the soldier's is more pleasant than the scribe's profession[11]

As intended Inena decided to become a scribe instead of a soldier, but this description may represent the early experiences of Horemheb when he joined the army. He would have entered into an apprenticeship scheme at the age of nine years old, remaining an apprentice until he was able to start military service at twenty years of age.

The soldiers were paid in food rations whilst on campaign, which was enough to survive on, but when they returned to the barracks they received the excess which

7 Horemheb receiving shebyu collars, Saqqara. *Drawing by the author after Martin 1991*

they could exchange for other goods. From the Middle Kingdom fortress of Uronaroti, in Nubia, wooden tokens have been discovered which the soldiers exchanged for bread. There were different shapes, each representing a certain number of loaves of bread (e.g. 60 or 90) which they could be exchanged for. In addition to these official payments the soldiers acquired a large amount of wealth in the form of plunder from conquered enemies which would have included gold, cattle and even men and women to take home as servants. The officers received the best of the booty but the ordinary infantry soldier also returned from campaign with a full backpack. This possibility of wealth no doubt persuaded a number of young boys to enter the army.

There was a formalised system of awards for the bravest soldiers in recognition of their work, comprising of golden flies (a sign of endurance and persistence), as well as the gold collars of valour, known as *shebyu* collars. Not only were the recipients made wealthy by these gifts, but also gained recognition from the Egyptian community for their services to the crown. In the tomb of Horemheb at Memphis, Tutankhamun is shown giving shebyu collars to Horemheb, showing he was greatly valued in his role as solder and government official (7).

Soldiers were not always on campaign and spent a great deal of time guarding desert trading routes. This was a boring post to hold, and lasted for 20 days at a time. The soldiers marked off the days until their shift was over on the rocks surrounding the guard posts. The military were also used for transportation of large blocks of stone for sarcophagi and obelisks, which required numerous strong men. Soldiers helped with the harvesting for the same reason. Whether they were allowed to return to their own village to help with the harvest or were allocated a place is uncertain. The early years of Horemheb's career probably consisted of these activities, which although hard work may have enabled him to return home to Hansu to visit his parents for the harvest season.

When the soldiers were sent out on campaign they probably dreamed of the quieter guard duties, as the journeys to get to the battles were long and hard and could be as dangerous as the battle itself. However for a young recruit the excitement of a foreign battle would possibly outstrip the hardship suffered. A journey from Memphis to Thebes, if travelled in daylight by river took between twelve and twenty days by boat, beset along the way by sandbanks, hippopotami and thieves. As a deterrent to would-be attackers, the soldiers placed their cow-hide shields alongside the cabin on the boat, showing it was a military ship. The journeys were made more arduous by the equipment which was required, all of which was carried upon their backs including weapons (spears, shields, bows, arrows) (8), and food. An average soldier was given less than ten loaves of bread a day, which was to be carried in bags and baskets, either as bread or as raw ingredients, which were cooked along the way. They either made ovens from mud at temporary camps, or whilst on the march they used the village ovens as they passed through.

8 Weapons and model shields (Luxor Museum). Photograph by the author

A King is Born

By the New Kingdom and the time of Horemheb's recruitment, there was a permanent army, with a clear hierarchy of military positions with the higher positions passed down from father to son. Since the reign of Thutmosis III, and the emphasis on military kings this military hierarchy offered an extra route to the throne, especially for the uneducated, when previously power could only be obtained through the bureaucracy or the priesthood. Horemheb, both educated and military trained, used the position to his advantage.

Throughout the ten years of Horemheb's military apprenticeship he would be trained in all the skills required in the New Kingdom army, including chariotry and horsemanship which were essential for any solider. The chariots were small and light and were designed to carry two men, the driver and the weapons expert. It would be important for Horemheb to learn the skills needed for both of these tasks. Although it was rare for a soldier (or indeed anyone) to ride horses, a soldier would need to know how to, as well as how to tether the horse to the chariot correctly. There would generally be stable hands to do this, but a soldier never knew when he would be required to carry out the task at short notice. Whilst moving at speed in the chariot, Horemheb needed to show skills at archery, and the use of a spear. This required extensive target practice; by shooting arrows or thrusting the spear at a wooden or copper target whilst on the move (9). Stick fighting and target practice prepared the young Horemheb for sword fighting, and lessons in how to locate suitable missiles and how to use them prepared him for using throw sticks and sling shots.

As many campaigns and missions were abroad or in the desert Horemheb was trained in backwoodsman survival skills, and he no doubt was able to build a fire

9 Amenhotep II practicing with a copper target and chariot (Luxor Museum). *Photograph by the author*

10 Ostacon showing military training (Luxor Museum). *Photograph by the author*

using a fire drill, was able to hunt and prepare the kill for cooking, locate wells, and prepare basic food. Once soldiers arrived at a camp site, the leather tents needed to be erected, and although as a *General* servants prepared his for him, in the early years, Horemheb would have erected his own as well as dismantled and maintained the leather. Brute strength and stamina were essential, especially for the long marches to battle sites as well as for the tasks they were given during peace time. These were developed and maintained with a course of weightlifting using sand bags, wrestling and boxing, and no doubt running or marching for long periods over rough terrain in hot and uncomfortable weather (*10*).

Although the training was harsh, because the soldiers lived and trained together there was a highly developed sense of camaraderie with the men in each team, and this was encouraged through grouping of the army into divisions of about 5000 men, who were further divided into hosts, companies, platoons and squads of about ten men. These ten men trained together and would feed off each other's skills creating a fighting team that could not be beaten. The members of the squad protected each other, and there would be competitions against other squads, or at the larger end of scale, between divisions. This created a loyalty close to family. Bearing in mind many members of the army had grown up in this environment, these men *would* be their family; or at least the only family they had really known.

In addition to the military training, Horemheb also received his scribal training, giving him skills which were invaluable. Literacy levels in Egypt were very low, and soldiers on the whole were not amongst the literate; so from the very beginning Horemheb stood out from the crowd. He stood out enough to attract the attentions

11 Amenia and Horemheb detail from Saqqara (British Museum). *Photograph courtesy of Brian Billington*

12 Dyad of Horemheb and Amenia. Saqqara (Luxor Museum). *Photograph by the author*

13 Sementawy from Saqqara. *Drawing by he author after Martin 1991*

of a woman called Amenia whom he fell in love with and married (*11*). Unfortunately we do not know very much about her, other than she died before Horemheb became king, and was buried in his Memphite tomb (*12*). She was possibly a woman from his town, who supported him throughout his rise through the military and political ranks. She held the title during the reign of Tutankhamun of *Chantress of Amun* which was probably given to her by the king as a reward for Horemheb's loyalty. On a stela fragment from the Memphite tomb, under her chair is seated a monkey on a cushion eating a piece of fruit with one paw and reaching for another one with his other paw, and this was probably one of her pets. In April 2009 one of the only complete statues of Horemheb and Amenia was identified. The statue, in the British Museum, was acquired in 1839, in the Memphite area and shows a couple seated holding hands (*colour plate 3*) and was thought, by later scholars to have originated in Horemheb's tomb. The hands themselves were missing but were discovered in the tomb in 1976 and in 2009 were matched to the statue by René van Walsem clearly identifying the statue as Horemheb and his wife, Amenia. The statue was greatly admired by the sculptor Henry Moore (1898-1986), who used it for the inspiration for his King and Queen (1952-3) in the Tate Gallery, London; perhaps he could see what was to be Horemheb's royal bearing.

Amenia and Horemheb did not have any children, which would cause problems for Horemheb. As he started to rise in his career he needed a son to pass the position to. This led to his adoption of two men; Sementawy who was to be later replaced by Ramose (*13*). Sementawy was his army scribe, or secretary, and it appeared he died and was replaced by Ramose, who was a *Documents Scribe* or *Private Secretary*, as well as:

Scribe of the army of the hereditary prince, who is close to him. Whenever he goes, confident of his lord in every mention of the king, Ramose

The name of Sementawy had been erased and replaced by that of Ramose. Some have suggested that this may even be Ramses I,[12] who later became king after Horemheb.

Amenia died during the reign of Ay only a short time before Horemheb came to the throne, but she seems to have supported him throughout his rise in power from a scribe, to soldier, until he held the coveted title of Deputy King under Tutankhamun. She died a wealthy but childless woman. Her husband Horemheb, may have been an unusual man, raised in the army from five years old, totally indoctrinated into the military lifestyle, viewing his squad as his family and maybe even putting them before her at times. However, would he have been any different from anyone else in the army at this time, as his education and training would have been the same? We can tell he would have been a loyal, brave and strong man, and someone that Amenia stood by for many years, through the early years and then the later, wealthier and more powerful years where she was present at the court of Tutankhamun, mixing with the elite. Was this why she stayed with Horemheb? Or was he an intelligent, interesting, brave and loyal man, whom she was in love with? Sadly questions we cannot answer, although we are able to try and build the character of Horemheb a little more by looking at his career in more detail.

CHAPTER 3
HOREMHEB'S EARLY CAREER

Although in the previous chapter we have pieced together Horemheb's training and education, prior to the reign of Tutankhamun, there is very little information regarding his early military career. Most of Horemheb's military life is recorded in his tomb at Memphis starting when he was the *Great Commander of the Army* during the latter years of the reign of Akhenaten. However from the list of titles and the progression route, it is possible to present an image of his early career.

One of the earliest expeditions that probably involved Horemheb was an expedition in year one of Akhenaten to the quarries at Khenu (Place of Rowing), modern Gebel el Silsila, 65 km north of Aswan, to quarry sandstone and limestone for Akhenaten's early building works at Karnak. At this point Akhenaten was constructing a temple to Ra-Horakhty at Karnak, and there is an inscription at Gebel el Silsilch that refers to the quarrying of the benben (pyramidian) at the site.[1]

This site was used to quarry granite from the Middle Kingdom until the Roman period, and in this time eight million tonnes of stone were extracted.[2] The *General* during the reign of Akhenaten was a man called Mai, but Horemheb as a 17-year-old recruit, may have accompanied the military to this region. All soldiers were part of a company of approximately 250 men, and in his later tomb at Saqqara he mentions the *Beloved of Aten* company which may have been the one of which he was a member.[3] There are images from the quarry decorated with Akhenaten worshipping the Aten. The talatat blocks used in all of his later structures were quarried of Silsila sandstone although no blocks of this particular size have been discovered at the site.[4] Gebel el Silsila was an interesting site, comprising sandstone cliffs, which narrowed the river acting as natural barrier to riverine traffic,[5] and to Nubia in general, perhaps by a natural chain of rocks across the river, or as some people believe an actual chain hung between two jagged rocks.[6] Although the quarrying was not an act of warfare, Horemheb's role probably was one of protection, as the roads to the quarries were dangerous and open to attack.

As a literate man he may also have held an administrative role, perhaps recording the men employed and the quantity of stone returned to Thebes. Many expeditions were large-scale affairs and one records more than 1000 men and donkeys used for the work;[7] including the army for protection and a series of men conscripted into the work or convicts sentenced to work the stone. There would be a few specially trained individuals on the expedition, and it is likely the chief sculptor of Akhenaten, Bek, was responsible for opening the quarry here, and choosing the ideal stone for Akhenaten's monuments. A record of a quarrying expedition to the Wadi Hammamat during the reign of Ramses IV shows there were 170 administrative staff, 130 stonemasons, 800 Asiatic prisoners, 2000 temple personnel for transporting the blocks, 5000 soldiers and 50 guards. This is likely to be the type of expedition Horemheb was on, being simply one of the faceless soldiers. However Horemheb showed promise in this expedition and later held the title *Overseer of Works in the Granite Quarries of Gebel Ahmar*, east of modern Cairo.[8] It is currently beneath the Cairo-Abbassiya region, that houses a sports stadium, amusement park and gardens, leading to a name change from Gebel Ahmar (The Red Hill) to Gebel Akdar (The Green Hill). This quarry was used from the Old Kingdom onwards for royal statues and monuments,[9] and during the pharaonic period up to ten tonnes of stone may have been extracted. The quarry itself was closely associated with the solar cults and was popular with kings who were solar oriented such as Djedefra, Amenhotep III and Akhenaten.[10] The Colossi of Memnon of Amenhotep III were thought to have been made from quartzite from this quarry.[11] The solar connection was due to the sun shining on the stone in the hill illuminating it in an ethereal way. This quarry was clearly in full working order during the reigns of Akhenaten and Tutankhamun but not as popular during the reign of Horemheb, who was slowly moving away from the solar cults.

The expedition to Gebel el Silsileh may also have introduced Horemheb to the *Master of the Royal Horse*, Ay, who was later to be king. In the Amarna tomb of Ay, he and Mai are rewarded for their services to the king, with golden shebyu collars. Once the stones were brought back to Thebes they were recorded and placed under the jurisdiction of the *Vizier*, Ramose. This expedition seemed to have made an impact on the young Horemheb and later, when he became king he built a temple at the site.

Although Akhenaten is reputed to have been a pacifist, evidence suggests he was constantly surrounded by personal bodyguards (*14*). Soldiers and policemen appear in many Amarnan tomb scenes, often accompanying the king, and there are still a number of visible tracks surrounding the Amarna plain, indicating patrols were regularly placed here. Akhenaten clearly felt unsafe, and it appears many high positions at the royal court were filled by military men.[12] The boundary stela surrounding Amarna indicates the complete withdrawal from Thebes was due to an unspecified incident making it impossible for him and his cult to remain there. As a revolutionary, Akhenaten upset many, not only the priesthood of the abandoned Amun cult but also the general populous whose religion and belief system was outlawed by the new king.

14 Royal Body Guard from an Amarna tomb. *Photograph by the author*

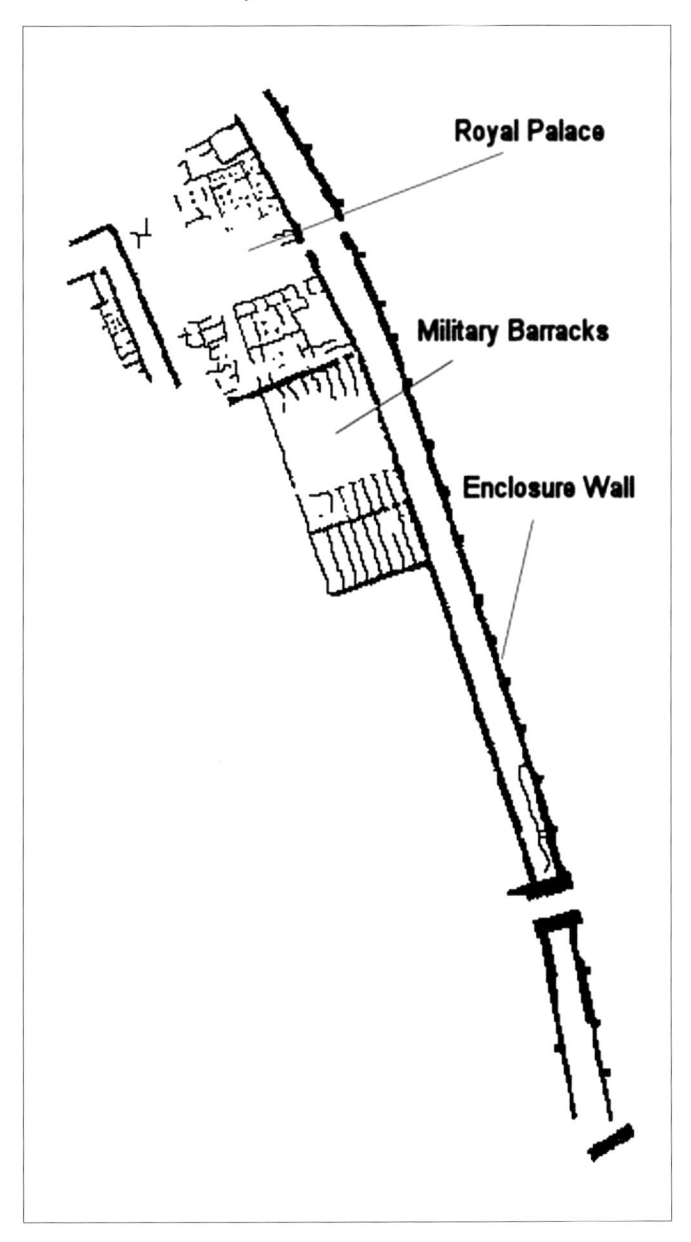

15 North Riverside Palace of Amarna and the military area. *Drawing by Brian Billington*

He was therefore under threat from institutions and individuals. Although Akhenaten protected himself by remaining in his new city, surrounded by hand-picked officials, archaeological evidence shows the Aten cult was not accepted by everyone at the city. There were numerous statues and murals dedicated to the traditional gods in the homes of many of Amarna's residents, ironically including the house of the *High Priest* of the Aten showing the religion was perhaps seen as a royal cult. Therefore Akhenaten may have needed protection from those within his own, self-created world. The importance of Amarna as a military encampment both during the reign of Tutankhamun and later is supported by excavations which show the workman's village here was used for the entire reign of Tutankhamun for a contingent of guards, and evidence shows it was used for this purpose for 20-25 years.[13] It is quite likely that Horemheb supervised this contingent of guards during his early military career, ensuring standards and loyalty were maintained.

Horemheb, being literate and a trained military expert, was in control of recruiting the bodyguard of Akhenaten, controlling the rotas, dossiers and records of the bodyguard in addition to other regiments of the army. He also supervised the training of new recruits. His skill as *General* and *Administrator* was such that when Tutankhamun and subsequently Ay ruled he still held a high-status position within the administration despite the very different manner of their rules. This suggests Horemheb was a great diplomat, who did not get involved with political controversies, and continued performing his job to a high standard, making himself indispensable. It is clear that Horemheb was a particularly prominent figure in the court of Akhenaten towards the end of his reign, but at the beginning he was simply just another face in the sea of soldiers at Amarna.

It was not for another seven years that the threat of war was upon Egypt and this must have been a time of great anticipation for the army and the 24-year-old Horemheb, who was hoping to have his first taste of battle. From the Amarna letters, it is recorded that in year 12 there were political problems and impending war with the Hittites, who were gradually gaining control over the Near Eastern region. The Hittite army were marching closer to Egypt slaughtering any Egyptian vassal rulers who did not surrender. Those they did not slaughter were accommodated into the army. During this period the most feared in the region, Abd-Ashurta and his son, Aziru, rulers of the Amorite Kingdom, defected and joined the Hittite forces. The Egyptian vassals and the Hittite rulers, both in turn appealed to Akhenaten to aid them in their campaign, and requested he send them an army. One letter from the town of Tunip to Akhenaten states:

> If his soldiers and chariots come too late, Aziru will make us like the city of Niy (*which was destroyed*) if ... we have to mourn, the king of Egypt will mourn over these things which Aziru has done for he will turn his hand against our lord! ... for 20 years we have been sending to our lord, the king of Egypt but there has not come to us a word, no not one

Aziru wrote to Akhenaten requesting help against the Hittite forces even though he had joined them and participated in the slaughter of those loyal to Egypt. He states he destroyed the city of Simyra, which was under Egyptian rule, to prevent the Hittites from destroying it. Understandably Akhenaten did not know who was being loyal to him, so refused to send a supporting army to the area. However he sent a messenger to Aziru demanding he rebuild the city. Aziru avoided the messenger, and stated this was because he was in the north fighting the Hittites.

The last of the Egyptian vassal rulers to fall in the north to the Hittite army was Rib-Addi from Byblos, despite a number of letters to Akhenaten asking for an army to be sent to the region to protect the city. Akhenaten refused this request, and as the letters from Rib-Addi stopped it can be assumed he was murdered and Byblos fell under the rule of the Hittites.

A similar problem was also happening in Southern Palestine with the Khabiri Aramaean Semites who were also requesting help from Akhenaten. This letter from Jerusalem states:

> The Khabiri are occupying the King's cities; there remains not one prince to my lord, the king. Everyone is ruined ... let the king take care of his lands, let him send troops. For if no troops come in this year the whole territory of my lord, the king will perish

The replies sent by Akhenaten seem to have been inadequate, and it appears he did not send the military force required to alleviate these problems. It is suggested that he either ignored the pleas for aid entirely, concentrating on his religion and new city, or he sent a small army or diplomatic scouting party to attempt to diffuse the Hittite threat. The situation really needed the focus of the entire Egyptian army as well as a mighty king at the head leading them into battle as was traditional. Any campaign, whether a scouting party or full scale expedition, to the Palestinian region at this time may have been led, and planned by Horemheb, who had been promoted to *General*. As these letters were received from all vassal states in the Near East Horemheb carefully followed the situation, preparing the army for potential warfare, which never came.

It is clear Horemheb's early career was primarily administrative and many of his early statues show him as a scribe. His dedication to Thoth, the patron god of scribes, was prominent throughout the reign of Tutankhamun and the re-establishment of the traditional religion (16):

Praise to you Thoth, Lord of Hermopolis (*modern el Ashmunein*), who came into being by his own accord and was not born. Unique god, lord of the netherworld ... who distinguishes the tongues of foreign lands ... may you place the scribe Horemheb firmly by the side of the Lord of the Universe, in the way that you gave him life when he came forth from the womb.[14]

This inscription attributes the creation of the world to the patron god of scribes. The cult of Thoth was centred at the site of Ashmunein, almost opposite the city of Amarna, and during his reign Horemheb carried out building works at the site, using building materials from the site of Akhenaten's then abandoned city. There is very

16 Horemheb making offerings to Thoth from Gebel el Silsileh. *Drawing by the author*

little remaining of his work at the site, due to quarrying here through the Christian and Islamic periods. However, the foundations of a colossal pylon, leading to the eighteenth dynasty Thoth temple, built by Horemheb and added to by Ramses II have been discovered. This pylon was identified as his by the foundation blocks which were in their original positions. Part of the foundation deposit survived in the form of a quartzite grinder, but the rest of the deposit was robbed in antiquity.[15] Although there is very little visible above ground, the foundations surviving indicates the pylon was originally approximately 46m wide, comparable in size with Horemheb's pylons at Karnak. The core of the structure was constructed using blocks from Amarna, and numerous talatat[16] blocks of the Aten and the Amarna period have also been discovered here.

Thoth was a lunar god and Horemheb's dedication may have been the beginning of detracting the focus away from the solar cult of the Aten. As king, this was emphasised further and Horemheb often depicted himself praying to or in group statues with Ra-Horakhty, Thoth and Maat the goddess of truth. Horemheb may have been projecting the message that cosmic balance (Maat) can only be achieved by both the sun (Ra-Horakhty) and the moon (Thoth), in open retaliation to the 'monotheism' of the Aten cult, and was a clear indicator to the people of Egypt that Horemheb was a traditional king with traditional values.

Horemheb further emphasised the importance of the moon on a door jamb from his Memphite tomb, depicting him worshipping Osiris (*colour plate 4*). There is a unique hymn dedicated to the god, in his form as the nocturnal version of Ra the sun-god. The theme itself was not new, and was first found in the Middle Kingdom Coffin Texts, but this is the first time it was recorded as a hymn. Akhenaten's religion had dismissed the need for Osiris and the funerary deities, as he believed when the Aten set at dusk the world fell into the darkness of the time before creation. It was only through Akhenaten himself that the sun would rise again in the morning. After death the only chance of rebirth was through the king, and images of Akhenaten and Nefertiti replace those of the funerary gods in the noble tombs at Amarna. The re-introduction of the sun's nocturnal journey by Tutankhamun, gave hope for rebirth, and a new day. A further hymn in Horemheb's northern tomb emphasised the reintroduction of this nocturnal journey:

> The Hereditary Prince Horemheb, he says; I have come to you that I may praise your beauty, that I may honour your majesty as both daytimes [*morning and evening*]. May you place the royal scribe Horemheb with you in heaven ... may his name be among the great crew who drag Ra to the west ... you will seize the prow-rope of the night-barque when Ra sets in his going to the Netherworlds, the Westerners [*the deceased*] saying 'Welcome! Welcome' When he penetrates the Netherworld he dispels darkness, the sleepers [*the dead*] jump to their feet when he reaches them[17]

Although his emphasis is on the lunar deities, Egyptian duality meant that the moon could not be worshipped without the sun, and Horemheb does not neglect the solar deities. There are two stelae in his Memphite tomb dedicated to Ra-Horakhty a combination of the deities Horus and Ra, showing another favoured affiliation with the god Horus. One of these stelae is currently in the British Museum and the other was smashed by vandals and is in Cairo in fragments. The door jambs of the statue room, which are also in the British Museum revere the newly reinstated cult of Ra:

> Utterance of the hereditary prince, Horemheb, triumphant, when he worships Ra at his rising, saying, praise to you, who comes every day, who begets yourself each morning who comes forth from the body of your mother without ceasing, the two regions come to you bowing down, they give to you praise, when you rise, when you

have illuminated the earth with brightness, your divine limbs aflame as a mighty one on the heavens. Excellent god, eternal king, lord of brightness, ruler of light. Upon his throne in the Morning barque, great in brilliance in the Evening barque, Divine youth, heir of eternity. Who begets himself, who generates himself. The great Ennead worship you. The lesser Ennead exults to you. They praise you in your beautiful forms with your brilliance in the Evening barque, as when the sacred apes spy you. Rise you, your heart glad. With your diadems in the horizon of heaven, Grant you glory in heaven, Power on earth, that I may go forth among your followers of every day. That my heart may be satisfied with all offerings. May you receive flower-offerings, from the sanctuary. Upon the table of the lords of Heliopolis. By the hereditary prince, count, wearer of the royal seal, sole companion, privy councillor of the palace, superior in the whole land, fanbearer on the right hand side of the king, general of the lord of the two lands, real king's scribe, his beloved the hereditary prince Horemheb

This prayer shows Horemheb's reverence for Ra indicating he was a devoted follower of Ra of Heliopolis in additions to the other deities revered within his Memphite tomb. As it may have been dangerous for Horemheb to have such images and prayers of traditional gods in his tomb during the reign of Akhenaten, it suggests it was not completed during the Akhenaten's reign, but rather during the reformation period of Tutankhamun.

It was only during the reign of Tutankhamun that Horemheb really flourished. This could be due to the survival of the archaeological record, or it could be due to Horemheb's young age and lack of experience during the time before Tutankhamun. Previous to Tutnkhamun, in year one of Akhenaten, Horemheb was possibly only 12 years old and perhaps 29 at Akhenaten's death. These years were probably spent working hard and earning respect as a soldier. By the start of the reign of Tutankhamun, Horemheb held many titles, and by the end of the reign the revered title of *Deputy King*. Some titles may have been honorary without specific duties, and others were held by him earlier in his career, due to representing different ranks of the administration and military. It was quite common for all titles held over an entire career to be recorded in the tomb as if they were held contemporaneously. This seems to be the case here. Horemheb's titles can be divided into separate areas of officialdom, indicating he held positions of authority in many areas, as well as showing a clear path of progression through the ranks.

As we know he started his career in the army, initially as a military scribe and then as a soldier. We are able to trace the stages of his career, through the titles recorded in his Memphite tomb. He began his career as the *Scribe of Recruits*, responsible for enrolling the new recruits and keeping records of their training. This role was also responsible for the booty acquired from Asia including the capture of the northern enemies.[18] He quickly excelled at this and was promoted to *Overseer of Recruits of Lord of the Two Lands*, giving him control over recruitment and placements. He had clearly showed himself to be trustworthy as this position gave him control over who entered the army, and it was essential that he was loyal to the king as this ensured the army was too. He caught the attention of the king, and was given the additional title of *True Royal Scribe* (*colour plate 5*). This would see a change in work location, as he was required more at the palace for the royal administration. There was more than one *Royal Scribe* at any one time, and he no doubt started at the bottom of the ladder, and worked his way up. It is likely that by the time the restoration text of Tutankhamun was written, he may have been instrumental in drafting it, which could explain why Horemheb usurped it when he became king. By the time this was written Horemheb may have held the title of *Overseer of all Overseers of Scribes of the King*, whose role was to control all the record keeping of the royal administration and to ensure the standard was maintained. This led to the position of *One who had Authority over the Library*, which may sound mundane, but libraries in Egypt housed sacred texts, political documents and sensitive material that could be used against the throne. He was therefore responsible for protecting information and ensuring access was monitored.

His career then took a more practical turn, as he was given the title *General*, controlling a particular regiment of the army, and then promoted to *Overseer of the Generals of the Lord of the Two Lands*, giving him ultimate power over the entire army, and their *Generals*. This power put him in close communication with the king, and his advisors and it was not long before he held the title *King's Envoy*, and a fragment from his Memphite tomb (which has since gone missing), tells how he was sent as envoy to the region of the 'sun disc's uprising,' returning triumphantly. However no other details of this expedition are given.[19] This title of Envoy was probably combined with that of *Mouth who Appeases in the Entire Land*, a position of high esteem, giving Horemheb the power to speak on behalf of the king, when dealing with foreign dignitaries. The latter indicates he was a great diplomat, capable of calming any situation, and appeasing irate diplomats, uncertain priests and officials or traumatised farmers. A scene in his Memphite tomb shows him acting as an intermediary between Syrian dignitaries as they appeal to Tutankhamun. They had travelled by horseback from the region of the Sinai and their horses were being cared for by their grooms, to one side of the image. They speak through an interpreter, (17) who is thought perhaps to be Sementawy, the adopted son of Horemheb, in Libyan, Akkadian or Canaanite, who relays it to Horemheb who then speaks to the king, who replies through him:

> Word spoken to his Majesty when the chiefs of every foreign territory came to beg life from him, by the hereditary prince, sole companion, royal scribe Horemheb. He said making answer to the king ... foreigners who do not know Egypt, they are beneath your feet for ever and eternally. Amun has handed them over to you. They entered every foreign territory
>
> Thus said Pharaoh to ... all his officers, ... and it has been reported that some foreigners who do not know how they may live are come from ... their countries are hungry, and they live like animals of the desert ... the great strength [*the king*] will send his mighty arm in front of his army ... and will destroy them and plunder their towns and set fire ...[20]

The text is badly damaged but it appears these rebels had conspired against Egypt only to be defeated by the Egyptian king. Here they are asking for clemency from him. This position was open to corruption, as messages between the king, the interpreter and the dignitaries could be abbreviated or exaggerated depending on the agenda of the envoy. Horemheb was trusted enough not to abuse this position. By looking at the nature of Horemheb's own rule, we can understand why he was so trusted as his entire rule was based on truth and justice (Maat), with severe punishment for corrupt officials and soldiers.

It is often overlooked that during the reign of Tutankhamun, there were military campaigns, and these are recorded by Horemheb in his Memphite tomb, as well as by Tutankhamun himself on talatat blocks used to decorate his temples. Horemheb records a northern campaign, and he parades a number of Asiatic prisoners before Tutankhamun. The accompanying text describes Horemheb's role in the battle and states:

17 Interpretation scene from Saqqara. *Drawing by the author after Martin 1991*

his name was renowned in the land of the Hittites[21]

As is typical with any battle reports, they are full of pomp and pro-Egyptian propaganda; meaning every battle is a victory and the enemy quakes in the presence of the king or the tomb owner. Therefore although we are unable to read a great deal into this statement, we can ascertain that Horemheb was at least in battle with the Hittites.

Evidence suggests there were two campaigns in the later years of Tutankhamun, one against the Asiatics and one in Nubia. These were recorded at his mortuary temple on the west bank at Thebes. These talatat blocks were originally Akhenaten's, recarved by Tutankhamun and further reused by Ay. They were discovered in Horemheb's pylons

18 Chariot battle of Tutankhamun, from a reused block at the mortuary temple of Horemheb. *Drawing by the author after Johnson 1992, fig 15*

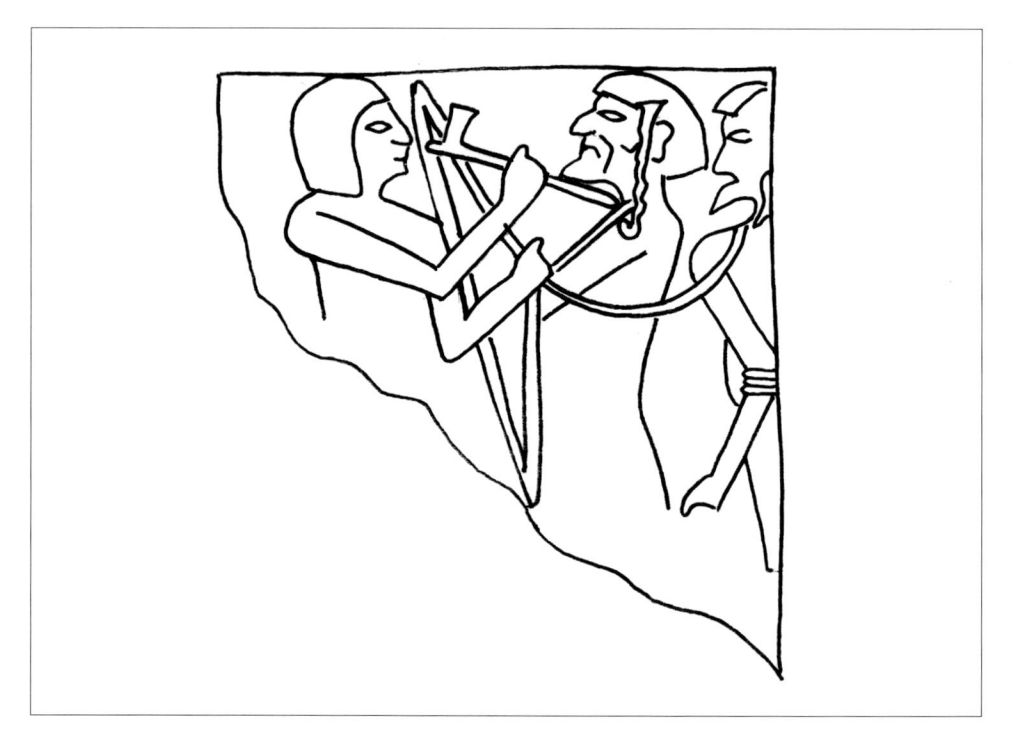

19 An Egyptian soldier tying up a Libyan captive. Reused blocks from the mortuary temple of Horemheb. *Drawing by the author after Johnson 1992, fig 11*

at Karnak temple.[22] The talatat blocks record four episodes from these battles, and although they are fragmentary, the Asiatic record is preserved quite well. It is likely that both these campaigns were led by Horemheb, who depicts similar scenes in his Memphite tomb.

> Greater than the great ones, mightier than the mighty ones, great chieftain of the subjects ... who follows the king on his journeys in the southern and northern foreign land ... chief of the most important courtiers, who listens to the confidences of the unique ones ... master of the secrets of the palace ... messenger of the king at the head of his expedition to the southern and northern foreign land ... elected by the king above the Two Lands to carry out the government of the Two Shores [*Two Lands*] overseer of generals of the Lord of the Two Lands ... the unique one who counts the troops ... one who was in attendance on his lord [the king] on the battlefield on this day of smiting the Asiatics.[23]

This indicates that Horemheb was definitely in the battles with the Nubians and the Asiatics but also suggests that Tutankhamun himself was on the battlefield. The Asiatics are depicted as coming from two different groups; Canaanites with mushroom-shaped haircuts and beards and Syrians with cropped hair and full beards. The scenes start with the battle itself which was on land using chariotry. The Egyptian chariot corps is followed by the running infantry.

The Asiatics are terrified of the Egyptian army, and the Asiatic chariot corps flees closely followed by the Egyptians to a walled citadel. The Egyptians then use scaling ladders to penetrate the fortress. Hundreds of dead Asiatics are depicted, and one image shows three Asiatic women and a small child wailing, holding their arms aloft in fear of the Egyptian army. The battle ends in victory, and the enemy dead are counted by having their hands cut off and recorded by the Egyptian military scribe. Some of the soldiers have enemy hands threaded onto their spears as grisly trophies, perhaps demonstrating how many Asiatics they personally killed.

The Nubian battle was very similar although the blocks are far more damaged. There was also a chariot battle which followed the same 'plan' as the Asiatic battle (*18*) ending in a victory parade, where booty and prisoners are presented to the king. In the Nubian campaign a number of Nubian bound captives, and in the Asiatic battle scenes, Asiatic captives, are given to Tutankhamun (*19*) who then presents the prisoners and booty to the god Amun. A corresponding scene in Horemheb's tomb shows Asiatic and Nubian prisoners, recorded by military scribes and may represent the post battle activities of these campaigns.

The victory procession at the end of both battles is twofold; one on land and the other by river (*20*). During the Nubian parade the soldiers marching in victory are depicted wearing the tasselled helmets of the Asiatics defeated in the previous battle, and the soldiers from the Asiatic battle have spears threaded with enemy hands. The charioteers all walk alongside their plumed horses, clutching the reins, whilst accompanied by infantry, holding battle axes and open fans.

After the land procession, the Egyptian army made a spectacular, victorious return to Thebes by boat (*21*). The royal barge with numerous rowers, with four towboats in full sail aiding, led the procession. The barge was accompanied on both sides of the Nile by rows of running infantry. A cage was hung from the royal barge with a Syrian prisoner within; its prominence indicating it was a chieftain. Who captured this Chieftain is not recorded, but bearing in mind how well Horemheb is rewarded with shebyu collars, it may have been him. A further block from the Memphite tomb, currently in Bologna depicts a feast in honour of Horemheb and it has been speculated that this banquet was to welcome Horemheb back to Memphis[24] after a battle such as this one (*22*).

20 Victory parade of Tutankhamun after the Asiatic battle. *Drawing by the author after Johnson 1992*

Middle and below: 21a & b River parade of Tutankhamun. *Drawings by the author after Johnson 1992 figure 28*

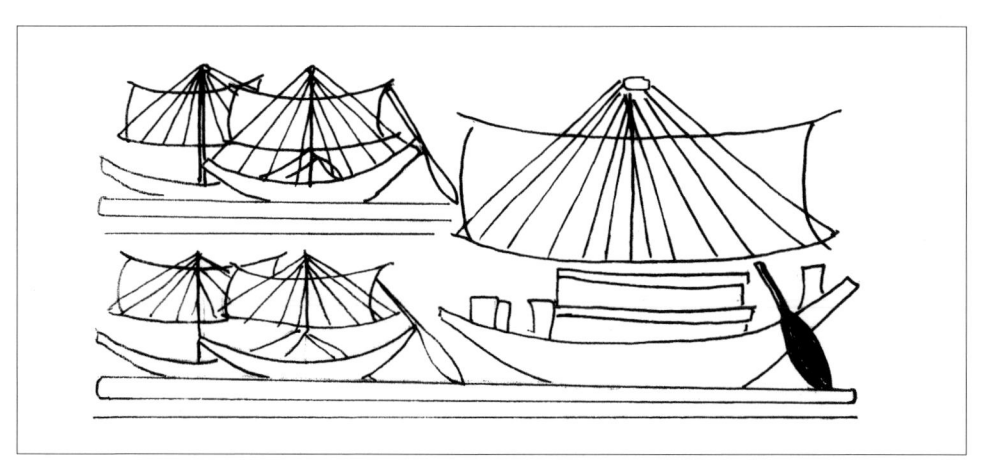

22 Feasting from the Memphite tomb of Horemheb. *Drawing by the author after Martin 1991*

In addition to Horemheb's military role, he held a series of positions in royal administration after his promotion to king's envoy, each more important than the last including those of *Chief of the Entire Land, Overseer of All Works of the King in Every Place* and *High Steward*, which rendered Horemheb responsible for all the workshops, military, taxes, and building works. It would be impossible for him to actively participate in the day-to-day running of all these activities, so instead he would simply give a summarised report to the king, perhaps weekly or monthly based on the reports of the Overseers on the ground. This required him to be in close correspondence with Tutankhamun, and much of the time acting on his behalf. In order to facilitate this he was given the role of *Sealbearer of the King of Upper and Lower Egypt*, enabling him to act on behalf of the king, through possession of the royal seal. In addition to the positions of general governance, just discussed, Horemheb also held two religious titles, that of *Overseer of all Divine Offices* and *Overseer of Priests of Horus, Lord of Seby* giving him supervisory power over the newly appointed priesthood in Tutankhamun's newly re-established religion.

His royal administration and central government titles held the highest status and provided Horemheb with a great deal of wealth and opportunities. These titles were probably obtained later in his career as each brought him in close proximity to Tutankhamun. These included the honorary title of *rpat*, or *Hereditary Prince*. Although no real duties were attached to this title it was one of high status which would be passed down to his son, should he have one, showing royal favour was not just bestowed upon him but his entire family. Another honorary title was that of *Foremost of the King's Courtiers*, which was simply a title of status. He also held the advisory positions *Sole Companion* (to the king), *Fanbearer on the Right of the King* and *Master of the Secrets of the Palace*. The role of *Sole Companion to the King* also ensured Horemheb was in close contact with the king. This may have been a natural progression from the *Fanbearer on the Right Hand of the King* which although sounds like a mundane position, was not, as it enabled Horemheb to be present in all meetings of the king, and in the presence of foreign and Egyptian dignitaries. This role may have also led to promotion to *Master of the secrets of the Palace* which like the fanbearer, meant Horemheb was privy to state secrets, and advised the king accordingly. Horemheb was clearly considered a trustworthy official which no doubt influenced Tutankhamun in his decision to appoint him *One Elected by the King Above the Two Lands to Carry Out the Government of the Two Banks* and *Overseer of All the Offices of the King*; both practical positions giving Horemheb the authority to act on behalf the king throughout Egypt, overseeing all officials and activities, ensuring loyalty to Tutankhamun. In order to catch the attention of the king it was clear Horemheb was the man to impress. This was even more apparent when Horemheb was promoted further to the position of *Deputy of the King in the Entire Land*; the highest position of state and the heir apparent to the throne.

As such an important figure in the royal court, Horemheb would be called to attend state events on behalf of the king. Such events included the funeral of the *High Priest* of Ptah at Memphis, Neferonpet, recorded on the Berlin Trauerrelief, which took place during the reign of Tutankhamun. There were twelve official mourners at the funeral, who are only identified by their titles, although making a clear identification of some of these officials has been possible. These officials were positioned in order of importance with the *Royal Scribe*, *rpat* and military officer taking the lead. He was followed by the overseers of cities and viziers, the *Royal Scribe* and *Steward*, the *Royal Scribe* and *Chief Treasurer* (identified as Maya), *Overseer of the Law Court*, the *Military Officer* (Nakhtmin), the *Chamberlain*, *Overseer of the Treasury*, the *High Priest of Ra at Heliopolis*, the new *High Priest of Ptah at Memphis* and the *Governor* bringing up the rear.[25] It is the man at the front, closest to the funerary bier that is of interest to us, as he is titled *rpat*, (*Hereditary Prince*), and is likely to represent Horemheb as he is the only one who held all these titles, and was the first individual to hold the title *rpat*, and not be a king's son since Thutmosis IV.

The tomb of Tutankhamun (KV62) has an image of his funeral, which is similar to that on the Berlin stela, as it also shows twelve officials, labelled 'The companions and the officials of the house of the king, who are dragging the deified king and Lord of the Two Lands, Nebkheperure, to the west'.[26] Again the names of the individuals are not recorded but it is thought Horemheb was also at the front of this entourage. However, although he seems to be present in the image of the funeral, there is nothing in the tomb bearing his name, and this is interpreted as meaning he was not in fact present at the funeral. There were objects within the assemblage dedicated to Tutankhamun by Nakhtmin, the military officer and Maya the *Treasurer*, and it is thought they attended the funeral, and the images on the wall indicate Ay carried out the burial rites,[27] in the role of 'eldest son'.

Although the funeral may have been the final act of a loyal servant to Tutankhamun, Horemheb was continually at the beck and call of the young child during his kingship. On one occasion Horemheb was called to calm down the king [*the palace*] 'when it had fallen into a rage.' It appears Tutankhamun was having a tantrum and only Horemheb, in his role as *Deputy King* and mentor, could calm him down. This intimacy with Tutankhamun is further emphasised on a stela within Horemheb's tomb with the inscription:

> May you cause Horemheb to stand firmly by the side of the sovereign, just as you yourself are by the side of the Lord of the Universe [*Thoth*], as you foster him when he comes forth from the womb of his mother

Horemheb compares himself to the god Thoth, as well as a proxy father to the young boy king.[28] This shows his relationship to the king was intimate and personal, far more important than that of advisor, or royal administrator; in fact that of family.

Although it is difficult to identify which of these titles were held together, the vast list displays the diverse role of Horemheb during the reign of Tutankhamun in particular, and also during the reign of King Ay as he continued adding to his Memphite tomb until he took over the throne rendering his nobles' tomb obsolete. Many of these titles would be recompensed with status and wealth and Horemheb probably owned a vast amount of land and property. The most valuable piece of land was that of his tomb in Saqqara, a prominent part of the Memphite cemetery. This was a boon of the king, and he was likely rewarded further with the workmen and materials to build it for some service rendered to the king. If the tomb in Amarna inscribed with the name Paatenemheb belonged to Horemheb it was quickly abandoned, as he started building his Memphite tomb. Even the very wealthy would not have the wherewithal to build such monumental sepulchres, and the site, access to stones from the quarries, stonemasons, draftsmen and painters are testament of his status and closeness to the *King*. He was able to employ the best in their field to produce his tomb.

The site was carefully chosen, although at this point the cemetery at Memphis where the tomb is situated was not virgin land, and the tomb was built over the site of two Old Kingdom mastabas, with the original burial incorporated into the monument. Many stones used to block the entrance to the burial chambers were quarried from the pyramid of Djoser nearby.[29] At the bottom of shaft (i) in the north-west corner of the courtyard the burial of the judge, Khuywer from the fifth or sixth dynasties (2375-2345 BCE)[30] was still in situ as the tomb was built. The other shaft (iv) in the second courtyard was also from the original mastaba tombs but the burial was not intact, and therefore this was used to bury Horemheb's two wives. The area chosen for the tomb was relatively private, and Horemheb's tomb was not surrounded by other monuments, as it was situated further west than the other New Kingdom burials.

The tomb itself was an innovation of the period known as a temple tomb, which was laid out like a traditional temple with a forecourt, pylon, open courts, chapels and store rooms. These temple-tombs were impressive but difficult to protect from robbers and the elements as most of the monument was above ground. The open courtyard for example would quickly fill with windblown sand, and one of the roles of the priests responsible for maintaining the cult of the deceased Horemheb, was to keep it clear. Once the cult was no longer practised the temple filled with sand gradually hiding the structure. It was royal in plan and was adopted by very high officials and minor royals

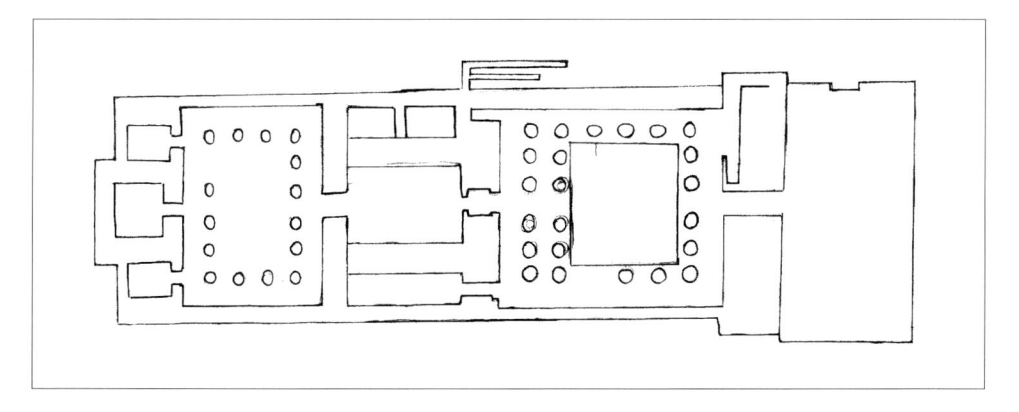

23 Memphite tomb of Horemheb. *Drawing by Brian Billington after Martin 1993*

throughout the nineteenth dynasty. It appears from the excavations that the tomb was built in three stages; at the success of the Nubian, and Syrian campaigns; at the success of the Libyan campaign and at the end of the reign of Tutankhamun, although the building works from the latter period are incomplete with the outlines of the images drawn but not carved.

These temples were utilised as mortuary temples for the deceased who were buried beneath them and there was possibly a ceremonial approach to the tomb from the cultivated area, as attested by the remains of a paved forecourt. The entire tomb was made of mud-brick, which was faced internally with Tura limestone making a good carving surface for relief decoration and externally with plaster. The pylon on Horemheb's temple was seven metres high, and to show the difference between a religious temple and the temple-tomb, it was left undecorated. Instead it was encased with limestone blocks polished to a high shine. The rest of the walls within the tomb were also encased in limestone and we are fortunate many of these have survived. Behind Horemheb's pylon was a pillared courtyard with 24 rectangle limestone pillars, although only ten are *in situ*,[31] which originally stood three metres tall forming a pillared colonnade. These pillars were decorated with images of Horemheb and the deities. All the images faced the inner temple following the journey of the sun, which moved from east to west from the pylon to the statue room at the rear. The courtyard was designed with the centre slightly lower than the colonnade to drain away rain water. The courtyard was being extended eastwards but the construction was abandoned when Horemheb ascended to the throne. There was a statue room, which housed statues of Horemheb and Amenia, and these statues were placed in niches in the walls. Long rooms on either side of the statue chamber were used as chapels initially, and in the Coptic period the monks from the nearby Monastery of Apa Jeremias used them as anchoritic cells, and several Christian symbols including crosses and fish have been discovered on the walls and ceiling.[32] At the rear of the temple was the sanctuary which was the intended focus of the funerary cult of Horemheb, which was utilised by the Ramesside family after his death for worship of the deified Horemheb.

When Horemheb became *King*, this Memphite tomb was near completion, and it was no doubt quite difficult for him to give it up, to abandon it to the sand as it had stood a sign of his wealth and status for so long. The decoration recording his life as a soldier has proven invaluable. The work was carried out by a number of different workmen as there are clear differences in styles and artistic ability displayed in the reliefs.[33] He had already built a burial suite for himself in the tomb, and obviously had every intention of being buried there. This suite was reached by a third shaft and corridor which opened into a pillared hall, with palace façade cornicing carved into the walls, which were painted red and black.[34] This decoration was normally used to decorate coffins, and in effect the burial chamber was a giant sarcophagus to protect Horemheb's remains for eternity. A door led from this room to another pillared hall, which had carved images of windows just beneath the ceiling and the door frame was decorated with ankh and *was* sceptre symbols. There was a red and black colour scheme throughout the tomb with most of the subterranean chambers showing traces of this paint.[35] The tomb was not complete, and the workmen abandoned work, possibly when Horemheb became *King*. The diorite pounders and chisels were discovered near this doorway during the excavations of the tomb exactly where they had fallen. It is uncertain whether he continued adding to the tomb after his accession to the throne.

The most unusual aspect of Horemheb's early career before his ascension to the throne, was that although he held the title '*Deputy of the King*' and *rpat* (*Hereditary Prince*) it was not he who took over the throne from Tutankhamun, but rather

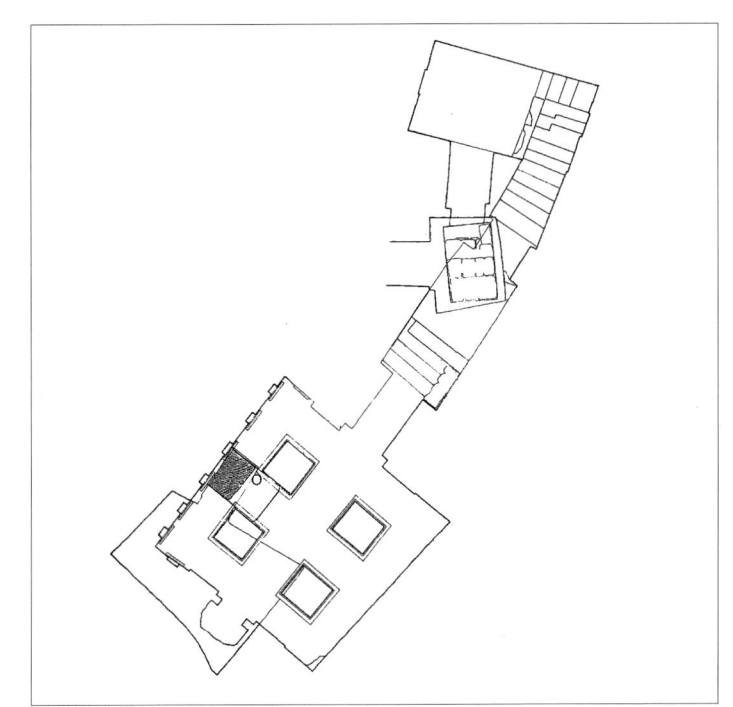

24 Internal structure (upper level) of the Memphite tomb of Horemheb. *Drawing by Brian Billington after Martin 1978*

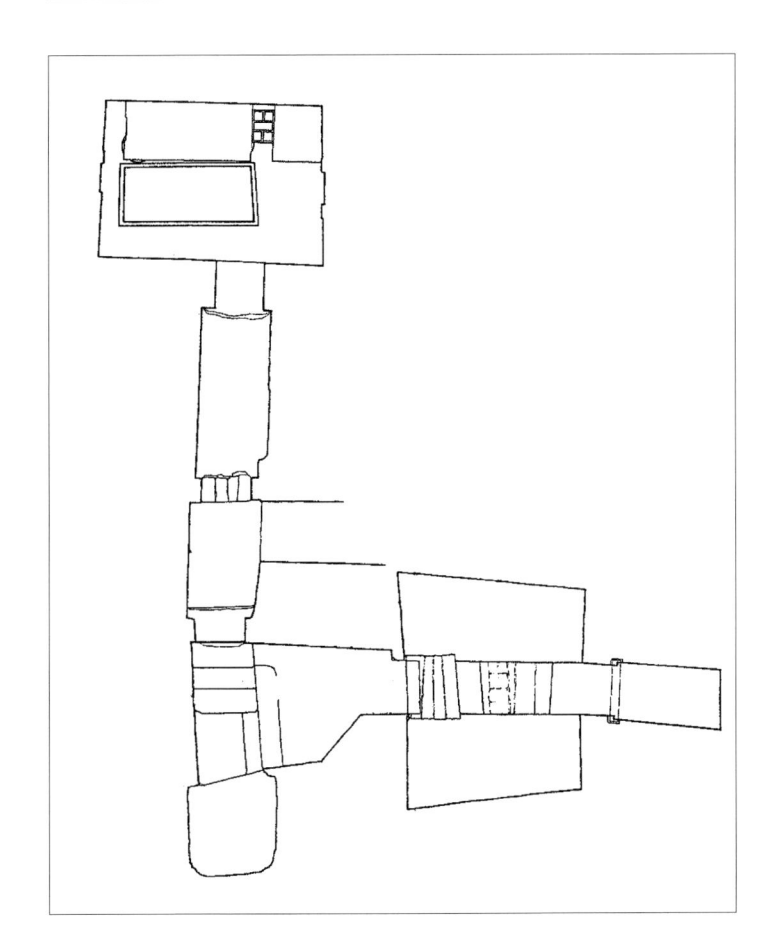

25 Internal structure (lower level) of the Memphite tomb of Horemheb. *Drawing by Brian Billington after Martin 1978*

another official, who was of almost equal status to Horemheb, Ay. Ay also held a high status in the royal court and it has been suggested he co-ruled with Tutankhamun before his death[36] although there is no strong evidence for this. As the importance of Horemheb's position in the royal court of Tutankhamun only comes from inscriptions commissioned by Horemheb himself, some scholars believe he exaggerated his position to legitimise his right to the throne, as Ay was probably higher in rank throughout the reign of Tutankhamun.[37]

CHAPTER 4

ASCENSION TO THE THRONE

Horemheb held a very important position within the royal court of Tutankhamun, bearing the title *rpat* or *Hereditary Prince*, and acting as *Deputy King*. One would think, therefore, that the transition to *King* upon the death of Tutankhamun would have been straightforward. Most historians believe this was not the case, as instead of the designated heir becoming *King* as was traditional, an elderly relative, and *Vizier* of Tutankhamun, Ay, usurped him. This in itself has caused a great deal of debate with many theories as to how and why this happened. Perhaps Ay diverted Horemheb away from Thebes, taking the role of the eldest son at Tutankhamun's funeral and ascending to the throne in his absence, perhaps a diplomatic arrangement was made between Horemheb and Ay so they both could rule in turn, or maybe Ay took the throne under duress, due to the continuing problems with the Hittites in the Near East. Without a clear record of the events from the period these questions cannot be answered with any degree of certainty although it is possible, using the available evidence, to discuss the likelihood of each scenario, producing the most probable sequence of events.

When researching the succession after Tutankhamun's death it is necessary to examine closely the titles not only of Horemheb but other officials in the royal court. As other men appeared to hold the title *rpat* or *Hereditary Prince*, it suggests perhaps, in some instances, it was an honorary title with no rules of accession attached, or even a modern misinterpretation of the title. A major hindrance to the study of the individuals of this period is that many monuments were later intentionally destroyed, either by Horemheb himself or Ramses II. The purpose of this destruction was to erase the names of individuals, preventing them from being remembered and therefore denying them an afterlife. To a large extent the protagonists were successful as there are many gaps in the history of this period, but some evidence regarding certain individuals has survived. It is with these officials that our investigation starts, as the evidence indicates that although Horemheb was named as heir during Tutankhamun's lifetime, albeit perhaps upon his own advice[1] there were other contenders for the throne.

Ay was the main adversary, even though this was not necessarily obvious during Tutankhamun's reign. From the records it is clear that Ay was an important member of the royal court, holding a position close to the *King* as well as being his elderly kinsman. As with many members of the Amarna royal family, the family tree of Ay is uncertain and nowhere are his parents' names recorded. From the examination of Ay's titles, it is interesting to note that many of them are the same as Yuya's, the father of Queen Tiye the wife of Amenhotep III, and the mother of Akhenaten. Most positions, whether military, administrative or kingship passed down from father to son, so identical titles can often be interpreted a sign of filial connections.

There is no doubt in the royal court of Akhenaten and Tutankhamun, Ay was a man of great importance. He was *General of the Royal Chariotry*, *True Scribe of the King*, or private secretary, and *Fanbearer at the Right of the King* under Akhenaten; all positions which gave him close contact to the king. As Akhenaten's secretary, Ay was no doubt responsible for recording Akhenaten's religious utterances, which goes

26 Amun Min and Horemheb (British Museum). *Photograph courtesy of Brian Billington*

some way to explaining why his tomb is the only one at Amarna with the Hymn to the Aten carved on the wall.[2] As *Fanbearer* he was privy to the secrets of the *King*, and his discussions (private or political), as was Horemheb. Ay was a close advisor to Akhenaten, although during the reign of Tutankhamun he seems to have been surpassed in this role by Horemheb. However he was still a prominent character as attested by a small piece of gold-foil found in the Valley of the Kings, bearing the title of *Royal Chancellor, Vizier* and *Doer of Right*,[3] the latter title was kept and incorporated into his royal titles once he became *King*.

The only title held by Yuya, but not Ay was *High Priest of Min at Akhmim*, although it is generally accepted that Ay was born in this town, and once he was *King* he dedicated a temple to Min here (26). This discrepancy could simply be a case of timing. When Ay was a man of prominence, Akhenaten's cult was primary and therefore maintaining religious titles such as this would damage his career. Due to the similarity in titles, and their name, it is generally accepted that Yuya was Ay's father. As queen Tiye was the daughter of Yuya and Tuya it is therefore accepted that Ay was her brother, and therefore great uncle to Tutankhamun; a true contender for the throne in the absence of a direct male heir.

The most intriguing title held by both Yuya and Ay, and one that is important to our discussion is *it ntr* or God's Father. This title is often interpreted to mean 'father in law' to the *King*, as Yuya was the father of the wife of Amenhotep III. However in what capacity Ay was the 'father in law' to Akhenaten, Smenkhkare or Tutankhamun needs to be explored further. The title is mentioned in his tomb created no earlier than year nine of Akhenaten, so it is likely referring to a connection with Akhenaten. However it is necessary to explore all possibilities.

For the title to be literal, Ay needs to be the father of the wife of one of the Amarna kings although his use of the title became more prolific during the reign of Tutankhamun. This poses a number of problems. Tutankhamun's only recorded wife is Ankhesenamun, the daughter of Akhenaten and Nefertiti, but it is clear he had more wives than this. The sister of Huy, the Viceroy of Nubia was the *Matron of the Harem of Tutankhamun*; without a harem of wives this title would be unnecessary. It would be impossible for Ay to be Ankhesenamun's father, but as it would be very unusual for an Egyptian *King* to have only one wife. Could one of these other brides have been the daughter of Ay? We know that Ay's wife Tiy had at least one child, although whether a boy or a girl, or even if the child survived is not recorded. Ay's wife, was royal wet-nurse to Nefertiti, as recorded in his tomb at Amarna. This was a revered position and Tiy was one of only two women who received the Gold of Honour based on her position (27).[4] She is shown prominently alongside Ay beneath the Window of Appearances with Akhenaten and Nefertiti throwing gold shebyu collars to their favoured courtiers. It has been suggested the prominence of Tiy in the Amarna royal house helped Ay rise to power and she may have come from a superior ranking family than his;[5] although this would not be the case if he was truly Queen Tiye's brother. As a wet-nurse, Tiy would have given birth to a child in order to be able to nurse, but who this child was or whether it survived is lost to us. However, if his child survived, could *she* have been in the harem of Akhenaten? Assuming the child died at birth, coupled with no mention of a second wife able to bear children, Ay would not be the father in law of anyone, royal or otherwise and this has led to the assumption that the title *it ntr* was in his case, an honorary title related to his wife being the wet-nurse of the queen.[6]

Another suggestion which is not often considered is that Ay may have been the father of Kiya, the secondary wife of Akhenaten, and accepted mother to Tutankhamun. The origins of Kiya are as obscure as most other characters from the Amarna period, but should Ay be her father he would be the 'father in law' to Akhenaten and grandfather to Tutankhamun; therefore in this instance, the title *it ntr* could mean father-in-law of the *King*. If this is not the case then another interpretation needs to be found for this rather obscure title.

Alan Gardiner[7] suggests the title *it ntr* was given to a priest of a 'certain age' and standing; an honorary title, but one showing a close connection to the *King*, embracing a filial attitude towards him. The title is often accompanied by the epithet *mry ntr* beloved of the god and may mean simply Elder Statesman. There are various reasons why this does not apply to Ay and his use of the title. Ay, as mentioned above

27 Ay and Tiy; Ay's tomb, Amarna. Photograph by the author

did not hold a priestly title, he held administrative and military titles, and therefore *it ntr* could not be a title given to the priesthood. This issue has also been raised of the *King*'s relationship with the *it ntr*. It is certainly surprising that the divine *King* was obliged to give filial respect to a man simply because of his age. A *King* is not obliged to act in this way towards anyone other than the gods, and it is them he appeals to in times of need; although it must be considered that in the case of Tutankhamun he relied heavily on the advice of his statesmen due to his young age and inexperience. However this was for practicality, not obligation and tradition. It also needs to be considered that Ay kept this title of *it ntr* even when he became *King*, incorporating it into his royal titles. This indicates it means so much more than 'Elder Statesman' because, as pharaoh he would not need to accentuate his non-royal administrative roles. As *King* he was no longer an *Elder Statesman*, but divine. This suggests the title is associated with royal relationships rather than administration.[8]

One of the most accepted interpretations of the title *it ntr* is that of *Tutor to the King*, and this could apply to both Yuya and Ay. Yuya is believed to have been the tutor of Amenhotep III, who his daughter Tiye was to marry. As they married at a young age it is quite acceptable that the young *King* was still being tutored. This suggests the young Tutankhamun may also have been tutored by the *it ntr*, in this instance Ay. This ensured Ay was close to the boy *King*, training him in his royal duties, and appropriate behaviour, as well as guiding him on essential matters of politics.

Some scholars have gone as far as to suggest that Ay was regent for the young Tutankhamun and the real power behind the throne.[9] Excavations from the Temple of Nebkheperure in Thebes, built by Ay for Tutankhamun, have uncovered 52 architraves, 13 pillar fragments, six wall fragments, five lintel fragments, and one cornice fragment, bearing titularies, cartouches, and dedications of both Tutankhamun and Ay. However 12 architrave blocks bear the titles of both Tutankhamun and Ay together,[10] and have been used as proof of a co-regency between the two kings, leading to the implication this temple was a joint project. On closer inspection Ay states he built the temple 'as his monument for his son,' not as a joint project. The idea of co-regency does not quite stand up to scrutiny despite this apparent building collaboration. Co-regencies were normally announced in the instance of a king not having an heir, which *is* the case with Tutankhamun, but normally when the *King* was of a greater age than the co-regent. It would seem somewhat surprising that Tutankhamun would name an elderly man as co-regent, on the off-chance he would die without an heir before the elderly man. Tutankhamun could not have foretold his own early demise and at 18 years old or younger it would be assumed he would father a number of heirs before his death. If he were to name an heir surely it would be someone a little younger than Ay; perhaps someone of Horemheb's age. Evidence suggests this is what he did.

However, with Ay's long-standing royal connections; being the brother of Queen Tiye, possibly the father of Kiya and the great uncle or even grandfather of Tutankhamun his claim to the throne outstripped that of Horemheb whose success lay in the hands of the boy king and the titles bestowed upon him. With the boy king gone, the throne went to the person with the strongest claim; Ay, despite the titles held by Horemheb when Tutankhamun was alive.

Another individual often believed to be involved in the fight for the throne was possibly the son of Ay and Tiy; perhaps their only child or the brother of Kiya should Ay be her father. Other scholars do not think Tiy was his mother, and suggest perhaps he was Ay's grandson.[11] This man, Nakhtmin, was *First prophet of Min-Isis*, or *High Priest*, at Akhmin and is first attested in the tomb of Ay at Amarna and is depicted on Ay's temple at Akhmin. The priest, Nakhtmin from Ay's hometown is often confused with another man of the same name, who was a soldier in the army, and donated five shabtis to the burial of Tutankhamun. Both Nakhtmins were closely involved in the royal court in one way or another, one as a priest for the newly re-established cult of Min-Isis and the other as military leader under the reign of Tutankhamun.

They are however, not the same man, clearly two individuals, as the priestly Nakhtmin has no military titles, and the military Nakhtmin has no priestly titles.[12] It is however the military Nakhtmin, who is of interest here as he holds some intriguing titles; *rpat*, or *Hereditary Prince, Royal Scribe, Military Officer of the Lord of the Two Lands, General and King's Son*. For many years scholars have debated over this title of 'King's Son' which coupled with *rpat* suggests he was the heir apparent to the throne.

Nakhtmin's first appearance in the records is on the shabtis from Tutankhamun's tomb making it unlikely he was the son of Amenhotep III as he would have been too old to father a son at his death, or Tutankhamun who died too young to bear a son of military age. The records also do not show any sons of Akhenaten, although Tutankhamun and Smenkhkare are believed to be his. This has led some scholars to the conclusion that Nakhtmin is the son of Ay, and heir apparent to the throne after his death. However, upon examination of Nakhtmin's various monuments, his mother is named as Iuy, the *Votaress of Min*, and *Musician of Isis*, and his father was a *Judge, Royal Scribe* and *Overseer of the Mountains of Nubia*, a man called Pennesutowe.[13] The known names of his parents obviously affect the arguments regarding him as a genuine king's son. So who was Nakhtmin and why did he hold such an eminent title?

The key to the mystery is in the title of *Overseer of the Mountains of Nubia*, held by his father, which places him in Nubia. This indicates perhaps Nakhtmin's role was also in Nubia, in control of the southern army. Some scholars have tied this in with the so-called hostility between Ay and Horemheb. They state Horemheb's military associations were mainly in the north, as the battle scenes in the Memphite tomb have indicated, with titles given to him by Tutankhamun. This indicates that Nakhtmin controlled the military in the south, under the patronage of Ay, showing an apparent north-south divide.[14] Both Horemheb and Nakhtmin were titled *rpat* indicating Nakhtmin was designated as heir to the throne of Ay and Horemheb to the throne of Tutankhamun before Ay usurped it. This explains why both held the title *rpat* but does not explain why Nakhtmin is named as *King's Son*. Had Ay given him the title in an honorary capacity? Or is there some other explanation?

It is commonly accepted that Nakhtmin's title of *King's Son* is incomplete and it should read *King's Son of Kush*,[15] a title closely associated with the Viceroy of Kush, an important semi-military administrative position at the Egyptian frontier in Nubia. This is supported by his father's Nubian connections and neatly explains both the *rpat* and *King's Son* titles. This has instigated studies regarding Nakhtmin's placement in the line of known viceroys from this period. Amenhotpe-Huy was the Viceroy of Kush under Tutankhamun and died or retired before his death. He seems to have been replaced before Ay ascended to the throne by Nakhtmin, already in a position of power and wealth at this point,[16] but no Viceroy of Kush was a royal prince until the reign of Herihor (twenty-first dynasty).[17] During the reign of Horemheb, Nakhtmin was replaced by Paser, who was appointed this position by Ay. After his death the statues of Nakhtmin were mutilated, denying him an afterlife, which has been accredited to Horemheb, citing Nakhtmin's claim to the throne as the potential reason. However there must be another reason, as Nakhtmin had no royal claim to the throne and therefore would not incur wrath for this reason.

Others have claimed Ay gave Nakhtmin the position of Viceroy of Nubia as a means of limiting the power held by Horemheb and his army, and this was the reason he was held in contempt by Horemheb, but there is no evidence for this. The Viceroy under Tutankhamun, Amenhotpe-Huy held a chariotry rank in addition to being Viceroy, indicating this position incorporated military training, and it is thought Nakhtmin was trained under him, serving as infantry commander, until Huy died passing the role to him. This seems to be a straightforward promotion into the position of Viceroy, with no links to the throne and certainly not a position to out-rank Horemheb. As this position was hereditary, Huy named Nakhtmin as his *rpat*, or heir apparent. Upon his ascension to the position of Viceroy Nakhtmin also gained the titles *The Two Eyes of the King, Controller of the Nobles*, and *Leader of the Nobles*, giving some indication of the importance of this role, of acting for the *King* on the Nubian frontier.[18] If Horemheb had indeed been jealous of the promotion of Nakhtmin by Ay, and took it as a personal infringement on his power and influence, then surely he would have felt the same about Amenhotpe-Huy under Tutankhamun, and later Paser, who was also appointed by Ay? In fact Paser remained in office throughout the reign of Horemheb, to be followed by his son, the stablemaster Amenemopet.[19] This in itself indicates that there was no rivalry between Horemheb and Ay, as it may have been dangerous to keep one of Ay's men in such an important position, who could potentially invade Egypt with a Nubian pretender and steal the throne. Neither Huy's nor Paser's tomb and statues were deliberately mutilated after his death in the same manner of Nakhtmin indicating promotion was not the reason for the destruction and there was another reason why Nakhtmin fell from royal grace in the years following the death of Ay. Whether the destruction was really carried out by Horemheb is not known, although it has been suggested it was simply because he was the son of Ay, an Amarnan king and his first wife.[20] Perhaps Nakhtmin committed a crime and was punished for it? Maybe he was an embezzler, a tomb robber, or even planned the assassination of the *King*? Perhaps as some people believe, it was jealously, or that

Horemheb felt threatened by him but when one considers the power and experience held by Horemheb, in addition to his intimacy with the royal family it seems unlikely he would feel threatened by a politician based in Nubia. In addition to that, on the Berlin Trauerrelief, showing the funeral of the *High Priest* of Memphis, Horemheb is clearly Nakhtmin's superior,[21] and therefore would not be threatened by him. However Horemheb recognised the power held by the Viceroy of Kush, and divided the role between Kush and Wawat, with two men each in control of a specific area of the Nubian region.

From the evidence available there were only ever two real contenders for the throne of Egypt upon the death of Tutankhamun. The Deputy King, Horemheb and the final surviving royal male relative, Ay. There should have been no problem, as according to tradition the surviving male heir takes the throne and should he have no heirs upon his death it should go to the named heir. To confuse the issue of ascension even further Tutankhamun's widow decided to get involved, bringing another potential heir into the equation.

One of the most discussed and controversial issues regarding Ay's ascension to the throne is the letter sent to the *King* of the Hittites, Supplilumas, from an Egyptian royal widow requesting a Hittite prince be sent to Egypt to be king. This letter is widely believed to have been written by Tutankhamun's widow Ankhesenamun. She was still a young girl, perhaps only 21 years old upon the death of her husband, Tutankhamun, and clearly did not want to relinquish her position as 'King's Wife' and the power that accompanied it.

Perhaps it was clear to her that her great uncle, Ay was to take over the throne and had voiced his desire to wed her as a means of further legitimising his right to the throne, preventing her from marrying someone else who could try to usurp the throne from him. She was not keen, as he was a great deal older than her, and as there were no other princes to marry (whether sons, brothers or uncles) it is believed she wrote a letter to the Hittite *King*, requesting one of his sons be sent to marry her, making him *King* of Egypt.

She stated in particular she did not want to 'marry a servant' which could refer to her prospective marriage to Ay, the tutor to her deceased husband, Tutankhamun:

> My husband has died. A son I have not. But to you they say the sons are many. If you would send me one son of yours, he would become my husband. Never shall I pick out a servant of mine and make him my husband ... I am afraid

The Hittite *King* was naturally suspicious and sent an emissary to Egypt to report on the Egyptian political situation. The emissary returned to the Hittite *King* and reported that the situation was as the queen had written. The queen, in her eagerness to marry a Hittite prince sent her messenger to the *King* with another letter. The records show the messenger Hani, speaking on her behalf stated:

> Oh my Lord! This is ... our country's shame! If we have a son of the king at all, would we have come to a foreign country and kept asking for a lord for ourselves? Nibhururiya, (*Tutankhamun*) who was our lord, died; a son he has not. Our Lord's wife is solitary. We are seeking a son of our lord for the kingship of Egypt, and for the woman, our lady, we seek as her husband! Furthermore, we went to no other country, only here did we come! Now, oh our Lord, give us a son of yours[22]

Such a request from an Egyptian queen was unheard of and the Hittite *King* did not initially believe it was a genuine request, but he was finally convinced by the words of the messenger. Eventually he sent his son Zennanza to Egypt, which he would not have done if there was any indication there was a royal son or contender for the throne. Unfortunately Prince Zennanza died before he reached the Egyptian border; although whether he was murdered, died of an accident or succumbed to plague is unknown although Supplilumas chose to believe the worst.

Academic debates have continued regarding the possible murderer of Zennanza, and both Ay and Horemheb have been accused; with the assumption there was a rivalry between them. It is suggested Horemheb murdered the prince as he was a threat to the throne, named by Tutankhamun as his. An ensuing war between the Egyptians and the Hittites would make the army and the *General* Horemheb indispensable even under the new *King*, Ay.[23] However if Ay was threatened by Horemheb as many people suggest, it seems ludicrous Ay would name his rival as heir. It has been suggested that the comment on the coronation statue stating Horemheb with a word placated the *King*, is in reference to the fall-out of his act of killing the Hittite prince.

> He being summoned before the sovereign when it, the Palace, fell into rage, and he opened his mouth and answered the king and appeased him with the utterance of his mouth[24]

Soft words and a threat on Ay's life[25] ensured he did as he was told. There is of course no evidence to prove this or any other murder theory, and often simply because Horemheb was a soldier he was considered violent and ambitious. He had no need to murder to achieve the throne as Tutankhamun had already named him as heir, giving him a legitimate claim to the throne.

Ankhesenamun is believed to have eventually married Ay, although this is also uncertain and based solely on the discovery of a ring bearing both their cartouches.[26] This in itself is not proof, as there is no mention of a wedding, and she is never referred to as Ay's wife. She disappears from the records at the death of Tutankhamun, other than this ring, and even in the tomb of Ay she is not depicted. This is a particularly interesting turn of events, which has led at least one scholar to suggest something more sinister; execution for treason, and would go some way to explain why her image and name have been hacked from some monuments.[27] If she had written the letter and the prince had arrived safely, as Ay was already *King* before the funeral of Tutankhamun, she would need to get rid of him, and the only way would be assassination.[28] This scenario relies on many 'what ifs' and therefore should be dismissed in favour of the evidence and the facts as they stand.

Various questions are raised by this letter; probably more than it answers. The main one concerns the logistics of the letter being sent in the first place. The next *King*, Ay, had a vested interest in this letter as a prince from Hatti would obviously affect his plans to ascend the throne. This suggests, had he known about it, the letter would not have been sent. The same argument could also be used in regard to Horemheb, as a foreign prince on the throne would also affect his position at court and his right to the throne. Therefore if Ankhesenamun wrote this letter without the knowledge of Ay or Horemheb, it is very surprising that the letter got sent at all. Ay, as the *Vizier* had access to all messages leaving the palace and would have been able to intercept it.

It has been suggested the letter was actually written by Ay not Ankhesenamun, designed to keep Horemheb in the north, pushing him to intercept the Hittite prince before he reached Egypt. This again relies on the assumption there was a bitter rivalry between Horemheb and Ay, and keeping Horemheb in the north would prevent him from taking the throne from Ay before he was crowned. Horemheb was therefore stationed in the north to protect the northern borders, with Ay in the south with the *King*, showing their different spheres of influence.[29] If such bitter rivalry existed the question needs to be asked as to why Ay named Horemheb as his heir rather than banishing him from Egypt and destroying his monuments as happened to others who did not have royal favour.

One solution is that Ay had no designs on the throne, and supported Ankhesenamun in her correspondence viewing it as the last hope for Egypt which was without a *King* or legitimate heir. If Zennanza had been sent straight away he would be in Egypt in time to perform the funerary rights for Tutankhamun and then would have been crowned. Ay may have been waiting in anticipation for the arrival of the prince and only took the throne upon Zennanza's death in preparation for the retaliation by the Hittites[30] and to prevent Horemheb from ascending to the throne. Perhaps he only initially took the throne on a temporary basis to oversee the crisis. However this resulted in him ruling permanently until his death.[31]

However, this does not really stand up to scrutiny on a number of points. One, Ay was the great uncle of Ankhesenamun, and therefore of royal blood, the only surviving member of the royal family and the legitimate heir, and two, never in Egyptian history had an Egyptian princess married a foreign prince, so why would it be encouraged in this case? Tutankhamun had already named his heir, the *Hereditary Prince* or *Deputy King*, Horemheb, so it seems most unlikely that there would be an official appeal abroad. This went against the laws of Maat, where an Egyptian 'commoner' is better on the throne than a royal foreigner.

Whether the letter was physically written by the queen or not, it was written in her name. However the queen's name in the letter is Dahamunzu, the vocalisation of the title *King's Wife tA Hmt nsw*, rather than her personal name. Some scholars have argued this could refer to Nefertiti rather than Ankhesenamun.[32] However the name Dahamunzu could also be a vocalisation of Sankhamun, a shortening of Ankhesenamun. As Nefertiti disappeared from the records a number of years before the death of her husband it seems unlikely to be her.

The timing of the letter, and when it was sent, has also been the subject of much debate. Calculations have determined that Tutankhamun died in January, when his widow sent the letter. The Hittite *King* sent his envoys to Egypt to check the information and it is believed by some that the messenger returned from Egypt the second time in spring.[33] Zennanza was sent to Egypt shortly after, coinciding with the funeral of Tutankhamun in April, after the traditional seventy day period of mummification. However some scholars have devised more convoluted time scales for this, suggesting that Tutankhamun died in mid-late August, and was not buried for six months.[34] However, the body of Tutankhamun does not show any sign of a delayed burial, with the pollen amidst the wrappings and the flowers in the tomb support an April burial immediately after mummification (28). The reason for this supposed six month delay is not clear.

Variations on the timing of the events of this, include, the first correspondence from Ankhesenamun arriving at Hattusha (modern Bogazköy in Turkey), the Hittite capital, in the late autumn, some nine to ten months after Tutankhamun's death, with a further six months before Zennanza reached Egypt[35] in the spring of the year following his death. This is however problematic on two counts; one, that the correspondence was negotiated in secret by Ankhesenamun for a period of fourteen months, and two, for the Hittite *King* to believe the request for a son for the throne of Egypt was genuine, the throne of Egypt would have stood empty for this period. Both of these are improbable.

A Hittite source[36] which is possibly a draft of a letter from Suppiluliumas to the Egyptian *King*, although the names are missing, indicate there were a number of months between the Hittite attack on Amka, an Egyptian territory and the death of Prince Zennanza. The letter is very fragmentary and the reading of many sentences is in question[37] but the nature of the draft indicates there was a series of letters between

28 Tutankhamun's death mask. *Photograph by Clare V. Banks*

the rulers, and it responds to complaints of statements made by the Egyptian *King*. It appears in a previous letter Suppiluliumas threatened the Egyptian *King*, who tried to maintain the peace between the two countries by not accepting responsibility for the prince's death. It is therefore clear the Hittite *King* did not attack immediately, as a knee-jerk reaction to his son's death but engaged in semi-polite correspondence first; either in the hope the Egyptian *King* would exonerate himself or to buy time whilst he organised an offensive. How long this took we can only guess. One of the Amarna letters (EA41) however, indicates the relationship between Egypt and Hatti had deteriorated badly since the time of Amenhotep III, with an Egyptian attack on Kadesh, and a retaliatory Hittite attack on Amka. This suggests that the death of Zennanza only made this conflict worse, but was not the reason for it. EA41 suggests the reason was financial, and the Hittites were angry that the gifts of gold from Egypt were diminishing:

> My father sent foot soldiers and charioteers who attached the country of Amka, Egyptian territory. Again he sent troops, and again he attacked it. When the Egyptians became frightened, they asked outright for one of his sons to (take over) the kingship. But when my father gave them one of his sons, they killed him as they led him there. My father let his anger run away with him, he went to war against Egypt and attacked Egypt.[38]

The *Deeds of Suppiluliumas*, the Hittite ruler, records problems during the period directly after Tutankhamun's death, although this is not supported by the archaeological record. Perhaps this was a continuation of the Hittite problems during the reign of Akhenaten, and the confrontation with Tutankhamun and his army. Records further indicate the Great Hurrian War, where Suppiluliumas fought the Hurrian troops of the defeated Mitanni as they defended their territory, took six years before they were defeated, and the Hittites captured Carchamish. They then marched southwards to the Egyptian territory of Amka. The news reached Egypt just after the death of Tutankhamun. Some believe Horemheb was in Syria at the time and the Amka defeat probably affected his status within Egypt, securing Ay's ascension to the throne.[39] Whether the plan was to attack Egypt itself is unknown although possible, but the archaeological evidence does not support any Hittite offensive on Egypt.

The majority of the research about this letter concerns who sent it, when and for what purpose, but the possibility that the letter of Dahamunzu may not have been written at all is not considered. The only copy of the letter is from the Hittite capital Hattusha; but even this is not the original letter or even a copy of the letter. This correspondence is recorded as part of a narrative written by the son of Suppiluliumas, Mursilis II known as the *Deeds of Suppiluliumas* and it could be argued it is propaganda promoting the Hittite *King* to the detriment of the Egyptians or even to support a claim to the Egyptian throne. It is also mentioned in two prayers of Suppiluliumas again written by his son Musilli II. The entry on the 'Seventh Tablet' describes receipt of Dahamunzu's letter beginning:

> While my father was down in the country of Carchemish, he sent Lapakki and Tarhunta … Zalma forth into the country of Amka. So they went to attack Amka and brought deportees, cattle and sheep back before my father. But when the people of Egypt heard of the attack on Amka, they were afraid and since, in addition, their lord Nibhuruiya had died, therefore the queen of Egypt who was Dahamunzu, sent a messenger to my father and wrote to him thus[40]

This introduction does not suggest she wrote the letter out of fear of her destiny in Egypt but rather her fear of the increasing power of the Hittites. This therefore suggests this act was not the final act of a desperate widow but rather an attempt to gain the Hittites as allies and settle the treaty with a royal wedding. This therefore places this letter into a completely different context, and potentially casts doubt on its existence. If a letter *was* written, how much was taken out of context when placed into this propagandistic narrative about the might of the Hittite *King*? It also needs to be considered that the attack on Amka from the Hittite sources happened both before and after the letter was written showing inconsistencies in their record keeping.

Mursillis, the author of the annals within which the letter is recorded, makes it clear the events he is recording occurred when he was a child and there are several times where he does not have information about the event because he could find no reliable sources or he was not there.[41] Normally in an archaeological context such a record would not be taken at face value, not without further evidence. Other than this report there is no further evidence; just a record of a past event reported through oral tradition and hearsay.

In order to make the letter believable small details were added, such as times of arrival and the name of the Egyptian messenger, Hani, are recorded. Hani may have been at the Hittite court, but bringing a very different letter or message; perhaps one informing the *King* of the death of Tutankhamun with no mention of sending his widow a husband. The Hittite advisors were therefore able to use his presence, putting the words of the Egyptian royal plight into the mouth of the messenger, ensuring there were no written records, and only very carefully chosen witnesses to his monumental speech.

Viewing this so-called letter from Ankhesenamun as a piece of propaganda, devised by the Hittites to prove their own might immediately eliminates the other problems the letter has raised; for example the timing of the correspondence, the fact that Ay or Horemheb allowed the letter to be sent, or even their ignorance of the letters as well as the exact identity of Dahamunzu. None of these issues are relevant if the letter was a simple correspondence informing the *King* of her husband's death, paraphrased into something more monumental, displaying the Egyptian's fear of the Hittites.

Even the reference to Ay as a 'servant' does not sit comfortably. Ay was possibly Ankhesenamun's great uncle, the *Vizier* and the heir to the throne. He was hardly a 'servant'. Even Horemheb, as the army *General* and *Deputy King* under her husband held one of the highest positions in the country. It is therefore possible that this turn of phrase was chosen by the Hittite advisors through a lack of understanding of the familial connections between these men of power and the Egyptian royal family, in addition to presenting a deterioration of Egyptian royalty.

The letter also gives the Hittites a perfect excuse to wage war on the Egyptians. The apparent murder of Zennanza:

> But when my father gave them one of his sons, they killed him as they led him there. My father let his anger run away with him, he went to war against Egypt and attacked Egypt. He smote the foot soldiers and the charioteers of the country of Egypt. But when they brought back to Hatti land the prisoners which they had taken, a plague broke out among the prisoners and they began to die. When they moved the prisoners to Hatti land, the prisoners carried the plague into Hatti land. From that day on people have been dying in the Hatti land[42]

Further doubt is cast over the reliability of these texts in the record of Zannanza's death:

> When they brought this tablet, they spoke thus; the people of Egypt killed Zennanza and brought word: 'Zennanza died' And when my father heard of the slaying of Zennanza, he began to lament for Zennanza and to the gods ... he spoke thus' Oh

gods! I did no evil, yet the people of Egypt did this to me, and they also attacked the frontier of my country[43]

The Hittite *King* was told only that Zennanza had 'died' not that he had been murdered. The Egyptian *King* denied it so this could have been another aspect of an over-imaginative Hittite offical. As propaganda, the text suggests if the request had not been sent, they would never have sent the prince to Egypt to be murdered. If he had not been murdered war would not have been waged and the plague would not be killing the Hittites; hence it was all the fault of the Egyptians.

However, the texts could also be interpreted another way; Zennanza may have died of plague, which we know for certain was present in the Amarna workman village at the end of the reign of Akhenaten. The constant Egyptian presence of messengers at Hattusha may have already condemned the young prince to death before he even left for Egypt. Therefore the comment that the Egyptians killed him does not necessarily mean murder but through disease; which is indeed mentioned later in the record.

Using correspondence as a propaganda tool was not new, as during the Hyksos period (1663-1555 BCE) the Sallier I Papyrus records a letter from the Hyksos *King* to King Seqenenre Tao II in Thebes complaining his hippopotami in the Theban pool were keeping him awake in the Delta. A totally unreasonable and unbelievable proposition; Seqenenre Tao retaliated by waging war on the Hyksos *King*. The Ankhesenamun letter, seems to have been used in the same way; an unreasonable request leading to war, and therefore should be treated in the same way.

However, although this theory may fit on some points it fails on one major one. Although the Hittite narrative clearly states they attacked Egypt and killed a number of soldiers, there is no evidence of any hostilities between the Egyptians and the Hittites during the reign of Ay, or the early reign of Horemheb. We know the Hittites were growing in power and marching across the Near East during the reign of Akhenaten, and we also know both Sety I and Ramses II had problems with the Hittites until year 21 of the latter's reign when the peace treaty was signed.[45] This suggests the problem was an increasing one even during the reign of Horemheb despite the lack of open hostility at this time.

Despite the apparent absence of war, the theory that this entire event was orchestrated to place blame at the Egyptian door for a plague sweeping Hatti is quite possible and once this odd letter is taken from the equation of the history of this period the transition between kings at the death of Tutankhamun is almost straightforward.

Could the whole record be one to justify a war that never took place? Is there lost evidence to be uncovered which will clarify this somewhat confusing issue? Or are we back at the beginning wondering about the sequence of events which led Ankhesenamun to write the letter requesting the Hittite *King* send his son?

So from this jumbled mass of evidence, with large gaps and confusing contradictions we can attempt to put together a scenario regarding the sequence of events leading to Ay becoming *King of Egypt* instead of Horemheb. We can list the known facts and work on the theory from there. Tutankhamun died, aged 18, possibly from a chariot accident in 1325 BCE, to be followed on the throne by Ay, his great uncle, and only surviving male relative. The only two events which confuse this rather straightforward transition from one *King* to another is the named heir, the *rpat* Horemheb, and the letter sent by Ankhesenamun to the Hittite *King*; the latter causing more problems than the former. However, as discussed, this letter seems so highly unlikely and is only recorded in secondary sources, created to explain how the plague spread to Hattusha and to justify an offensive against Egyptian territory. Once this confusing episode is erased we just need to evaluate why Ay and not Horemheb came to the throne upon the death of Tutankhamun.

This can be answered in the light of the type of *King* Horemheb later showed himself to be (see Chapter 5). Horemheb dedicated his reign to the restoration of the traditional religion, politics and culture of ancient Egypt, emulating Amenhotep III who ruled what was viewed as a Golden Era. This traditionalism would not have allowed him to rule directly after Tutankhamun because there was a surviving male heir. To usurp the throne from a true heir, no matter how old or indirectly related would go against the law of Maat and would not be an auspicious start to his reign. By waiting until the death of Ay, only four years later, meant he made a smooth transition to the throne, upheld the law of Maat (cosmic balance, truth and justice) and started a new dynasty independent from the Amarna heresy. This would have been an easy transition to orchestrate. Ay was elderly and realistically knew he would not survive for many years, and with no surviving son, needed to name an heir to the throne. Horemheb was named as heir, chosen by none other than Amun himself, showing it was his divine right to rule (29).

Before Ay came to the throne Horemheb may have pointed out the reality of the situation. He was a *General* of the army, and *Deputy King* and could, should he desire it, take the throne that was rightly his by the decree of Tutankhamun, but in order to uphold the law of Maat he was willing to acquiesce allowing Ay to rule in his twilight years on the condition he named Horemheb as heir. However, this threat may not have held any sway as Ay also would have had loyalty of the army in his earlier role of *General of the Royal Chariotry* and therefore seems unlikely to have been made. Rather than a life-long conflict between these two great men I suggest there was instead a long-term collaboration between them starting under the reign of Tutankhamun when both men were responsible for advising the *King* on political decisions. There seems to be no conflict of interest in Tutankhamun's policies, indicating these two men worked together in advising him. Their goal was the same, and their methods similar, as is attested by the activities throughout the reign of Ay and then by Horemheb. That is not to say that neither *King* had their own ideas, it is just they had a common goal; to restore Egypt to its former glory. If there had been a bitter rivalry between them this would have been detrimental to their cause; which could result in civil war between the followers of Horemheb (attributed the north) and the followers of Ay (attributed to the south). This did not happen and their 'deal' or collaboration regarding the succession of the throne after the death of the boy-king ensured this goal was reached.

In 1325 BCE, 70 days after the death of Tutankhamun (*colour plate 6*), Ay became *King*. The coronation was like any other, and the south wall of Horemheb's Memphite tomb displays the active role he held during the ceremony. His main role appears to have been to organise and control foreign dignitaries, including Libyans, Western Asians, Nubians and Aegeans who travelled to Egypt to pledge allegiance to the new *King of Egypt* (30). The coronation probably took place at the capital of Memphis, and there is some indication in the image of the coronation that some of these foreign visitors were captives and therefore not there of their own accord. Others however were travelling dignitaries and there are images of what could be tents set up in the capital to temporarily house them.[46] The newly crowned *King*, Ay, is depicted at the 'Window of Appearances' showering honoured guests and officials with tokens of appreciation; Horemheb was undoubtedly among the recipients.

The only known regnal years of Ay are those of years three and four, despite Manetho giving his Achernes (Ay) a 12-year reign. It is possible he ruled for longer than four years but as yet, no evidence has yet been found.[47] The four years of his reign (1325-1321 BCE) were relatively peaceful with little happening by way of warfare or uprisings. One inscription hints at the continuing Hittite problems and some have interpreted it as showing that a Hittite offensive did take place after the letter of

29 Horemheb protected by Amun (Luxor Museum). *Photograph by the author*

30 Foreign delegation at the coronation of Ay from Saqqara (Louvre Museum). *Photograph by the author*

31 Cartouches of Ay

Ascension to the Throne

Ankhesenamun. The stela currently in Cairo (34187) dates to year three of his reign, and describes land Ay gave to an overseer called Isutta and his wife Mutnodjmet. The land was called 'Mound of the Hittites' and it is suggested this was where the Hittite Prisoners of War were housed, somewhere in the region of the Giza necropolis.[48] It has also been suggested Ay's adoption of the title 'Subduer of Asia' or 'Expeller of Asiatics' is in connection with the Hittite advance over Syria[49] (31). Although intriguing it is unfortunately not enough evidence to prove there was a Hittite war against the Egyptians.

There was a muted building programme, which no doubt would have gained momentum had he ruled for longer. He built a shrine at Akhmin, his home town, and there are images of Ay and his wife, Tiy on the façade. Ay stands before Horus, Mehit, Min and Isis, and a stela emphasises his role in the restoration of the sanctuaries of the gods and the celebration of their festivals,[50] a campaign started under the reign of Tutankhamun.

Ay also began work on his mortuary temple (*colour plate 7*); or rather usurped that of Tutankhamun on the west bank of the Nile, near modern Medinet Habu, enhancing it for himself. It is evident he built new structures at the site, as foundation deposits dated to his reign have been discovered at nine points throughout the temple including the corners of the structures and at other points throughout the building. These deposits consist of the typical items such as pots, bronze tools, wooden brick moulds, faience beads, faience models of food, and faience tiles inscribed with the name of Ay, at the base of the pit, and bowls of food offerings. A number of the items still retain the names of the workmen who created them and possibly worked on the temple itself. There was very little of Ay's temple remaining when it was excavated in 1931-33, due to centuries of floods running through here unhindered, despite the temple being built as a terrace to try to counteract the natural terrain, as well as havng been used as quarry for building materials. Remaining evidence suggests Ay built the pylon and a ceremonial palace of mud-brick, in addition to a small stone temple at the rear of the structure, which was built entirely during his reign. However the decoration was usurped by Horemheb, through replacing the cartouches of Ay with those of his own. There is only one cartouche of Ay that seems to have been missed.[51]

The mortuary temple comprised a courtyard reached by a pylon ending in a pillared hypostyle hall with twenty open papyriform columns[52] similar to those of Amenhotep III at Luxor temple, measuring 42m in length and 10.5m wide. The colour has survived from these columns showing the shaft to be white with a rectangular frame in the centre bearing the names of the *King*, as well as colourful edging to the top and bottom of the columns. The hypostyle hall led to the inner temple which was divided into three sections; the middle incorporated the cult rooms for the worship of the Theban triad (Amun, Mut and Khonsu) with two smaller hypostyle halls, with stemmed papyrus cluster columns, with closed capitals, and the sanctuary which has since been completely destroyed. The series of rooms to the left was possibly for the worship of Osiris, or the deified Ay, and the rooms on the right for the worship of other deities although these are now unknown. The palace here was a temporary residence for the *King*, comprising a reception hall with eight columns, with vestibules on either side and the four-pillared throne room behind it. There were a number of other rooms surrounding these but their use has not been determined, although two were separated by a low wall and possibly housed the shower and latrine. Another may have contained the staircase to the roof. The whole palace only filled an area of 21.6m by 22m and was therefore quite modest in size. One strange structure appears to be a temporary wooden structure 7.5m before the front of the palace, with a canvas or linen lining stretched over a series of wooden poles. The post-holes indicate that the structure had been repositioned at least once,[53] what this was used for is uncertain.

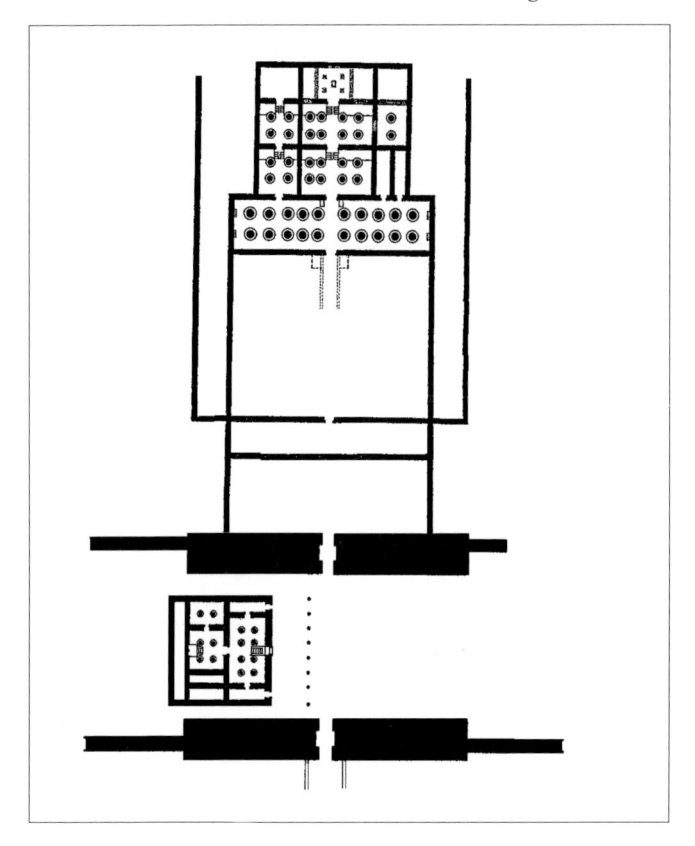

32 The mortuary temple of Ay, Medinet Habu. *Drawing by Brian Billington after Hölscher 1939*

Ay wanted to associate himself closely with the previous *King*, proving he was a legitimate heir to the throne, and built a memorial chapel for Tutankhamun at Karnak where he named Tutankhamun as his father, which whilst being a physical impossibility was appropriate to the ideology of kingship. Inscriptions from the 'Temple of Nebkheperura in Thebes' which was primarily decorated by Ay states:

He (Ay) made this as a monument for his son ... Nebkheperure [Tutankhamun]

So not only does Ay claim Tutankhamun is his father, but also his son, his cartouche is displayed regularly alongside that of Tutankhamun.[54] Whilst associating himself with Tutankhamun he wanted to disassociate himself from the Amarna heresy and started the campaign of destruction against the temples of Akhenaten and the Aten at the temple of Karnak, helping to further restore it to the glory of Amun. He also moved the colossal lions of Tutankhamun to the temple of Amenhotep III at Soleb in Nubia. It is these lions and the inscription which has fuelled the discussions of Tutankhamun's parentage, as he names Amenhotep III as his father here.

One act of Ay during his reign which belies all theories of hostilities between himself and Horemheb is his official naming of Horemheb as heir. Some claim perhaps this was performed under duress; with Horemheb threatening to kill him should he refuse. This is based on conjecture and the records actually state Ay accompanied Horemheb to Karnak for the Opet Festival, one of the most important Theban festivals which had been reinstated during the reign of Tutankhamun. This festival started with a procession along the Sphinx Avenue between Karnak and Luxor temples along which Amun was transported. After staying at the sanctuary of Amun at Luxor temple for

33 Dancers at the Opet Festival of Tutankhamun usurped by Horemheb, Luxor Temple. *Photograph by the author*

34 Soldiers at the Opet Festival of Tutankhamun usurped by Horemheb, Luxor Temple. *Photograph by the author*

eleven days Amun was accompanied back to Karnak with a splendid river parade, followed by the *King*, soldiers, priests, dancers, musicians and singers (33 & 34); a great public event with the populace lining the river banks hoping to catch a glimpse of the god Amun, or even the *King*. This was a time for Ay to celebrate naming his heir, not a time for forced actions; it was too public.

Ay, accompanied by Horemheb, entered the oracle of Amun at Karnak and addressed the god. Amun announced he chose Horemheb to follow Ay on the throne. This was a traditional means of announcing heirs and was considered infallible. This was an ideal opportunity, should Ay and Horemheb have been enemies, for Ay to gain the support of the gods, through his priests, and have Amun name someone else. Horemheb would not have been able to go against the divine will without jeopardising his future. To go against the god was to usurp the throne and risk being erased from history by future kings. This he wanted to avoid. This indicates Ay willingly named Horemheb as heir as someone who would continue the work of restoration without personal ambition. Horemheb as heir to the throne was common knowledge and the Trauerrelief from the Saqqara tomb of the *High Priest* of Ptah, Ptahemhat-Ty shows Horemheb, entitled *rpat*, under Tutankhamun or Ay (35).[55] This has been interpreted by some as showing he was heir to the throne of Ay. They worked together for many years and had the same goals for Egypt. The only problem was Horemheb did not have an heir, although he was still young enough to produce one. He was a wise choice; in fact one worthy of the gods.

Horemheb further emphasised this divine intervention and records how he was chosen by the deities to rule Egypt, although he does not credit Amun with this. Instead he claimed the local god from his hometown, 'Horus of Hansu', chose him as *King* before he was born and was placed under special protection until he was ready to rule:

> His father Horus placed himself behind him, his creator made his protection. One generation passes, another came ... he knew the day of his good pleasure to give him his kingship. Lo, this god distinguished his son in the sight of the entire people, for he desired to enlarge his gait until should come the day of his receiving his office ...[56]

An interesting piece of propaganda paralleled in the *Contendings of Horus and Seth*. After Isis was impregnated with Horus by Osiris before he went to the Underworld, she raised the infant Horus in the marshes of the Delta under special protection until he was old enough to take his rightful place on the throne. In the interim, the god of chaos, Seth ruled Egypt. The parallels between this myth and the Amarna period are clear. Horemheb

35 Scene from tomb of Ptahemhat-Ty (Berlin Museum). *Drawing by the author*

presented himself as the true Horus, biding his time until he came to the throne, dispensing of chaos (represented by the Amarna kings) and bringing the land of Egypt back to the way of Maat (cosmic balance and truth). As an additional piece of propaganda by accrediting a deity other than Amun, Horemheb was sending a message to the populace that although there was one supreme god, Amun, he was not the only god. Almost as if he was making the statement that replacing one god (Aten) with another (Amun) was not much of a change; he wanted to bring back the full pantheon of deities in *all* their glory.

During the reign of Ay, whilst gaining the prestigious title of heir, Horemheb also suffered a personal tragedy when his wife of many years, Amenia, died. She was buried in his Memphite tomb, only a short while before he became *King*. The seals to her burial chamber bear the cartouche of Ay, placing her death firmly within this four year period.

Her burial was robbed in antiquity and the shaft leading to her chamber has grooves in the stone from the ropes used by the robbers. Her body was ransacked, but fragments of her wooden coffin and some small scarabs have survived from her funerary assemblage, showing she was given a rich and befitting funeral. Her burial chamber comprised a barrel vaulted ceiling with two lines of painted decoration, and two carved reliefs of false doors on the walls, as well as a limestone offering table, with scalloped columned legs, and a libation bowl inset into the surface. The front of the shelf bore a cavetto cornice as would normally adorn a temple. This was unique to this burial. The coffin was placed in a burial pit cut into the floor of the chamber, and although it had disintegrated over the centuries, there was evidence in the pit of unguent which had been poured over the coffin by the funerary priests during her funeral.[57] A funerary suite was dedicated to her in the temple above the tomb, and a block was discovered depicting her funeral. Her mummified body is supported by the goddess Nephthys, showing a full restoration of the traditional funerary beliefs by this point; something Horemheb was keen to promote. The funerary rituals intended for Horemheb are also depicted within the tomb and are the most complete in Egypt. Although intended for his own burial it is possible some of these rituals were carried out for his wife Amenia and then later his second wife Mutnodjmet. There are a series of professional mourners who lined the streets leading to the cemetery during the funerary procession, wailing and beating their breasts in grief (*colour plate 8*). These were hired especially for the occasion. The funerary feast is being prepared and comprises a series of butchers slaughtering animals as well as a number of jars filled with food and drink lined up in preparation. Some of the jars are painted red, and are later smashed in a ceremony dating as far back as the Old Kingdom, known as the *Breaking of the red-ware vessels* (36). This ritual is closely associated with the slaughter of the bulls, and the blood of the animals and the red pots symbolise Seth and the destruction of enemies.[58] The names of traditional enemies are often inscribed on these vessels to reiterate the act of breaking the vessels as 'breaking' and destroying the enemies.

What Amenia died of is unknown as her body was destroyed by robbers. As she possibly lived at Amarna during the latter years of Akhenaten, perhaps she was weakened, but not killed, by the plague virus spreading throughout the town. Perhaps the danger had not quite passed, and if the letter to Suppiluliumas is to be believed, the plague was rife at the Hittite capital at the end of Tutankhamun's reign, and it may still have been affecting people in Egypt at this time.

Ay on the other hand died of old age. He was well into his sixties, which in ancient Egypt was considered elderly. His body has not been discovered, but we know he was buried in his tomb in the Western Valley of the Valley of the Kings (WV23). The tomb is a larger version of Tutankhamun's, decorated in similar fashion, with a yellow background, and one wall dominated by the twelve baboons who welcomed the sun-god (and the *King*) into the underworld. Some scholars have suggested it may have been originally built for Tutankhamun or Nefernferuaten, one of the daughters of

Akhenaten.⁵⁹ An unusual element of his tomb, which shows his more humble origins, is the traditional fishing and fowling scene; the only one to be found in a royal tomb. One issue causing some debate is the image depicting Ay's wife making offerings of water to his deceased form; as this is not Ankhesenamun but rather his wife Tiy, wet-nurse to Nefertiti. Many people assume, based solely on the record of the letter of Ankhesenamun to the Hittite *King*, that she was married to Ay, becoming his Great Royal Wife. There is no evidence, other than the ring showing their cartouches side by side, that they ever married, and Tiy is the only woman recorded as his wife; both before and after he became *King*. It is likely that Tiy pre-deceased her husband and was buried in his tomb, although her remains have also not been discovered.

The tomb of Ay was ransacked after his burial, and his funerary assemblage was destroyed. Horemheb is normally accredited with this destruction, as part of his later campaign to destroy the kings of the Amarna period. However, the evidence in the tomb suggests it was desecrated during the Ramesside period; the damage by Horemheb being mainly cosmetic.⁶⁰ It is clear Ay had been given a proper burial, according to tradition with Horemheb carrying out the rituals in the role of eldest son. The burial goods discovered in the tomb are poor in comparison with the burial of Tutankhamun and later Horemheb's burial, and this has been taken as proof that Horemheb disliked him. His body was placed in the sarcophagus, but the lid was not in place, and had been left propped up against the wall. The body was probably covered in a linen pall similar to that of Tutankhamun with gold rosettes stitched onto it. He was provided with guardian statues, similar to those of both Tutankhamun and Horemheb, and was also adorned with the uraeus, and a wooden flail. He was also given food for the afterlife, and two fragments of jar labels have been discovered from meat jars. Perhaps the measly funerary goods are a matter of preservation after the robbers ransacked the tomb.

As with all things Horemheb adhered to tradition, so he could not be criticised and reviled for his actions. He buried Ay,⁶¹ as he would his own father, becoming *King* in his place.

36 Breaking the Red-Pots, Saqqara. *Drawing by the author after Martin 1991*

CHAPTER 5

HOREMHEB – LORD OF THE TWO LANDS

In 1321 BCE Horemheb became *King* not long after the Opet Festival at Karnak which was held in July. One of the first events of his ascension to the throne was his marriage to Mutnodjmet, believed by most to be the sister of Queen Nefertiti. Some scholars however believe this woman to be independent of the Queen's sister. The confusion really occurs in the reading of her name. Most people accept Mutnodjmet as a correct reading of her name although some scholars read the name of the sister of Nefertiti as Mutbenret. Those who read it as Mutnodjmet believe this to be the same woman who married Horemheb but those who read the name as Mutbenret believe them to be two different people.[1]

In the Amarna tombs of Ay, Panehsy, Parennefer, Tutu and May[2] dating to the early years of the reign of Akhenaten (prior to year nine)[3] a woman appears accompanied by two dwarf companions, Mutefpre and Hemetnisu-weternehneh.[4] She is clearly a lady of importance and bears the title *snt n Hmt nswt wrt*, Sister of the Great Royal Wife. It is thought that as she is often accompanied by the royal princesses she may have acted as their chief nurse and governess (37).[5]

There is no doubt this woman was the sister of Nefertiti, but that does raise the problem of her parentage. Is she the 'milk sister' of Nefertiti; i.e. the true daughter of Ay and Tiy, and therefore also nursed by Nefertiti's wet-nurse? Or full sister? As the parents of Nefertiti are unknown then this must be the same for Mutnodjmet. Some scholars believe her to be the daughter of Ay although she does not hold the title of 'King's Daughter,'[6] but Ay and Tiy's tomb is one of the few places that mention Mutnodjmet. If she was Ay's daughter, marriage to her would have further legitimised Horemheb's right to rule.

Although this may seem a moot point it is in fact quite an interesting element to the story of Horemheb's rise to the throne. If he did marry Mutnodjmet, as is commonly believed, then she is one of the last surviving female members of the Amarna household, after the disappearance from the records of Ankhesenamun, the widow of Tutankhamun. Some scholars who believe in the 'royal heiress theory' (i.e. the royal blood-line runs via the females, and therefore a contender for the throne must marry a royal woman) believe Horemheb married Mutnodjmet in order to legitimise his reign. However, it has long been proved the royal succession ran through the male line. This means as Mutnodjmet was not royal, but of noble blood, and as only the sister of a Queen she never held any royal titles herself. Therefore if this was a political marriage, it was not to secure the throne for Horemheb but perhaps to prevent any ambitious young men marrying her and attempting to usurp the throne through her. Horemheb had a legitimate claim to the throne; Ay had pronounced him heir apparent based on the oracle of Amun at Karnak. Horemheb had effectively been chosen by the gods themselves to rule Egypt. On the coronation statue the marriage to Mutnodjmet was also recorded as a divine act:

> He proceeded to the palace, He [*Amun?*] brought him before Him to the shrine of his revered eldest daughter. She did obeisance to him, she embraced his beauty, and placed herself before him.[7]

37 Mutnodjmet and her nieces. *Drawing by the author after Tyldesley 2005*

Her royal connections are not stated as the reason for the marriage but rather her divinity as the daughter of the god Amun. Her divinity is further accentuated by her titles of *Divine Consort, High Priestess of Amun* and *The Divine Mother, Beloved of Isis*. Horemheb wants to make it clear that the throne is his by divine right;[8] not by royal succession and connection to the previous royal family. This propaganda, describing the gods' intervention with the succession, ensured Horemheb was accepted by the people of Egypt as a *King* the gods supported in contrast to the way they abandoned Egypt during the reign of Akhenaten.

Mutnodjmet was not young when she married Horemheb. She was already an adult prior to year nine of Akhenaten so to err on the young side she was at least 11 years old in year nine. She was 19-20 when Tutankhamun was *King* and 34 when Horemheb ascended to throne. Her existence prior to year nine of Akhenaten have led some scholars to the conclusion that the bride of Horemheb cannot possibly be the same woman, as she would have been too old.[9] On the coronation statue of Horemheb she is even entitled *Advanced in Years* and as she lived until year 13 of Horemheb's reign, she died at approximately 49-50 years old. She was an interesting choice of bride for what was to be a great *King*. She was potentially too old to bear children, and in her early years at Amarna she had lost all of her teeth; although whether to illness or a congenital disorder is uncertain. This meant that for most of her life she was on a liquid diet. For someone who is reported to be the sister of Nefertiti, whose name means the *Beautiful One has Come* and living at a palace which overindulged with banquets of fine food, this may have been an unhappy, or at best a frustrating existence. Did Horemheb marry her for political reasons? Or did he marry her for love? Surely if he married purely for political reasons, he could have married someone younger and more suitable for the title of Great Royal Wife, but she remained his consort for most of his reign. She is displayed prominently throughout his reign alongside him, as his consort indicating he valued her input as well as re-emphasising the duality of kingship and the importance of male-female collaboration. On the coronation statue she is presented as equal size and status to Horemheb, showing an equality which was first displayed between Amenhotep III and Tiye, and Akhenaten and Nefertiti.

Despite her age and tooth loss, an inscribed statue of her placed in the Memphite tomb refers to her as:

> Noble lady, great of praise, Lady of the Two Lands of Upper and Lower Egypt, Great in graciousness ... beautiful of face at the side of her Horus, when she answers him ... who appeases the god with her voice, Great Royal Wife, may she live, be youthful and healthy, life, and dominion like Ra for eternity

A wonderful epithet that gives some insight into the relationship between them. She is described as being alongside her Horus (i.e. her husband), whom she appeases with her voice, suggesting she offers advice to him which he acknowledges, and that she is able to calm him; perhaps in the same manner as Horemheb calmed Tutankhamun 'when he had fallen into a rage'. Mutnodjmet's titles have been compared to those of Nefertiti further supporting the theory of their close relationship.[10]

Horemheb's Memphite tomb was used for the burial not only of his first wife Amenia, but also for Mutnodjmet. It was not until the nineteenth dynasty that royal wives were buried in the Valley of the Kings or Queens. Instead they were buried in simple undecorated rock-cut tombs or shaft burials, without impressive superstructures. The burial of Mutnodjmet was 28m below ground, also in shaft iv, which was backfilled with limestone blocks and the entrance plastered over and stamped with the seal of Anubis, the protector of the cemetery. This tomb, like most others in the Memphite cemetery, was ransacked by tomb robbers who tunnelled through the entrance into her burial chamber. In order to search the body thoroughly it had been dragged into the chamber above, where she was discovered three thousand years later. Her body shows she was in her forties and was buried with a stillborn or unborn baby.[11] It is therefore assumed she died in childbirth, a dangerous time in any woman's life but especially for a woman of her age. Examination of her pelvis shows she had given birth numerous times, but as no children (or at least no male children) survived Horemheb, it is thought that they were stillborn, or died in infancy. A further personal tragedy for Horemheb and his queen.

Mutnodjmet was given a traditional royal burial, but as her death was unexpected her burial chamber was not ready and there was just enough room for the coffin, a few funerary items and some jars of food and wine. One of the wine dockets which was probably from her funeral is dated to year 13 of Horemheb's reign:

> Year 13, month 3 of the inundation. Very good quality wine from the vineyard of the Estate of Horemheb, Beloved of Amun, Life Prosperity and Health, in the house of Amun[12]

This is a good indicator of the year she died. Wine was an integral part of the royal lifestyle as reflected by its inclusion in the tombs of Mutnodjmet and Horemheb in the Valley of the Kings. Each wine jar bore the name of the *King*, the year of his reign and which vineyard produced it, indicating that, like Tutankhamun before him, Horemheb governed a number of vineyards. We have a great deal of knowledge about the wine trade in Egypt and studies are being made on the remnants left in tombs to determine the ingredients. The process of wine making started with the grape harvest, when the grapes were picked at the moment of ripeness and suitability. The baskets of grapes were then emptied into vats of clay, wood or stone, which whilst being absent in the archaeological record, have survived in New Kingdom tomb images. The clay vats were plastered with gypsum making them watertight and to compensate for the low acidity in the grapes. The grapes were crushed by foot by four to six men who held onto straps hanging from a frame above them, treading on the grapes until they were liquidised. The colour of wines varied, and to produce white wine the red grape skins were removed. Middle Kingdom (1900 BCE) tomb scenes from Meir show greenish brown grapes, indicating that they may have produced white wine, which may have been available in the wine cellar of an eighteenth dynasty *King*.[13] The crushed grape mulch from these vats was then placed into a large sheet of linen tied to an upright pole, which was twisted clockwise squeezing the liquid out into pottery vessels. This process required great strength and in the tomb scenes there are sometimes five individuals involved in the twisting of one cloth. The juice in the pottery jars is then left to ferment before being transferred to racked jars which were stoppered up with perforated seals to allow the carbon dioxide to escape. After the fermenting process was complete the wine was ready for consumption or, as was the case here, was placed in the tomb of the queen for her afterlife. As part of the funerary cult of the queen numerous statues of her were placed within the tomb structure and fragments of these have been discovered. One such statue shows her in a close fitting pleated garment to her ankles, a tripartite wig and plumed headdress mounted with the sun disc. There is a collar around her neck comprising three strands; one of triangles, one of petals, and one of mandrakes. She originally held a flail in her left hand but this is now missing. Although the statue was damaged, it seems it was originally incomplete and there are traces of red sketch lines on the sandals on her feet. The inscription on the front of the statue bears the inscription 'Great King's Wife, Lady of the Two Lands, Lady of Upper and Lower Egypt, Mutnodjmet, may she live, remain youthful and healthy like Ra for eternity.'

The burial itself was ransacked by robbers, who exposed her body, increasing the rate of decay until only a skeleton remained. They destroyed the burial, stealing most of the valuable objects (38). However remnants have survived indicating the splendour of her burial including a canopic jar (*colour plate 9*), currently in the British Museum (BM36635), and an alabaster vase decorated with blue hieroglyphs:

> You have put your arms round what is in you the Osiris, Chantress of Amun, the king's wife Mutnodjmet. May your corpse be united with the earth, may your *ba* be deified within heaven, may your *sah* be august in the earth eternally so that one lives in the necropolis for eternity

As the coronation inscription indicates Horemheb married Mutnodjmet just prior to his ascension to the throne. His wife Amenia had recently died, during the four-year reign of Ay, and it was essential he married again in order to beget an heir. This he would have done whether living as a civilian or as a *King*. As he was to be *King* he needed a wife of noble background. He may have known Mutnodjmet from his time at Amarna and agreed to the marriage as a convenience. Horemheb obtained a wife with royal bearing, who would be a suitable consort and Mutnodjmet would sit on the throne of her sister as Great Royal Wife, something she thought would never happen.

Shortly after the marriage Horemheb's coronation took place. The coronation inscription of Horemheb is recorded on a dyad statue of Horemheb and Mutnodjmet now in the Turin Museum, as well as on a stela discovered by Petrie in front of the pylon at the temple of Ptah at Memphis.[14] The statue is made of dark grey granite and was found in tomb of Roy (TT255).[15] On the side of the throne of the queen is an unusual representation of a winged female sphinx worshipping her own cartouche (39).[16] This area on the side of the royal throne is normally reserved for images depicting the unification of Upper and Lower Egypt so this in itself is unusual. There

38 Mutnodjmet shabti figure (British Museum). *Photograph courtesy of Brian Billington*

39 Mutnodjmet as a sphinx from the Coronation statue in Turin. *Drawing by the author*

is a similar image on a bracelet of queen Tiye with her arms holding the cartouche of *Neb-ma't-re* (Amenhotep III).[17] The imagery itself has caused some debate as the overlapping wings are characteristic of the *rekhet* bird or lapwing. The *rekhet* birds are often thought to represent the people of Egypt under the power of the pharaoh, although one scholar suggests they represent captured Libyan tribes. Couple this with the positioning of the sphinx here, over a papyrus swamp representative of the Delta, tends to support his theory. Were queen Mutnodjmet and Tiye represenended like this in recognition of their *rekhet*, non-royal, origins, or as an indication they were in fact foreign, or Asiatic descent. Tiye is known to be non-royal, the daughter of Yuya the *Lieutenant General of Chariotry*,[18] who many believe to be of Asiatic origin. As Mutnodjemet is the sister of Nefertiti who could in fact be the daughter of Ay, the brother of Tiye, shows she has potentially the same foreign origins as Tiye. Although an interesting aside, the true purpose and message of this imagery will remain uncertain, although it does provide a link between Mutnodjmet and queen Tiye.

The timing of the coronation was carefully orchestrated to fall not long after the Opet Festival celebrations had finished in July. The Opet was followed by the wedding celebrations and then the coronation, ensuring the first 'memories' of the new *King* were fun and frivolous; a time of celebration, feasts and public holidays. This immediately endeared the population to the new *King*.

The beginning of the Petrie stela is missing, and there are only 12 lines of text remaining, which can be matched up with those on the Turin statue. Prior to this it was believed to belong to Amenhotep III. The end of the stela emphasises Horemheb's devotion of Ptah, whereas the Turin statue does not do this.[19] This could be to show allegiance to the cult of Ptah even though Memphis was abandoned as the place of the coronation. The coronation was undoubtedly an elaborate affair, with spectacular feasts and public celebrations; a public display of the future that the new *King* would bring to Egypt. The coronation statue (*colour plate 10*) describes the event taking place in Thebes, rather than the more traditional Memphis. Memphis was the centre of the traditional solar cult of Ra, whereas Thebes was the cult centre of the cult of Amun; the cult hit hardest by the iconoclasts of the Amarna heresy. Horemheb wanted to make a public display of the re-establishment of the traditional deities, state gods and personal deities and used his coronation to do this.

The emphasis in his coronation propaganda of his local god, Horus of Hansu, was a means of showing a connection between the *King* and a local god; presenting Horemheb as 'one with the people'. Others have interpreted this aspect of the coronation stela as a metaphor for Horus (i.e. the *King*, Ay) who was an incarnation of the god, naming him as *King*.[20] Although the local form of Horus is closely associated with the mainstream god,[21] he is still a local deity, recognised by the people. Not only did this local god name Horemheb as heir to the throne, but it is recorded he travelled to Karnak and Luxor temples, personally introducing Horemheb to Amun as the rightful heir to the throne of Egypt:

> Then did Horus proceed amid rejoicing to Thebes, the city of the Lord of Eternity, his son in his embrace, to Ipet-esut [*Karnak*] in order to induct him into the presence of Amun for the handing over to him of his office of king and for the making of his period (of life).[22]

Horus handed Horemheb over to Amun who 'was filled with joy when he saw him coming on the day'[23] and crowned him immediately, finalising his divine right to rule and announcing the support of the gods of the new *King of Upper and Lower Egypt*.

The procession leading Horemheb to Karnak was accompanied by a statue of Horus of Hansu, sealed within a shrine, and was a metaphor of Horus handing over or the presentation of Horemheb to Amun. It was believed in ancient Egypt the statues of the gods contained the ka or spirit of the deity, rather than simply being a representation of them, so in this way the god *did* escort Horemheb. This procession was aimed to impress, and was witnessed and accompanied by the army, dressed in parade uniforms, beating drums and blowing ceremonial trumpets, statesmen, administrators and magistrates in ceremonial robes, as well as priests, bearing the bark of the god, and the songstresses of Amun playing instruments and singing. The procession would have been noisy, colourful and one witnessed by hundreds of people lining the streets hoping to catch a glimpse of the new *King*.

Once the *King* entered Karnak temple, accompanied by the *High Priests* of Amun, he was taken to the *pr-wr* (the Great House) for the purification rituals. This is thought to be at Luxor temple rather than Karnak, as this was called the southern harem of Amun, and this was probably within the Great House.[24] He would have been ritually cleansed by priests wearing masks of the gods Horus and Thoth. As with the priests, before entering into the most sacred parts of the temple, Horemheb was washed and shaved, and ritually anointed with fragrant oils and unguents. This ensured he was physically and mentally pure before entering the presence of Amun who was waiting to crown him. He was given a fresh loincloth of pure white linen and escorted by the priests to the *pr nsw* (or King's House)[25] where he was greeted by a priestess dressed as the goddess Mut who placed the golden ureaus upon his freshly shaved and anointed head. This was the first sign of his new status, as the uraeus or hooded cobra was only ever worn by kings or gods and represented the goddess Wadjet, hood raised ready to protect the *King* whose brow she adorned. At this point the boy from Hansu who spent his life as a scribe and a soldier realised his life had reached a totally unexpected turn; he was now a god. The living Horus (*colour plate 11*).

40 Horemheb and Amun, detail (Luxor Museum). Photograph by the author

Then Horemheb, wearing the golden ureaus, was escorted into the presence of Amun. The god placed each of the crowns of kingship upon his head, cementing his role as *King* in all its aspects. An inscription of Amenhotep II (1453-19 BCE) names nine different crowns, including the Red Crown of Upper Egypt, the White Crown of Lower Egypt, the Double Crown of Upper and Lower Egypt and the Blue War Crown. The coronation scenes of Hatshepsut (1498-83 BCE) at the Red Chapel at Karnak, show Amun placing each crown personally upon her head. We can therefore picture Horemheb kneeling before the statue of Amun as symbolically each crown is placed upon his head showing he is *King* in every aspect of the role. Exactly how this was symbolically enacted is uncertain, but the room was dark, lit only by the narrow light shafts in the ceiling and flickering oil lamps. The area would have been cleaned and purified by lighting incense and the air was probably thick with it. Combine this with the heat of the sun, and the incantation of the priests it would have been a very powerful and somewhat surreal event. Somewhere between reality and fantasy; making it almost possible to believe the ritual was turning him into a god.

The final part of the transition was the recitation of the names of Horemheb; the five titles unique to him which describe his relationship to the gods and the type of *King* he was likely to be (40). These were devised prior to the ceremony by a priest, in collaboration with the new *King* himself. Normally the name reflected the politics of the time, or the type of image needed to be projected to the populace. Horemheb's titles were no different; carefully chosen and as much a piece of manufactured spin as the coronation text describing the god's intervention. His five-fold titulary was:

41 Cartouches of Horemheb

42 Horemheb and Atum (Luxor Museum). *Photograph by the author*

1. Horus, Mighty Bull, Ready in Plans
2. He of the Two Ladies, Great in Marvels at Karnak
3. Golden Horus, Satisfied with Truth, Creator of the Two lands
4. King of Upper and Lower Egypt, Lord of the Two Lands: Djeserkheperure, Setepenre [Sacred are the Forms of Ra, Chosen by Ra]
5. Son of Ra, Lord of Diadems, Beloved of Horus in Festival [Horemheb][26] (41)

Each name tells a little about the *King* and with hindsight we can see how accurate they were; he was certainly 'ready in plans' for reform, and restoration, with truth and honesty playing an integral part. These plans, he claims 'astonished the people by that which came out of his mouth', showing they were good plans, in fact worthy of the gods themselves:

> His every plan was in the footsteps of the Ibis. His decisions were in accord with the Lord of Heseret (Thoth) rejoicing in accustomed usage like Thoth, pleased of heart therewith like Ptah.

Thoth was the god of wisdom, intelligence, and the written word; and a god closely worshipped by Horemheb. After the ceremony, the Coronation Statue claims:

> His Majesty sailed downstream as the image of Horakhte [*the sun-god*]. Behold, he organised this lands; he adjusted according to the time of Ra. He restored the temples from the pools of the marshes [*Delta*] to Nubia. He shaped all their images in number more than before, increasing the beauty in that which he made. Ra rejoiced when he saw them, which had been found ruined aforetime. He raised up their temples. He fashioned 100 images with all their bodies correct, and with all costly splendid stones. He sought the precincts of the gods, which were in the districts in this land. He furnished them as they had been since the time of the first beginning. He established for them a daily offering every day; all the vessels of their temples were wrought of silver and gold. He equipped them with priests with ritual priests and with the choicest of the army. He transferred to them lands and cattle, supplied with all equipment.

This suggests that from the very minute he became *King* he started his restoration programme which was to be the main goal of his reign. As the stela states he rebuilt the temples, including extensive building at the neglected Karnak as well as re-establishing the temple's wealth and rituals (42). He even supplied them with carefully chosen personnel and protection in hand-picked soldiers and one wonders how many of the priests were originally in the military. This was a way of ensuring the temple priests were under the control of the *King* as the threat of the priests gaining rivalry power was all too real. This is potentially what caused the problems in the first place. During the reign of Amenhotep III the power of the priesthood of Amun increased until it almost rivalled that of the *King* which is why the Aten was raised in power, initially during his reign, as a means of lessening their power. Akhenaten however took this 'new' deity too seriously and rather than diminishing their power he wanted to destroy them and the god altogether. Horemheb was to ensure this did not happen again.

CHAPTER 6
RESTORING THE GOLDEN ERA

Although in reality Horemheb did not leave the temple chambers immediately after his coronation to begin restoring the temples and the religion, it was the most important act during his first years as *King*. There was a great deal of work to do as Egypt was demoralised and on the 'verge of civil disintegration'[1] following the religious and economical upheaval of Akhenaten and his religious revolution. The Aten cult, through obliterating the gods, including Osiris who was known to teach law and order, wifely duty and filial piety resulted in a lack of moral guidance where all were concerned.[2] His self-centred religion did not reflect to needs of the majority of the population, leaving them drifting in a religious quagmire, uncertain of the new religion and forbidden from the old.

It was not simply a case of Horemheb re-opening the temples and diverting the revenue back to the temple coffers. During the time of Akhenaten's reformation many things had been neglected, each with their own consequences. For example, closing the temples put numerous people out of work and the neglected foreign policy affected the security of the Egyptian borders and her territories, resulting in the Hittites gaining control over Egyptian-owned land. This also affected the economy, which thrived on international trade. The collapsing economy affected the way the populace acted and with the *King* and militia stationed in Amarna, isolated within the city, law and order eventually broke down. Horemheb decreed to address these social issues as well as the economic, international and religious issues. Tutankhamun began the process with the relocation of the capital from Amarna back to Thebes, and the restoration of the pantheon of gods and Horemheb continued where he left off.

When Horemheb came to the throne the Egyptian people were looking for a leader who could regain all that had been lost. He needed a strong character who could control the military and the priesthood making it easier to restore the religion and foreign relations, so both a spiritual and a practical man was required. As a military *General* Horemheb already had the army under his control, and therefore the foreign policy and regaining lost territory would be easily achieved, as well as regaining control over law and order on home territory.

Through extensive restorative work and gifts to the main temples throughout Egypt Horemheb also gained the support of the priests; special attention to Karnak temple developed the support of the powerful priests of Amun. The way he guaranteed this support was to totally replace the staff with those who were loyal to him, ensuring that whilst appearing to be supporting the cult of Amun, and replenishing the temple of things lost during the Amarna period, he still had total control over them. This prevented the priesthood gaining too much power. Horemheb wanted them to have their power back, but not enough to be a threat. It was also a perfect way for Horemheb to reward those who remained loyal to him whilst he rose to the throne. Giving them powerful and well-paid positions ensured their loyalty even longer.

Horemheb's restoration programme was national, and did not focus only on the Theban cults. There are records of numerous gifts from Horemheb to the temple of Ra at Heliopolis; a usurped door frame bearing the epithet 'Hathor, Chief of the West at Memphis'[3] indicates he patronised a chapel to Hathor in the area. He also restored the gate to the temple of the Ram at Mendes, honouring this cult in addition to maintaining the cult of the Apis Bull at Saqqara, which was associated with the creator god Ptah. However, this deity had not been abandoned by Akhenaten and there is evidence of Apis Bull funerals associated with Akhenaten and Tutankhamun here. During Horemheb's reign he oversaw two Apis Bull funerals. They were buried in twin vaults at the Serapeum, separated by a plaster and painted stone wall. The Serapeum is an underground mausoleum, comprising a long series of burial chambers, initially built by Amenhotep III. Horemheb's burials, chambers D and E, were the first with decorated chambers, and the walls were plastered and painted with images of the Apis Bull greeted by the gods.[4] The burial had been ransacked in antiquity, as well as damaged by rock falls, but the lid of a canopic jar survived which is currently in the Louvre (N3943), as well as the burial itself, comprising a bulls head, without any flesh, resting on a pile of resinous black material, including bones, gold leaf and fine linen. Under the floor were numerous pots containing burnt bones and it has been suggested that at the funeral the flesh of the deceased Apis Bull was consumed in order for the *King* to absorb some of the divine powers.[5] This ritual was closely associated with the Cannibal Hymn of the Pyramid Texts which refers to the *King* absorbing the powers of the gods through devouring their flesh, and was perhaps a means of archaising the ritual to emphasise Horemheb's traditional roots:

> Bull of the sky is Unas, aggressive in his nature, living on the manifestation of every god. Eating the innards of them, who come, their bellies full of magic ... Unas it is who eats people ... and he removes for him what is in their bodies ... It is Unas who eats their magic, who swallows their souls[6]

Even the Aten, the god at the centre of the Amarna heresy, was not ignored during Horemheb's restoration, but was relegated back to the position of local god, rather than Supreme Deity. The Aten temple at Amarna was not completely neglected, although the town itself was all but abandoned, and there is evidence of a Horemheb cartouche at the temple indicating he made additions to the temple here in praise of the Aten. It is only in the latter years of his reign that he started his campaign of destruction against the Aten cult and temples. At the start of his reign he clearly did not wish to emulate Akhenaten in his destruction of gods or their temples.

Because Horemheb did so much during his reign it is best to look at each act individually so as to give each aspect of his reign the justice it deserves, even though the innovations were introduced simultaneously. He was a traditional *King* in many respects and 'tradition' was the buzz-word of his reign. If it went against tradition it was not to be tolerated. The kings who reigned before him who were against tradition were not to be tolerated either. Therefore Horemheb started his regnal years at the end of the reign of Amenhotep III, ignoring the reigns of Akhenaten, Smenkhkare, Tutankhamun and Ay. A nineteenth dynasty tomb at Thebes (TT19) belonging to the *First Prophet of Amenhotep of the Garden*, Amenmosi, includes a row of royal statutes, with Horemheb seated between Amenhotep III and Ramses I with no sign of the Amarna kings, showing he was viewed by the populace as following Amenhotep III. By ignoring the existence of kings between Amenhotep III and himself, Horemheb also ignored the changes that had occurred during their reigns. Therefore, it was essential for him to bring Egypt back to the glory of the reign of Amenhotep III. The re-establishment of the traditional religion was his first major task.

Horemheb was a religious man, as was shown when he favoured his local god, Horus of Hansu over the traditional state god Amun, showing he was a man of

1 Akhenaten (Luxor Museum). *Photograph by the author*

2 Nefertiti worshipping the Aten (Ashmolean Museum). *Photograph by the author*

3 Dyad of Amenia and Horemheb, from Saqqara (British Museum). *Photograph courtesy of Brian Billington*

4 Door jamb from the Memphite tomb of Horemheb (British Museum). *Photograph courtesy of Clare V. Banks*

Left: 5 Horemheb as a scribe. *Photograph courtesy of Robert Partridge, Egypt Picture Library*

Below: 6 Tomb of Tutankhamun showing the opening of mouth ceremony, and his wife Ankhesenamun making offerings of water to him. *Photograph by the author*

7 Medinet Habu with the mortuary temples of Horemheb, Ay and Tutankhamun outside of the enclosure wall. *Photogragh by the author*

8 Mourners at the funeral of Horemheb, from Saqqara (Louvre Museum). *Photograph by the author*

9 Canopic jar of Mutnodjmet, from Saqqara (British Museum). *Photograph courtesy of Brian Billington*

10 Coronation statue of Horemheb. *Photograph courtesy of Robert Partridge, Egypt Picture Library*

Left: 11 Detail of Horemheb (KV57). *Photograph courtesy of Robert Partridge, Egypt Picture Library*

Below: 12 Tutankhamun/Horemheb as Amun at Luxor Temple. *Photograph by the author*

13 Ankhesenamun/Mutnodjmet as Amunet at Luxor Temple. *Photograph by the author*

Above: 14 Rear of Pylon Ten at Karnak.
Photograph courtesy of Brian Billington

Left: 15 Opet Festival of Tutankhamun usurped by Horemheb, at Luxor Temple.
Photograph by the author

16 Horemheb as Hapy (detail) (British Museum). *Photograph by the author*

17 Sarcophagus of Horemheb in KV 57 with the Book of Gates in the background. *Photograph courtesy of Robert Partridge, Egypt Picture Library*

Above: 18 Horemheb making offerings to Hathor (KV57). *Photograph courtesy of Robert Partridge, Egypt Picture Library*

Left: 19 Horemheb making offerings to Osiris (KV57). *Photograph courtesy of Robert Partridge, Egypt Picture Library*

20 Canopic jar lid of Horemheb (KV57). *Photograph courtesy of Robert Partridge, Egypt Picture Library*

21 Coffin of Horemheb/Ramses I? (Cairo Museum). *Photograph courtesy of the Robert Partridge, Egypt Picture Library.*

22 Osiris bed lid bearing the face of Horemheb (KV57). *Photograph courtesy of Robert Partridge, Egypt Picture Library*

23 Tutankhamun/Horemheb statue from the the mortuary temple at Thebes. *Photograph courtesy of Robert Partridge, Egypt Picture Library*

24 Funerary Statue of Ramses I, Valley of the Kings. *Photograph courtesy of Brian Billington*

25 Abydos King List. *Photograph by the author*

personal religious conviction. There were two stages in his religious overhaul. One, in the first half of his reign was a slow and steady increase in religious building works, strengthening the temple economy and subsequently the local economy of Egypt. The second stage of his religious renovation occurred after the death of his second wife Mutnodjmet, in year 13. After this date he increased the work at Karnak temple for the priesthood of Amun, and continued the destruction campaign, started under Tutankhamun of the Amarna period monuments, erasing every mention of Akhenaten, Smenkhkare, Tutankhamun, Ay, and even including the image and the name of the god Aten in order to eradicate the 'criminal' Akhenaten.[7] Prior to this period there was minimal damage to Amarna monuments indicating there was some trigger, either religious, personal or political which started the process, or he was simply a cautious *King* who did not react without serious consideration.[8]

Dismantling the temples of Akhenaten at Karnak begun during the reign of Tutankhamun, and he used the blocks from these monuments for the construction of his own temples both on the east and the west bank at Thebes. Horemheb simply continued this programme of destruction. Like Tutankhamun he incorporated the blocks into his own building works, primarily at Karnak. This in itself, according to Egyptian protocol cannot be criticised as old temples and palaces were continually used as quarries by later kings.

There seems to be a distinct lack of malice in the method of destruction of the monuments of the Amarna kings before him, with the destruction of Ay's monuments being limited to the Theban region, with his Cairo and Gebel Shams monuments left untouched.[9] Initially Horemheb was comfortable to be associated with Tutankhamun and Ay, as this legitimised the rite of succession. At the Karnak shrine built by Ay for Tutankhamun, Horemheb erased the name of Ay replacing it with his own, which meant these inscriptions which named Ay as Tutankhamun's father, now named Horemheb in his place. It was only in the latter years of his reign that Horemheb defaced the images of Tutankhamun before destroying the temple completely.[10]

The defacement programme of Horemheb appears to have been carried out in two stages, initially the hacking out and rubbing smooth of the inscriptions and images, and then the reuse of the smoothed surfaces by recarving cartouches and images. The destruction of Ay's monuments were more thorough than that of Tutankhamun's. Initially Horemheb removed Ay's cartouches with a small-tipped chisel to break up the surface, before rubbing the surface smooth. Some were smoother than others, some have chisel marks still visible. The blocks were dismantled from the original monument before being reused. The figures on the Tutankhamun blocks are more damaged than the cartouches which are often only roughly carved out, and only on the pillars, indicating the temples were abandoned before destruction was complete.

One possible act of destruction that did not take place, and which has been the source of some discussion, is that of Tutankhamun's tomb. As we are all aware, this is one of the few intact tombs discovered in Egypt, and one that was not destroyed by Horemheb's men. Some have used this as proof that he was not at the funeral, hence he did not know where the tomb was. However, this does not ring true. If Horemheb wanted to destroy the tomb, whether he was at the funeral or not, he could have located it as many of the people who were at the funeral, or even those who built it would know where it was. Others have taken this lack of malice against the tomb as proof there was no hostility between the kings. However in 2009, research was carried out in the Valley of the Kings showing a more mundane reason why the tomb was left untouched. Directly over the entrance of KV62 is a flood layer three feet thick indicating there was a flood not long after Tutankhamun's burial. Above KV55, the reburial by Tutankhamun of an Amarna *King*, perhaps Smenkhkare (see Chapter 1), there are four feet of flood level detritus. It appears the same flood concealed both tombs and as there is no windblown debris; it indicates there was little time between burial, robberies and the flood.[11] Tutankhamun was buried in April, and the rains and flashfloods normally occur in October or November leaving only a 6-8 month period when the entrance to KV62 was open to view. This flood therefore occurred during the reign of Ay, and by the reign of Horemheb and his campaign of destruction the entrance to KV62 was well and truly buried by three feet of rubble and totally inaccessible to Horemheb and his men.

By ignoring the reigns of the previous kings Horemheb was not only able to re-use their monuments but also their deeds should he find them favourable. In this way he adopted the Restoration Stela of Tutankhamun, leading some to the conclusion he wrote the text originally, placing it in the name of the young *King*. The main theme of the Restoration Stela was the restoration of the old religion which suited Horemheb's plans. He adopted the stela as his own, replacing Tutankhamun's cartouches, although the image of Ankhesenamun was erased rather than simply replacing the text with the name of Mutnodjmet, the Great Royal Wife,[12] as was done on many images and statues at Karnak temple[13] (*colour plates 12 & 13*).

The Restoration inscription provides a good summary of Horemheb's vision for a traditional Egypt as well as giving an idea of the problems faced by Egypt at the collapse of the Amarna heresy:

> He restored what was ruined, creating everlasting monuments. Maat is back in her proper place, for he (*Tutankhamun*) put an end to wrongdoing throughout Egypt.
>
> When His Majesty's reign began, from the southern border to the northern marshes, the temples of the gods and goddesses were in ruins. Their shrines had crumbled into piles of rubbish choked with weeds. Their sanctuaries might never have existed, their chapels were little more than footpaths. The land was in chaos because the gods had abandoned it. Whenever the army was sent to Syria to extend Egypt's territory, it always failed. If someone called on a god in prayer, they got no response. In just the same way, if someone petitioned a goddess, they got no answer …[14]

This gives some idea of the chaos which had befallen Egypt as well as the ruinous state of the temples. Horemheb takes this as part of the theme for his Karnak text known as the Edict, where he states the vision for his reign:

> As long as my life on earth remains, it shall be spent making monuments for the gods. I shall be renewed increasingly, like the moon … one whose limbs shed light on the ends of the earth like the disc of the sun god[15]

When Horemheb refers to 'making monuments for the gods', not only does he mean stone monuments such as statues and temples but anything that glorifies the gods which included his works of justice and piety. His reference to the moon asserts his devotion to the lunar deity, Thoth, over and above the solar gods, and this is indeed prominent through much of his life.

Horemheb's Karnak building campaign was a huge undertaking, and his work dominates the temple even today; although he does not receive the credit for it. Any tourist visiting the temple of Karnak cannot help to be overawed by the wonder that is the Hypostyle Hall of Sety I and Ramses II. However, like the Ramesside dynasty as a whole, the Hypostyle Hall would not exist without Horemheb, as it was his original vision.[16] During his reign he planned it out and initiated the construction works by building a large courtyard but did not survive to see its completion. It was continued by his successor Ramses I (although there is only one cartouche of this *King* here), and his family (42). Sety I completed the northern part of the hall, and his carved raised relief can be seen here, but it is the large work of Ramses II which dominates the hall in the form of 134 columns, 24m in height with a circumference of 10m each. It would be interesting to know whether the finished monument reflects the ideas of Horemheb in any way.

Still standing, and a testament to the traditional building works of Horemheb, however, are the second, ninth and tenth pylons to the south of the Hypostyle Hall. Although he started the second pylon, he did not complete it. This was the work of Sety I (44). The pylon stands an impressive 99.88m in length, with eight flag poles fluttering in the wind. The ninth and tenth pylons were however entirely the work of Horemheb, which both stand over 66m wide and over 26m high,[17] slightly smaller than the second pylon, and decorated with traditional smiting and battle scenes (45 and *colour plate 14*).

Excavations of the ninth pylon have uncovered two foundation deposits in the west wing of the pylon in the far north and south corners (46). The southern deposit was more complete than the northern but there was no indication they were placed there at different times.[18] These deposits were traditional in nature, and include a small inscribed green faience brick bearing his name and title identifying the pylon as his. There was also evidence of gilded wood or bone items, although these have deteriorated leaving just the gold, showing they were realistic impressions of the blue and white lotus indigenous to Egypt, associated with creation and new life. Faience models of cattle, duck, wheat grains and vegetables up to 3cm in size were placed here as food offerings in the absence of real food. A millstone and rowel were also included for the production of food, as these were used to grind the grain into flour. A bronze hoe of 6cm and a wooden set square were also placed within the deposit, and are the types of tools traditionally used in the construction of a temple.[19]

Exploration of the internal structure of these three pylons since the late nineteenth century has uncovered over 60,000 talatat blocks from the Karnak temples of Akhenaten (47). Most pylons are hollow; with the space used for storage or temporary accommodation. In the case of Horemheb's pylons, the hollow space did not have a function but was greatly strengthened by these blocks. When building these pylons Horemheb's workmen dismantled the temples of Akhenaten, placing the blocks into the pylon to reinforce the structure, but this act also served to remove the temples and therefore all traces of Akhenaten. The tenth pylon contains large blocks carved in traditional artistic style while the ninth pylon was full of the smaller talatat in the Amarna style as well as blocks which appear to have originally belonged to a temple of Tutankhamun indicating Horemheb dismantled three temples at this time. In a few cases the talatat are in order but not all.[20]

The order of the placing blocks into the pylon was not recorded in the early excavations, but later studies have shown that as the blocks were removed from the Akhenaten temple, they were placed directly into the pylon, meaning theoretically when removed they could be placed back together in order. The blocks excavated in the late nineteenth century were stacked awaiting later removal, only to lose the initial sequence. The 'Akhenaten Temple Project' has been working at Karnak since the 1960s on removing the blocks from the ninth and tenth pylons, which are now in their thousands. They are currently working on a computerised system to match up these blocks into the correct order; a difficult task considering they are stored in at least six storerooms, full from floor to ceiling. There are further difficulties as some blocks were re-used by Tutankhamun and have therefore been carved on both sides. First it needs to be established whether the decoration belongs to Tutankhamun or Akhenaten, before they can be placed within a decorative sequence (48).

From the east wing of the ninth pylon over 35,000 blocks were discovered, some of which have been identified as belonging to the Benben Temple of Nefertiti. The

43 Second Pylon at Karnak. *Photograph by Brian Billington*

44 Hypostyle Hall of Horemheb, Ramses I, Sety I and Ramses II, Karnak. *Photograph by the author*

45 Back of the tenth Pylon at Karnak. *Photograph by the author*

46 Ninth Pylon at Karnak. *Photograph by Brian Billington*

47 Talatat blocks within the body of the ninth pylon at Karnak. *Photograph by the author*

48 Reconstruction of talatat blocks (Luxor Museum). *Photograph by the author*

blocks from this temple have undergone a great deal of damage, with the royal names and images hacked out. In addition, the rays of the sun disc Aten have been slashed, as they hold ankhs to the faces of the royal family.[21] This damage was inflicted once the blocks had reached the pylon, and there are numerous cartouches which were not destroyed, presumably because they were inaccessible.[22] As Horemheb knew many of the Amarna royalty and elite, the destruction was undoubtedly political rather than personal. However a hatred of Nefertiti might be surmised, as her Benben Temple seems to be the only one to be deliberately damaged.[23] However it may have been experimental at this point of the destruction, and was then abandoned due to being too time consuming. The blocks removed later and placed in the pylon last do not seem to have been destroyed so thoroughly, simply removed from their original location. The destruction campaign against the Akhenaten temples at Karnak was continued by Sety I and Ramses II as a number of talatat blocks were also discovered in the foundations of the columns in the Hypostyle Hall.

In addition to the pylons Horemheb reconstructed the 'Edifice of Amenhotep II', a low festival building with a pillared façade, which stood between the ninth and the tenth pylons. It was only a small structure standing 37m wide and 20m deep and originally comprised four separate structures, reached by a pylon, and portico, wth a number of pillared halls (49). Horemheb pulled the original structure down and then rebuilt it using the blocks. It was entered via a short ramp leading to a pillared portico. Once inside there was a large pillared hall, with smaller pillared rooms on either side. It was re-angled to match the axis of the two pylons and the processional way between them. Horemheb did not complete the decoration on this temple, as this was continued after his death by Sety I. Horemheb also started work on the ram-

49 Festival Hall of Amenhotep II between pylon nine and ten at Karnak. Photograph by the author

headed sphinxes which line the sacred avenue between Karnak and Luxor temples. Much of the stone for the Sphinx Avenue, and for other works at Karnak and Luxor came from the quarries at Gebel el Silsila,[24] which as we have seen was an important site for Horemheb (*50*). The Sphinx Avenue runs for 2km between Karnak and Luxor temples was used during processions including the important Opet festival and when complete comprised 1292 sphinxes, placed 13m apart. Modern excavations at the site are hoping to clear the whole avenue, and open it to the public, joining these two temples as they once were.

Not all of Horemheb's work at Karnak was such large-scale building work, and at the small temple of Thutmosis III dedicated to the god Ptah, he simply erected a stela to commemorate the Feast of Ptah in:

Year 1, month 4 of Akhet, day 22 of king Djoserkheperwra-Setepenra, Son of Ra, Horemheb beloved of Amun, vivified, day of the feast of Path, ruler of Ankhtawy [*Memphis*] in Thebes at her feast

This festival was celebrated on 20 November, in favour of the creator god of Memphis, who was able to create by using the power of the mind and spoken word. His cult centre was at Memphis but he was worshipped as a national god, and in Thebes in particular he was the patron deity of craftsmen; rather appropriate for a man who was rebuilding the religion of Egypt and their places of worship.

Horemheb wanted the festivals of the deities and their re-establishment into the pantheon to be a prominent and visible part of his early regnal years. He emphasised his role in the annual Festival, which not only marked the anniversary of his coronation

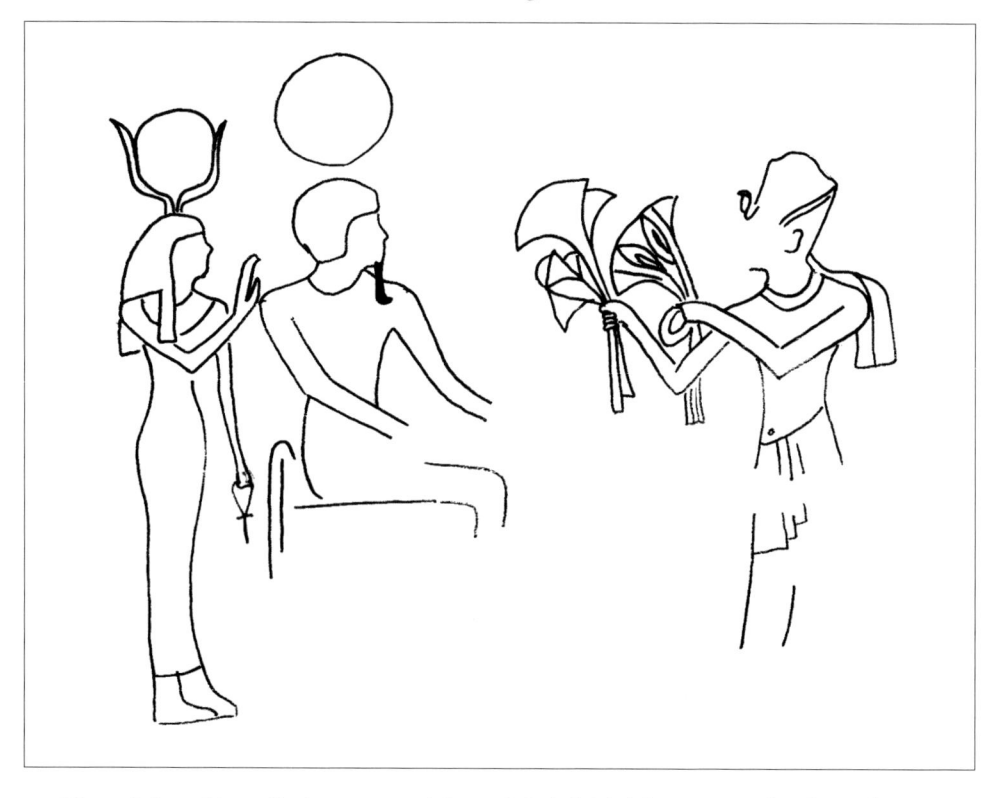

50 Horemheb making offerings to a god from Gebel el Silsileh. Drawing by the author

but renewed the importance of Amun. He usurped the elaborate illustrations of the Opet festivities (*colour plate 15*) created by Tutankhamun at Luxor, replacing the cartouches of the young *King* with those of his own, and those of Ankhesenamun with the name of his wife Mutnodjmet (*51*). He also made additions and improvements to the composition in recognition of his continuing restoration.

In the wider area of Thebes he started a restoration programme on the temple of Thutmosis III at Deir el Bahri, although very little was completed (*52*). This temple was just to the south of the main temple of Hatshepsut which dominates the site today and is located on higher ground on an outcrop of rock. Its high vantage point gave a clear view of Karnak temple and dominated the entire Deir el Bahri valley in the same way Hatshepsut's does today. It was originally called 'Holy of Monuments', and comprised three terraces joined by ramps flanked with two porticos. During the reign of Akhenaten the temple was attacked, and the name and images of Amun were hacked off the walls. This damage was restored twice, once by Horemheb and the second by Ramses II. The temple was dedicated to Amun-Ra and Amun-Ra-Kamutef, although Hathor was also worshipped at the site, and this is where the beautiful cave shrine dedicated to Hathor, complete with a limestone cow cult figure, currently on display in the Egyptian Museum, was discovered. The temple appears to have been used until the end of the twentieth dynasty. The restoration inscription of the upper colonnade of Hatshepsut's temple at Deir el Bahri intriguingly refers to Thutmosis III as 'Father of his Fathers' which has instigated some debate as to whether Horemheb was a descendent of Thutmosis.[25] However it is generally accepted to be a piece of propaganda associating Horemheb with the previous kings of the eighteenth dynasty. What better person to associate himself with, than the 'Napoleon of Ancient Egypt'?

51 Opet Festival of Tutankhamun usurped by Horemheb. Luxor Temple. *Photograph by the author*

52 Temple of Thutmosis III at Deir el Bahri (left of Hatshepsut's temple). Photograph by the author

53 The mortuary temple of Tutankhamun, Ay, and Horemheb at Medinet Habu. Photograph by the author

54 Horemheb as Atum (?)
(National Museum Alexandria).
Photograph by the author

He then turned his attention to repairing the door to the Hatshepsut/Thutmosis chapel which stands within the walls of Medinet Habu, and was close to where he was to build his mortuary temple indicating he rather wanted to be associated with the earlier Thutmosides (53). In year eight of his reign there was an inspection into the Valley of the Kings, perhaps as part of his campaign to locate a site for his own royal tomb. Part of this inspection took him to the tomb of Thutmosis IV, and a message was left written on the wall regarding their mission:

> to renew the funeral equipment of Menkheperura

It is not clear why this tomb was targeted or if there were others which were restored as well. Perhaps on their inspection of the Valley they noticed the tomb had been disturbed by robbers and they entered for damage limitation purposes. There is some speculation that perhaps he chose to restore the Thutmoside monuments and this tomb because he was a relation of the Thutmoside family, although this is unlikely. The Amarna kings were of the Thutmoside line, and there is no indication that he was related to any of the Amarna kings. It is more likely that he chose to restore this particular king's temple because Thutmosis III was the builder of the Empire that Horemheb was emulating and was hoping to be able to recreate.

Although Horemheb concentrated on the rebuilding of Karnak, he also wanted to re-establish the universal role of the King and the universal nature of the pantheon of gods, in direct contrast to the isolated, introverted religion of the Aten (54). Horemheb made a point of travelling the full length of Egypt, and whilst quarrying the stone for his numerous building commissions at Gebel el Silsila, 65km north of

55 Horemheb as Hapy (British Museum). *Photograph by the author*

Aswan he commissioned a *speos* (rock-cut temple) to be built here. In antiquity it was called Khenet, meaning 'The Place of rowing'; the modern name means 'Chain of Hills'. It was an important site and was believed to be the origin of the Nile, the area being sacred to the gods Hapy (55), Sobek, Amun and Ptah (*colour plate 16*). The quarry was a useful source for sandstone and this was used extensively from the New Kingdom to the Ptolemaic Period.[26] The Aswan Dam[27] (1906-09) was also built with rocks from this site; showing a 5000-year history of mining. Inscriptions from the site date from the pre-dynastic period with rock-art images of giraffes which once roamed freely in the area, alongside New Kingdom inscriptions of Amenhotep III and Akhenaten.

Horemheb's speos temple was on the top of the west bank quay, cut into a disused quarry, which is reflected by the five different sized entrances leading inside.[28] Quarries were often cut into a series of chambers with uncut plinths supporting the roof. This method gave the stone-masons access to the harder rock further into the cliff faces. Horemheb simply utilised one of these galleries. As the temple was not finished in his lifetime, as was traditional, later kings would complete such monuments and in this case the façade reliefs were carved by Ramses II and III with further additions by Siptah (1193-1187 BCE), with only a winged sun-disc and cartouche of Horemheb above the central doorway. Each entrance is a different width, leading to a T-shaped chapel with a vaulted long gallery on a north/south axis, with a central door, almost opposite the entrance leading to the sanctuary. This sanctuary held seven rock-cut statues, each representing one of the deities the temple was dedicated to Amun, Sobek, Horemheb, Mut, Khonsu, Taweret and Thoth (57).[29] There was a series of carved reliefs through the chapel, including on the pillars, but sadly today this is in poor state of repair, due to being occupied as a habitation until as recently as 1990. The interior walls are covered with dirt and soot from the hearth, and as it is away from the tourist 'trail' it gets somewhat neglected.

A further speos temple was built by Horemheb at Abahuda, modern Gebel Adda, in Nubia, just south of Abu Simbel on the east bank of the Nile. It was originally dedicated to Amun-Ra, Thoth, and local deities and was named *Amun's Heart is*

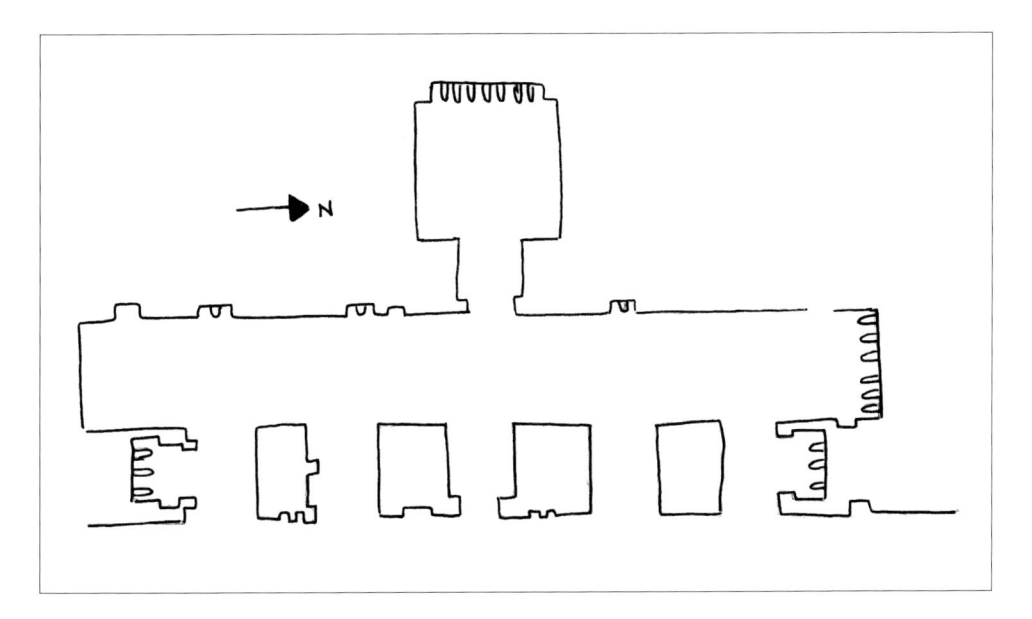

56 Speos Temple at Gebel el Silsileh. *Drawn by Brian Billington after Hari 1964*

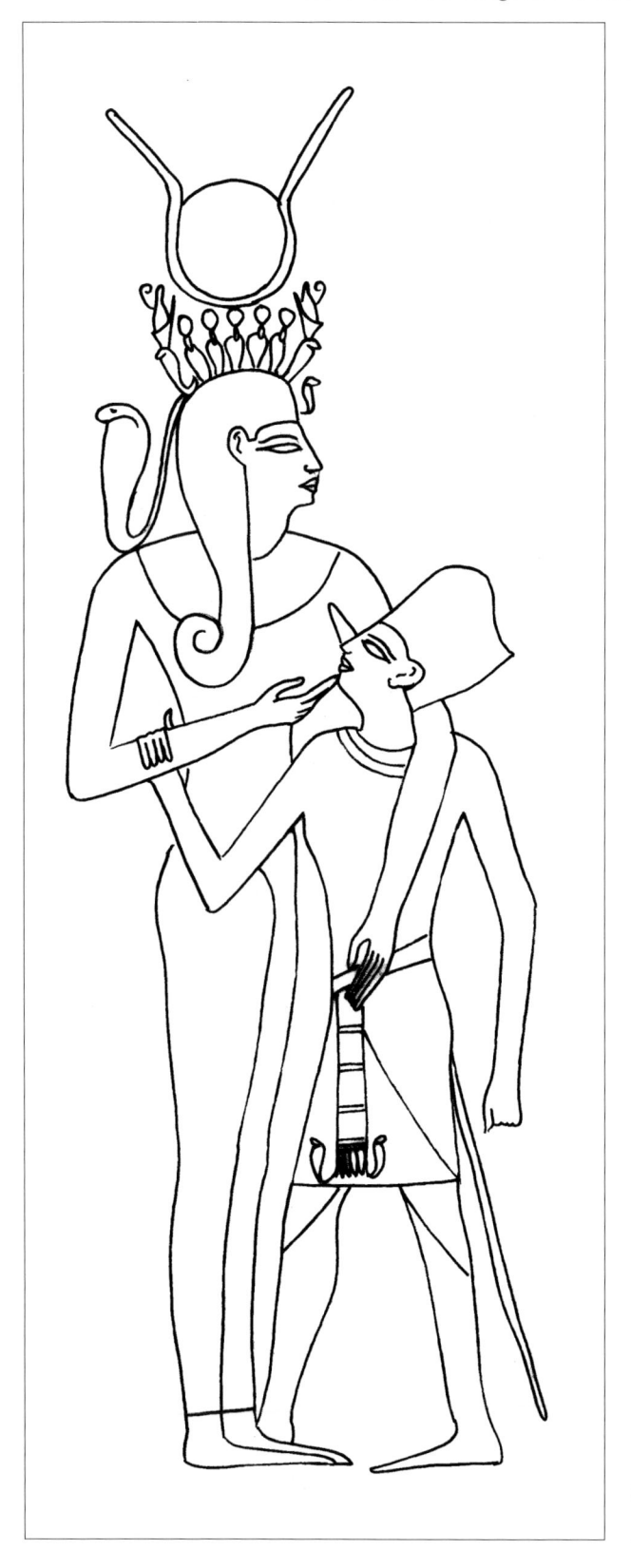

57 Horemheb suckling from Taweret at Gebel el Silsileh. *Drawing by the author*

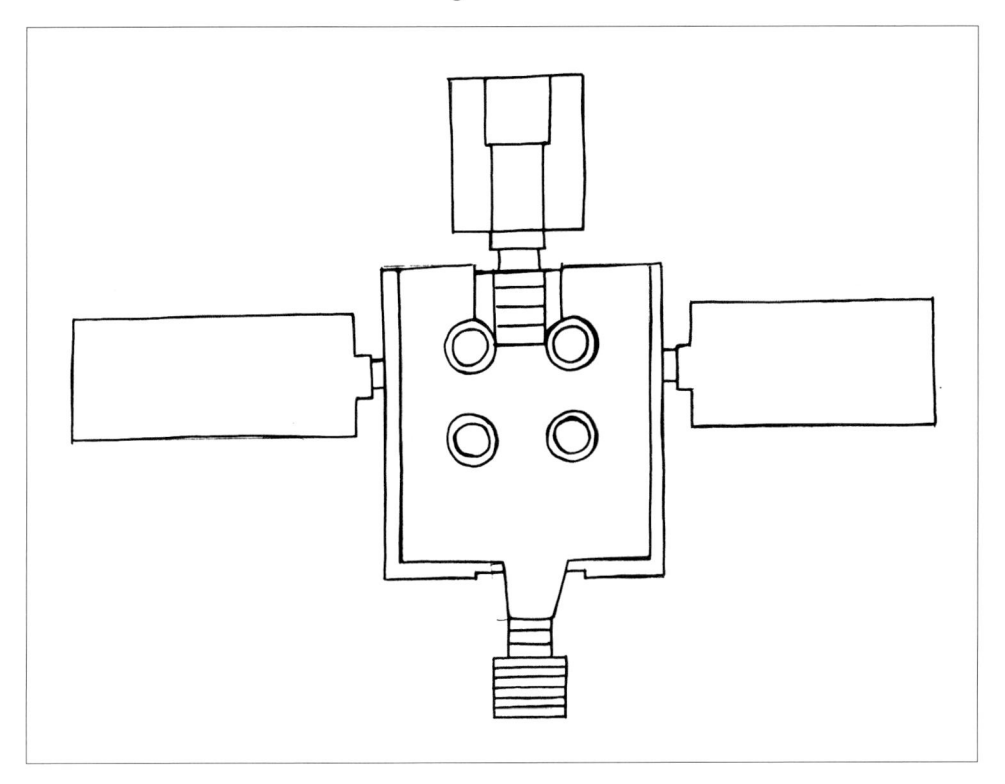

58 The temple of Abahuda. Drawing by Brian Billington after Sirdo 2006

Content. The temple was right on the water, and was reached by two short staircases of four steps leading to a longer staircase of eleven steps to the entrance.[30] At the time of inundation these steps were hidden beneath the water.

The temple itself was small, comprising an entrance hall with four papyrus columns (58), a sanctuary to the north and two undecorated side chambers, one to the east and one to the west.[31] The papyrus bundle pillars in the entrance hall support the theory that the temple was constructed at the end of his reign, as the pillar form is a transitory type between those of the eighteenth and nineteenth dynasties.[32] On the floor of the sanctuary is a shaft which leads to a subterranean chamber, although what this was used for is not clear.[33] It was converted into a church by the early Copts, who added graffiti and illustrations to the wall covering many of the original images, which showed Horemheb making offerings to the gods,[34] including Thoth, Horus and Anukis. However some of the scenes are still extant, including a coronation scene where Horemheb is crowned by both Seth and Horus (59), and is one of the few temples in Nubia where the image of Seth had not been replaced by Thoth. Another scene shows him being suckled by a goddess, emphasising his divinity. Normally the goddess in this scene would be Hathor or Isis, but in this scene it is Anukis, the consort of Khnum, the creator god worshipped in the region. Above the image the inscription states:

> Words pronounced by Anukis, Mistress of Sehel who resides in Amenheri I am your mother. For you, my milk that enters into you, in the form of life and of power; that it makes your body younger and strengthens your arms[35]

59 Coronation of Horemheb from Abahuda. *Drawing by the author*

One particularly interesting scene reinforces Horemheb's devotion to local forms of the god Horus, where he is standing before Thoth and four falcon headed deities, Horus of Maam, Horus of Buhen, Horus of Bak, and Horus of Maha.[36]

The temple has now been submerged under Lake Nasser, when the High Dam was built at Aswan, but blocks from the structure were saved and are in the Nubian Museum. It is thought to have been built in the later years of his reign due to the prominence of Seth in the decoration, which is suggested could be the influence of Prameses (Ramses I), who worshipped this deity and had even named his son after him.[37]

This devotion to Seth is further reflected in his temple at the Khata'na-Qantir-Tell el Dab'a site. On the highest part of the Tell, at a place called Es-Samana, the temple was constructed on the site of an old Hyksos temple. Surrounding the enclosure wall were a series of trees, laid out in a formalised pattern, identified in the archaeological record by pits.[38] The species of tree is therefore unidentified but it is possible they were palm trees, and the formation created a large sacred grove covering an area of up to 65m from the enclosure wall.[39] The temple itself was paved with limestone, and contained a round well and a door lintel inscribed with 'Seth, Apehti [*Great of Might*]' emphasising the temple was dedicated to him. Another temple, some 2.6km away, a similar distance as between Karnak and Luxor, along a similar orientation which was probably oriented with the river,[40] was also the focus of attention. This temple was surrounded by a 10m thick mud-brick enclosure wall, with a large stone gate or pylon in the east where the wall was thickest. It is likely this had stood on the site of an older temple, and additions were made by Horemheb and then later by Sety I.[41] This site of Qantir was important, and there is evidence of two huge harbour basins which could dock hundreds of ships. The northern edge of one of the harbours backs onto a fortification wall built by Horemheb, which protected the activation canal.

The second harbour was probably inactive during his reign, as it lay near a defunct canal which during the inundation created a seasonal lake. Some believe that this was the legendary site of Perunefer, a large port, which is often associated with the port at Memphis.[42] There was clearly a great deal of activity at the site of Qantir, and there is evidence of a large metal factory, with rooms for processing wood, leather, metal and stone. There were seven blast pipes worked by foot bellows. Examples of adhesive slag and crucibles have identified this as a bronze workshop. These types of structures are rare, and this was a particularly large example and surviving remnants within indicate that old weapons such as arrow heads and knives were melted down so the bronze could be reused (60). The factory was in use from the reign of Amenhotep II through to the reign of Sety I, when it was abandoned.[43] These Delta constructions finalised Horemheb's presence as national, covering the full length of the Nile from Aswan to the Delta. The next thing was to go international.

There is evidence that Horemheb made his presence known as far as Cyprus, where a faience sceptre, with the remains of an ivory handle, bearing his cartouches was discovered in 1977. It was found in a town near Halla Sultan Tekké, and was in a context 200 years later than his reign,[44] indicating the item was considered to be of some importance and value. It was probably a diplomatic gift between rulers which was kept as an heirloom. A vase fragment of equal standard, inscribed with the name of Horemheb in Ugarit may also have been of this same nature of exchange. The limited existence of Egyptian objects in Cyprus, which also include a wine jar of Sety I, intimates a commercial relationship only between Cyprus and Egypt.[45] It is, however, possible the object was sent to Cyprus after the reign of Horemheb when it was already an antique. However it is more likely that Cyprus was part of Horemheb's

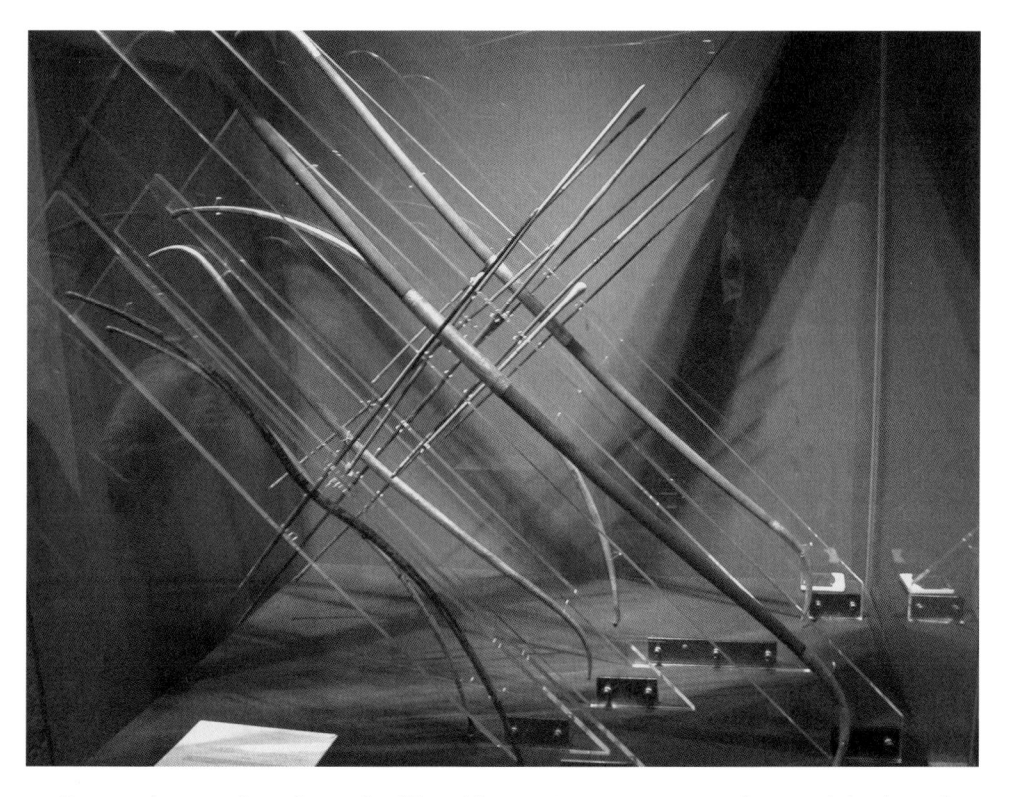

60 Bows and arrows form the tomb of Tutankhamun (Luxor Museum). *Photograph by the author*

international trade partnerships, and he probably sent a peaceful expedition there and this sceptre was part of the exchange of gifts preceding the trade activities. The natural resources and main trade items of Cyprus was copper (a major ingredient of bronze), as well as admirable artisans of gold and ceramics.[46] The exchange of opium, Moringa oil, small quantities of honey, and wine were also commonplace.[47] The Uluburun shipwreck, discovered near Kas in southern Turkey, dated to the late Amarna period, contained a large hoard of such Cypriot items, including fine and coarseware ceramics, jars containing pomegranates, and olive oil, and approximately 10 tons of copper in the form of 354 flat and 120 convex ingots. The ship itself, however, had the capacity to carry 500 tons of such copper ingots,[48] should it carry a full cargo. It is clear the items exported from Cyprus were luxury items rather than staples, necessary for the economy of Egypt. Although not an indication of the expansion of the borders of Egypt to include Cyprus and Ugarit, the reinstating of luxury-item trade indicates the economy was improving and the social hierarchy was once again stable.

While Horemheb was making his mark at home and abroad he also concentrated on law and order in Egypt. In order to restore law and order, as well as re-establishing and maintaining the neglected international relations, Horemheb needed to ensure he had full control *over* and loyalty *from* the Egyptian army. Although for all of his adult life he worked as a soldier, and then a *General* in the army, it must have been difficult to suddenly take a less active role; being the head of the army in an honorary rather than practical sense, having many other aspects of the royal administration to take up his time.

The *King*, although head of the army, did not have the hands-on experience he was used to and, therefore, needed to ensure that those he put into the roles of *General* and *Commander* were individuals who could be trusted. Horemheb, it seems, did not trust easily, and was perhaps aware that regardless of how trustworthy and loyal an individual was, temptation can sometimes be too much to resist. Therefore he divided the army into two divisions, the north and the south with a newly appointed commander for each. Before he came to the throne these two positions were held by one man; himself. Horemheb considered this too much power for a single individual. This division limited the power held by one person making it easier for him to control; no matter how remote. However one unusual element of Horemheb's reign was that he did *not* rule remotely and was a *King* very much involved with the lives of the people he governed and it was important for him to be viewed as a *King* for the people.

On the north face of the tenth pylon at Karnak Horemheb recorded his decree known as the Edict which outlined his new laws, designed to bring peace and harmony back to Egypt. The inscription is in very bad condition and not one line is complete, meaning some of the grievances and punishments are open to interpretation. There is also a copy of the Edict at Abydos too but this is equally damaged. As there is not a complete example of the king's name in the Edict other than on a lunette around the edge of the stela, it has led some to suggest that this document was penned by Tutankhamun, and usurped by Horemheb, and recorded events which he oversaw during the reign of Tutankhamun when he was an official.[49] The language used, however, indicates it was in fact written by Horemheb himself. The inscription lists the current abuses common in Egypt, which he denounced declaring a harsh punishment. Horemheb was an ambitious man, but 'his personal ambitions coincided with national interests',[50] which is expressed in his Edict. This list of abuses reflected the chaotic state of Egypt at that time and was part of Horemheb's effort in re-establishing order. However the Edict does not make a direct attack on the Amarna period, and he makes an attempt to reconcile the past and the present without making reference to the Amarna period in between.[51] He stated that he personally travelled throughout Egypt locating the problems and setting up groups of trustworthy officials to oversee law enforcement and listen to the appeals of the people:

> I have set this entire land in order – I have travelled through it thoroughly as far as the south; I have surveyed it entirely. I have learned its whole condition, having first toured its interior.
>
> I have sought out people ... discreet of good character, knowing how to judge thought, listening to the words of the palace and to the laws of the Throne Hall. I have appointed them to judge the Two Lands and to satisfy their inhabitants – I have set them in the great cities of Upper and Lower Egypt, every one of them without exception, enjoying the benefit of a stipend. I have given the, precepts and recorded laws in their journal ... I have taught them the right course of life by guiding them to justice. I have instructed them saying 'Do not associate with other people. Do not take a bribe from another. What shall one think of men in your station, appointed to replace others, as long as there is one among you who violate justice?'

It is clear he wants his law enforcers to be trustworthy and free from corruption as this is one crime he tried to eliminate from Egypt.

> But as for any lay official or any priest concerning whom one shall hear 'He sits there to administer justice in the court which has been set up for administering justice and yet he violates justice therein' it shall be reckoned to him for a great capital crime

Corruption was clearly an important issue and Horemheb was keen to stamp it out, emphasising that no one was exempt whether a layman or priest. This sent the message that on one hand although he was rewarding temples with gifts they were not above the law and should be inspirational to the population in general, so as to comply with his vision for Egypt:

> Then His Majesty took counsel with his heart ... in order to expel sin and destroy lying. The plans of His Majesty are an excellent refuge warding off the wrath all around ... cases of oppression ... which have been occurring among them. Now His Majesty was watchful day and night, seeking the benefit of Egypt and searching out excellent occasions. He took palette and papyrus roll; then he wrote down in accordance with all that His Majesty said

Horemheb was abundantly aware of the problems facing him, which were the result of neglect by the previous kings. He listed in detail the issues he identified as most urgent. They were theft, corruption and general dishonesty:

> If the commoner makes for himself a craft with its equipment in order to be able to serve pharaoh ... and the craft is taken away, so that he cannot deliver the dues, the commoner being deprived of his property, frustrated in his labours ... My Majesty has commanded to leave him alone because of his good intentions.
>
> Now if there is the man who wants to deliver dues for the breweries and abattoirs of Pharaoh on behalf of the two deputies of the army, and there is anyone who interferes and he takes away the craft of any military man or of any other person in any part of the country, the law shall be applied against him by cutting off his nose, he being sent to Sile. If however an official finds a commoner without a craft, then he shall get him a craft for his contribution, from another and shall send him off to bring the wood in his stead, for he will have to serve Pharaoh at all events.

> If there is an official who finds a commoner in possession of his craft but his goods taken away, the ship emptied of its cargo by an act of theft, and the commoner is deprived of his property and he has nothing – seeing that it is not good, this report of a very bad case, My Majesty has commanded to leave him alone.
>
> If there is anyone who interferes with those who ... and those who are supplying the harem as well as the offerings of all kinds of gods in that they deliver dues on behalf of the two deputies of the army, and he ... the law shall be applied against him by cutting off his nose, he being sent to Sile likewise.

In simplistic terms if someone was prevented, through no fault of their own, from doing the work of the *King*, then he was not to be punished as the intention was there to do the right thing. Serving the *King* was considered important as kingship and the economy were closely interlinked. If the temple and palace coffers were full this could be redistributed as rations or wages in the absence of a monetary system. A common crime seems to be the interference with boats on the way to the temple or palace full of goods. These were intercepted in one of two ways. Either the officers removed goods as a bribe in order to allow the boat free passage, or goods were confiscated to be sold or were bought from the boat-men at a decreased rate before it reached its desination which could then be sold for a profit. This was viewed as an abuse of their position and were targeted by the *King*, and punished accordingly. The Edict outlines the primary punishment as mutilation followed by hard labour or exile. A similar decree issued by Sety I, referred to those tampering with state boundaries and were punished with ear amputation followed by hard labour.[52] Perhaps he saw how well it worked for Horemheb and decided to maintain the regime outlined in the Edict. No one was free from the punishments of Horemheb, not even the army:

> The two divisions of the army which are in the country, the one in the southern region, the other in the northern region, are taking away hides throughout the land, without stopping for a single year so as to grant a respite to the peasants ... and seize those hides among them which are branded, while they are going from house to house beating and maltreating, without hides being left for the peasants and if the one who ... of Pharaoh goes to carry out the census of his cattle and he interviews them but the hides are not found with them, so that they are virtually in debt and they gain their confidence saying 'They have been taken away from us' seeing that this, too, is a wretched case, it shall be done accordingly. Now if the Overseer of the Cattle of pharaoh goes to carry out the cattle-census throughout the land – for it is he alone who shall collect the hides of the dead animals which ...
>
> My Majesty has commanded that the peasant shall be left alone because of his honest intention. But as for any military man concerning whom one shall hear 'He goes about and also takes hides away' starting from today, the law shall be applied against him by inflicting upon him a hundred blows, causing five open wounds, and taking from him the hide which he has seized as being something that has been unlawfully acquired.

Horemheb had identified a problem with dishonest soldiers travelling through the villages removing animal hides which they were keeping, or repeating the visit too often, meaning farmers were unable to replenish their stock. The soldiers were reported as collecting these hides in the name of the *King* under the pretext of tax collection. Not only was this clandestine tax collection preventing the farmers from breeding more animals but was also causing long-term issues. It was necessary for the farmers, should cattle die to keep the skin as proof when the next census for tax purposes was carried out. Without these skins they could not prove the animal had not been sold. Therefore Horemheb decreed only the *Overseer of the Cattle of Pharaoh* was entitled to collect such taxes and those who did it illegally were punished. However in the interim, if hides were stolen peasants were not to be punished as their intentions were once again taken into account. They would not be blamed for another's wrongdoing.

The reason for the theft of hides was tied in with a wider problem. At this time there was a leather shortage for both armour and weapons, and if soldiers were caught stealing it, they received a hundred blows and five open wounds as punishment. The leather shortage also affected the safflower industry which was grown in order to dye the leather rendering the safflower farmers redundant. Therefore both industries were protected by the *King* and those who abused the system were punished by mutilation, and exiled to the Sinai.

Tax amounts were also a major concern and the Edict addresses the falsification of the tax measures as a matter of urgency. Horemheb identified that many tax-collectors were collecting more than they should by changing the size of the measurement and holding back the excess for themselves:

> Now as for the these keepers of the monkeys who are going about taking ... in the southern region and the northern region and unlawfully taking corn from the inhabitants of the village, making the house-measure fifty *hins* (2.4 *litres*) in that they falsify the measure of the State granary and there are thereby unlawfully taking flax, vegetables. Seeing that this is a bad case, My Majesty has commanded to prevent this from being done ... in that they are unlawfully ... taking from the ships and other people are going about doing ... in the southern region and in the northern regions and unlawfully taking a house-measure of fifty *hins* from the commoners, But as for ... these honest ones ... they shall be rewarded.

Although this seems insignificant, when dealing with a non-monetary society Horemheb wanted to stamp down on all wrong-doing in order to bring Egypt back to the laws of Maat. He particularly did not want his people to be robbed by his officials, the very people in place to upload the laws. Horemheb punished those who falsified taxes but again rewarded those who were honest. It was important to his campaign that people acted honestly and without fear. Officials demanding bribes to pass inspection, or to avoid confrontation were also targeted by the Edict:

> But what shall one think of these new attempts to demand the 'something' of them now the mayors also shall take part in the royal journey for the sake of the commoners ... Seeing that this is a bad case, My Majesty has commanded to prevent this also from being done starting from today. But as for the ... who still seizes a ship which is in the harbour, he is the one against whom an inquiry shall be opened.

The *King* believed that through these reforms and law enforcement he would be able to restore Egypt back to the 'Golden Age' of Amenhotep III. Horemheb did not have time to oversee each court case individually, so it was necessary to appoint deputies and *Viziers* to work on his behalf[53] resulting in a complete overhaul of the judicial system with new judges and peers:

> Priests of the temples, officials of the residence of this country and wab priests of the gods forming every honourable court they shall judge the citizens of every town. My Majesty has taken great pains over Egypt in order to assure that the life of his

inhabitants may prosper while he appears every morning upon the throne of Ra. Behold the courts have been set up all over the country to judge everyman living to hold court in the towns according to the excellent plans of My Majesty.

Although on the one hand Horemheb limited the powers held by the priesthood, on the other hand he gave them the power of legal judges. This emphasised that once again the law of Maat was to be obeyed, and as the priests were servants of the gods, they were essentially doing the work of the gods; ergo the crimes of the people were judged by god. However, he was under no illusion that the judges were corruptible regardless of their religious posts and he wanted to ensure they would not open to bribery by exempting them from taxes of gold and silver; meaning they kept all their income. Although this meant they did not need bribes Horemheb was aware some might still be corrupt, so he made it a punishable offence. In order to keep a close eye on the officials, listen to their grievances, and reward them for their loyalty, he held monthly meetings accompanied by a feast, where officials were presented with golden shebyu collars and were addressed personally by the *King*. The tomb of Neferhotep at Assasif, dated to year three of the reign, indicates this act was more than just literary propaganda. Neferhotep depicts himself receiving shebyu collars from Horemheb who stood at a traditional Window of Appearances. Horemheb was rewarding the Amun priesthood and Neferhotep as *Amun's Divine Father* was of particularly high status and therefore favoured more than others. Strangely enough, whilst trying to eradicate all evidence of Akhenaten, this 'gift giving' system was the same tactic used by Akhenaten to appease his officials, thus ensuring their loyalty through gifts and elaborate banquets.[54] Horemheb clearly thought they were effective methods and therefore maintained this.

It was important to Horemheb to be accepted as a *King* 'of the people', someone who related to those he ruled. This was achieved through the Edict, and in addition to protecting the people he was also safe-guarding the assets of the state.[55] He wanted the people of Egypt to trust him to bring Egypt back to the glorious place it was before the Amarna period and its changes; one protected by the gods, safe from crime, free of corruption and abundant in food:

> I have issued the instruction because My Majesty wants to protect every ... Indeed they are taking with them provisions from the State Granary, every one of them being in possession of barley and emmer; there has not been found one who had not his share

The Edict is viewed by some scholars as a double-edged sword. Protecting the people and the assets of the *King*, but as well as a sweetener for what may have been a heavy-handed succession, especially with those who went against the laws of Maat and against the *King*. The work recorded in the Edict can be viewed in either one of two ways; as a necessary crack-down on criminals and corrupt officials in order to aid the poor and maintain economic and political disorder, or secondly evidence of his dictatorship and the doctrine associated with it. It needs to be considered that Horemheb was in a difficult situation. Whatever stance he took was going to offend someone, making enemies of them; whether it was the corrupt officials whose gravy-train had just left town, or the peasants who were to be taxed more whilst held under greater government control.

In order to implement these changes Horemheb needed assurance that his officials and army were loyal, honest and highly trained. As he was a *General* for a number of years he knew many of the soldiers personally and promoted men into positions of power as appropriate for their skills and ambitions. The army were also expected to defend the borders against the encroaching Hittite army, who even before the propaganda surrounding the so-called letter of Ankhesenamun, were taking advantage of the neglected vassal states under the reign of Akhenaten. The Egyptian army no longer held a purely administrative and idle existence.

However, evidence of battles and confrontations during Horemheb's reign is scarce. It is recorded there was a small-scale expedition to Kush which may have been an inspection of royal gold-mines. In the later eighteenth dynasty, gold became essential in the re-establishment and maintenance of international relationships with the Levant in particular, and the exploitation of gold mines in Kush, Wawat and the Eastern Nubian desert[56] were re-established during the reign of Horemheb which may have encountered resistance from the Nubians. The Kush campaign may have been against such a resistence, and is recorded in Horemheb's temple at Gebel el Silsila. As the scenes are very damaged due to modern graffiti and holes being drilled into the walls over the centuries, the year of the expedition is not recorded but the battle is depicted, with the *King* victorious in his chariot as Amun hands him the sword of victory. The scenes depict the victory parade, with numerous bound captives presented to the god Amun. The procession of captives is accompanied by Egyptian soldiers and a priest bearing an incense burner,[57] Horemheb is at the front carried in a sedan chair by twelve soldiers with feathers in their hair preceded by Nubian captives (*61*).[58] There is no doubt the expedition was an offensive, and there are images of Nubian captives presented to the *King*, and three Nubian men and one woman were crying in fear of Horemheb, referring to him as 'Lion entering into Kush'.[59] The supporting inscription shows the dominance of Horemheb over them:

> The Good God comes, he triumphs over the princes of every country. His bow is in his hand like the Lord of Thebes (Montu), puissant king, mighty in strength, who carries away the princes of wretched Kush, king Djeserkheperru (Horemheb), given life. His majesty came from the land of Kush, with the captives which his sword had made, according to his father Amun commanded him.[60]

Some have interpreted the campaign as the result of a Nubian demonstration against Horemheb who they perhaps did not view as the legitimate *King*.[61] There is nothing however in the inscriptions here to suggest this is the case and it is just as likely to be a dispute over the goldmines of Kush. Horemheb also appeared to carry out a northern offensive. The ninth pylon at Karnak depicts this northern campaign, where

61 Kushite campaign from Gebel el Silsileh. *Drawing by the author*

62 Acacia plaque from KV57. *Drawing by the author after Davies 2001*

Horemheb is offering three rows of Asiatic captives to the deities Amun, Mut and Khonsu. It is recorded that a mere two months after his coronation he travelled north to deal with political unrest and problems there. The captives greet the gods displaying suitable respect and fear:

> The wretched princes of the Haunebu; they say Hail to thee. Your name has encircled the two ends of the earth, among all lands; every land fears because of your fame; Your fear is in their heart

Amun is recorded on one inscription speaking to Horemheb:

> I have given to you triumph over the south, victory over the north

Although this is part of standard kingship propaganda it shows Horemheb was the undisputed *King of Upper and Lower Egypt* with military victories over both areas.

The northern campaign is further depicted on the north wall of the tenth pylon and in the adjoining courtyard, in the form of rows of prisoners identified as 'Vile Chiefs' of Syria and of Hatti. A stone fragment currently in Vienna depicts Asiatics whose cities were sacked and could be a record of the Northern campaign of Horemheb or possibly an earlier Hittite offensive, which diminished the Egyptian empire during the reign of Akhenaten.

A small sculptured acacia plaque fragment discovered in Horemheb's Valley of the Kings tomb, thought to be of Syrian origin,[62] depicting the lower half of two winged deities, may have been acquired on this Northern expedition (62). It had a number of small holes around the edge indicating it may have been nailed or stitched to something and was originally gilded. It was clearly an elite item, whether captured booty or a diplomatic gift is uncertain but it shows a degree of contact between Egypt and the Asiatic states during the reign of Horemheb.

On the connecting wall between Horemheb's two pylons at Karnak, a peaceful trading expedition to Punt is also recorded, showing not all foreign contact was aggressive. There is a great deal of academic discussion as to the location of Punt, or the 'God's Land' as named by the Egyptians. From images of Punt and the wildlife it is clear the route was along the Red Sea, and the images at Hatshepsut's temple at Deir el Bahri of the flora and fauna indicate it was in Africa somewhere, perhaps in Ethiopia, or Eritrea,[63] although many scholars place Punt somewhere in Somalia, Djibouti, or even as far south as Zanzibar.[64] The evidence suggests the Egyptians always reached Punt by sea, and the Puntites travelled to the Red Sea to trade, by means of rafts.[65] The chiefs of Punt present sacks of gold dust, ostrich feathers, exotic animals and precious woods to Horemheb, and are referred to by the Egyptians as 'Great Chiefs', showing a more equal relationship than that held between the Egyptians and the Nubians or Asiatics. Punt was never considered one of the enemies of Egypt, and although this scene is presented as a traditional tribute scene between a vassal ruler and the Egyptian *King*, this is not a reflection of the politics at the time. The Egyptians needed to trade with the Puntite rulers for their natural resources. The most famous expedition to Punt was that of Hatshepsut, earlier in the eighteenth dynasty, although this was not the first, with numerous expeditions in the Middle Kingdom, during the reign of Mentuhotep II, Senusret I, and Amenemhat II, which continued in the New Kingdom during the reigns of Thutmosis III and Amenhotep III. However there is no evidence of trade with Punt after the reign of Ramses III, and therefore can be associated with better times, when Egypt was economically and politically strong.

There is no doubt that Horemheb's reign was a busy one, but as he was unable to perform any acts purely for the sake of performing them, such as grandiose building works, or offensives against unchartered territory in order to extend the borders of Egypt, he is destined to be forgotten. Throughout his 15-year reign Horemheb dedicated his time, energy and resources to bringing Egypt back to the glory days of Amenhotep III, before Akhenaten and his revolution diminished all Egypt stood for. No government in history, responsible for the 'clean up' of a predecessor's neglect and bad management is ever given the credit they deserve. Horemheb in fact achieved a great deal in his 15-year reign; restoring the religion, and reinforcing law and order, as well as re-establishing international contacts so the Egypt he handed over to his successor was once again strong and powerful. This enabled the next generation of kings to expand the borders of Egypt, increasing her power and wealth beyond that of Amenhotep III. Horemheb may not have achieved these things himself but he created the foundations upon which a greater Egypt could be built; and this was no mean feat considering the delapidated state of Egypt when he came to the throne.

CHAPTER 7
THE END OF AN ERA

The death of Horemheb could potentially have thrown Egypt once again into turmoil, and even civil war, as he died without producing an heir. However due to his foresight and political shrewdness he had chosen an heir from amongst the *Generals* of his army; his close advisor, and *General*, Pramesses, who came from the Delta region. His rise in power and favour with the *King* can be seen when Pramesses was promoted from *General* to the position of *Vizier*, the highest administrative position in Egypt, before being named as Horemheb's Deputy King. Pramesses was carefully chosen, not only for his wisdom and age, as he was in his fifties when Horemheb was *King*, but also because he had a family comprising a son, Sety, a grandson, Rameses, and two granddaughters Hunetmire and Tia, who although would not inherit the throne could produce male heirs if necessary. This guaranteed his dynasty would continue for at least three generations.

When Horemheb died in 1306 BCE his *Deputy* and *Vizier*, Pramesses, became *King*, changing his name and ruling under the name of Ramses, the first ruler of that name, and the first *King* of what is known as the Ramesside period and the nineteenth dynasty. He continued to rule along the same path as Horemheb, returning Egypt back to the traditional ideology and culture, by building upon Horemheb's foundations.

Although the succession was straight-forward, there is a lot of controversy and academic debate regarding the reign length of Horemheb as there are a number of inconsistencies and contradictions in the available evidence. Manetho writing in the third century BCE gives Horemheb a reign of 12 years and three months. Manetho's sources however were flawed, as Horemheb is recorded twice; once as Oros (Amenhotep III of the collosi of Memnon) and secondly as Armais who the Greeks associated with the mythical Danaus.[1]

An inscription from the Tomb of Mes at Saqqara, contemporary with the reign of Ramses II, adds confusion to the debate by stating:

> In year 59 under the majesty of the king of Upper and Lower Egypt, Djoserkheperura Setepenra, Son of Ra, Horemheb, Beloved of Amun.[2]

The text refers to a law-suit which took place in that year and could therefore be considered a reliable source. However as it was written fifty years after Horemheb's death it is generally believed to be an error. It is thought these 59 years probably include the years from the end of Amenhotep III's reign to the end of Horemheb's reign, eliminating the Amarna kings. Through adding these years together we can produce two possible reign lengths for Horemheb. We know Akhenaten ruled for 17 years, Smenkhkare for two, Tutankhamun for ten and Ay for four years; a total of 23 years. For those who believe there was a co-regency between Akhenaten and Amenhotep III the reign length will be different to those who believe they ruled consecutively. For the former, subtracting 23 years of Amarna kings from a 59 years reign gives a difference of 36 years; for the latter assuming there was a twelve year co-regency there is a difference of 31 years. This would therefore suggest Horemheb ruled for between 31 to 26 years. Sadly the mathematics does not correspond with the archaeological evidence, making the issue even more complex.

Another point of conflict here is that Horemheb, personally, never added his regnal years to those of the Amarna kings, he simply erased them, beginning his year one at the death of Amenhotep III as if the next 23 years had not happened. Even in the early nineteenth dynasty, these reigns are simply ignored, and their combined regnal years were not added to those of Horemheb. Evidence shows when referring to events in the Amarna period, creative terms were used. A papyrus fragment for example refers to a death which happened in 'year nine of the rebel', and the inscription of Mes refers to negotiations happening during Akhenaten's reign, as happening in the time of the 'enemy of Akhetaten [*Amarna*]'. If Horemheb adopted these years as his own, then no references would be made to these times in this way as they would be all during his reign.

The archaeological evidence we have of his reign length however, is scarce and for many years only confirmed three regnal years; year 1, from the temple of Ptah at Karnak, year three from the Theban tomb of Neferhotep (TT50) and year eight from the graffiti in the tomb of Thutmosis IV in the Valley of the Kings. Three fragmentary stela attest Horemheb's year five or seven and year seven is recorded on two Ramesside ostraca.[3]

The latter part of his possible 26-/31-years reign is more difficult to prove with any certainty. Graffiti from a statue of the *King* from his mortuary temple at Medinet Habu states Horemheb entered the mortuary temple for the first time presumably on inspection in year 27. It was for a long time believed 27 years referred to the difference between the end of the reign of Amenhotep III and the reign of Horemheb.[4] The Inscription of Mes, and two Amarna dockets of year 28 and 30 of an undisclosed *King*, which some have accredited to him, also indicate a longer reign. However these dockets bear remarkable similarity to jar labels of year 28, 30 and 31 of Amenhotep III and are therefore more likely to be his. They are unlikely to be Horemheb's as there would be no reason for these dockets to be at Amarna, as after year three or four of Tutankhamun, the city was largely abandoned, and totally closed down before the middle of Horemheb's reign.

One particularly controversial piece of evidence is known as 'Redford's Bowl'; a mottled granite bowl discovered in a dealer's shop in Cairo in the 1970s. It had a diameter of 34cm and a hieroglyphic inscription running around the edge:

> Year 16, under the majesty of the Lord of the Two Lands, Horonemheb, ruler at the time of his first victorious campaign, from Byblos as far as the land of the vile chief of Carchemish. An offering which the king gives to Ptah south-of-his-wall, lord of the life of Two Lands, to Astarte Lady of Heaven, to Anat the daughter of Ptah, Lady of Truth, Reshef Lord of Heaven, Qudshu Lady of the Stars of Heaven, they may give life, prosperity and health to ka of the stable-master of the Lord of the Two Lands, Sennefer, repeating life.[5]

Not only did this evidence of a later year of Horemheb's reign close the gap between year seven and year 27, but also records the first evidence of Horemheb going into battle, the first instance of four Canaanite deities in connection with the Egyptian god Ptah, and the first mention in Egypt of the gods Astarte and Qudshu. It almost seemed too good to be true; which it was. It has since been discovered to be a fake. It is uncertain however, whether just the inscription or the bowl is the fake. There are numerous points about the inscription that have led to this belief, and it is now widely accepted the inscription was made in the 1940s, by a scholar between the two World

Wars, designed to undermine another scholar, Professor Seele.⁶ Many aspects of the inscription point to this period, including the unusual spelling of the name Horemheb (rendered Horonemheb) a common spelling in the 1930s and 1940s. Redford in his original article mentions the odd spelling but does not offer an explanation, but if it was genuine this would be another unique aspect to the artefact. The spelling of his name in this way incorporates the name of the Canaanite god Haroun, although the name of the god is not spelt out in this rendering, it was believed this spelling further emphasised the Asiatic connection.

There are two different inscriptions on the bowl which have since proved to be unconnected, with one half being a standard offering inscription and the other regarding the battle, with no natural connection between the two.⁷ Although the bowl was an interesting find, it is now ignored by Egyptologists in connection to Horemheb's reign length.

Recent excavations (2006-2007) in the tomb of Horemheb in the Valley of the Kings have discovered in the well shaft numerous pot shards originally from wine amphora. Over 200 of the pottery fragments bore hieratic inscriptions, many referring to year 13 of Horemheb for ordinary wine and year 14 for good quality wine. In total there are approximately 60 such labels indicating there were large quantities of wine in the tomb, each inscribed with the regnal year. Fourteen say 'regnal year' but the date is missing, 22 of Year 13, eight year 14, and there are a number where the date is not clear. Five could be year 10-19, three year 11-14, one year 13-14, five which could be year 13, 23, or 33. However the highest date of any clarity is year 14. All the wine from year 13 is from the same vintner, whereas the rest are varied.

Although these were all fragmentary there is a complete amphora jar in the Petrie Museum discovered in Sedment, which has been attributed to Horemheb bearing the inscription 'Year 12, Sweet wine of the Western (?) river [...] chief vintner Rurery (?).'⁸ Although there are no royal names in the inscription Petrie ascribed the year to Horemheb (63). Perhaps there was an indication on the inscription that it belonged to Horemheb which has disappeared since discovery. The name of the vinter is also

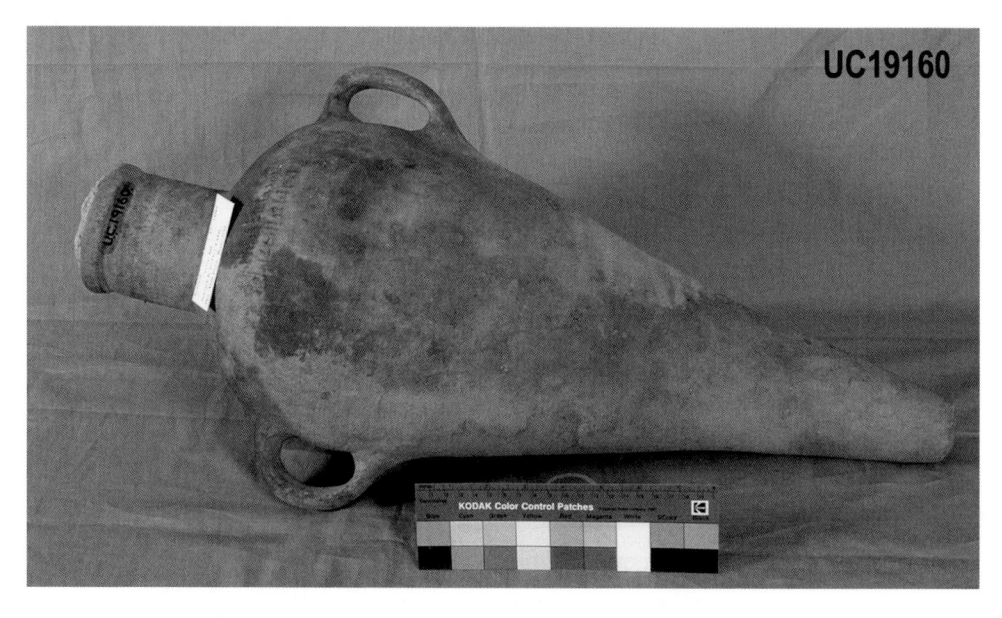

63 Amphora jar of Horemheb (Petrie Museum UC19160). *Photograph courtesy of the Friends of the Petrie Museum*

mentioned on a label from Deir el Medina dated to year 3, from 'the estate of Kheper-Djeser-Ra', with the name of 'chief vintner Ru[…]'. The vintner's name is unusual so they are possibly the same man. It was traditional to place wine in the tomb from the last of perhaps the last two harvests indicating he died before the harvest of year fifteen. Wine in Egypt had a limited life and the idea of vintage did not exist.[9] This is an important discovery bridging the gap a little between year seven and year 27, and is the first discovery since 1973 and Redford's Bowl. It is particularly significant as wine buried in the tomb was often the most recent and therefore the highest date from wine jars in a funerary context is often representative of the date of death of the tomb owner.

Circumstantial evidence can also be taken into account in support of a shorter than 26-/31-year reign. We know for a fact Horemheb participated in two Apis Bull funerals at Memphis (see Chapter 6). Some assume this indicates a rule longer than eight years to be able to reside over two such significant events. However using comparative evidence it is clear this is not necessarily the case. During the reign of Ramses II, for example, there were three Apis Bull funerals in the first 30 years in year 16, 26 and 30. In the 27-year reign of Ramses XI no less than five were buried;[10] an average of one every five years. Therefore in a reign of 8-15 years it is quite possible for two such bulls to die. It is also noted that although Horemheb usurped and added to temples of previous kings, his independent building work was not exceptional in volume, as one would expect from nearly thirty years on the throne. He has produced a little less than Sety I in his 13-year reign and far less than that of the 32 years of Ramses III. Although it is interesting to note his achievements in comparison to other New Kingdom reigns, the validity of such comparisons needs to be questioned.

Other factors should be considered when making such comparisons; such as the political and economical situation. When Sety I and Ramses III came to the throne they inherited a politically stable and economically sound country; even though both their reigns were beset with international conflicts. When Horemheb came to the throne he was not blessed with either of these. He inherited a politically unstable, morally corrupt and economically bankrupt country and needed to concentrate on these issues before concentrating on ego-boosting building projects. It would be more valuable to compare his reign to another *King* in a similar situation; for example Ahmose of the beginning of the eighteenth dynasty who ruled for 24 years and did not contribute greatly to Egypt's monuments as he concentrated on the politics and economy of Egypt throughout his reign.

Further evidence of a shorter reign can be found in the written texts regarding officials working during his reign. One such text is a letter from the Deir el Medina Chief of Police Mininiwy, to the *Vizier* Khay. He reminds the *Vizier* he has been in the post since year seven of Horemheb. Although the letter is not dated it is possible to ascertain that it is dated after year 16 of the reign of Ramses II, when the southern *Vizier* is known to be Paser. The earliest record of Khay as *Vizier* is in year 30 of Ramses II. Mininiwy is also mentioned in another text where he is a witness in a court trial regarding an event which occurred in year 15 of Ramses II.[11] From this it is possible to calculate that Mininiwy was a necropolis workman in year seven of Horemheb and worked as Chief of Police sometime until after year 16 of Ramses II, possibly even year 20 or 25. He was therefore a workman at 18-20 years old and allowing for the possible 26/31 years for Horemheb's reign Mininiwy would have died at 75-80 years old. Although not unheard of it is considered unlikely that he was this age at death; and even if he was at such an advanced age he would not still be the Chief of Police. However if Horemheb ruled for a shorter period of 15 years this would not be a concern as he would then be 53-58 years at death.[12] This so-called obstacle of Mininiwy's advanced age has been described as 'largely illusory'[13] as there are numerous mummies who died at a similar age, including Ramses II himself who was in his 80s when he died, Pepy II who ruled for between 60 and 90 years, as well as non-royal individuals such as Asru the Chantress of Amun who was almost 70 when she died. It was not unheard of, and if someone had access to good food, and medical care their life-span could be increased considerably, but the question needs to be raised as to whether he would still hold his position in the police force?

Another official whose age at death is a concern in this debate is the *Chief Sculptor of the Lord of the Two Lands*, Userhet also known as Hatiay or Pen–Ya. His career is mapped on a stela from the enclosure of the Great Sphinx at Giza, dated to Sety I, in addition to a votive shabti from the Serapeum at Saqqara commemorating the Apis Bull burial of either Year 16 or 30 of Ramses II.[14] Userhet also appears in the tomb of Maya the *Overseer of the Treasury*, dated to the reign of Tutankhamun. On the south wall of the tomb, Userhet is depicted in attendance of a funeral, under the title *Overseer of Works in the Place of Recurrence*, and *Chief Annalist*. It is thought to be the same man at an earlier point in his career. Study of the Leiden stela and Userhet's doorway has demonstrated that stylistically they can be matched to the late eighteenth rather than nineteenth dynasty. Userhet also emphasises in his biography his humble origins, a tool commonly used in the Amarna period but which disappeared by the reign of Sety I.[15] From these monuments it is possible to work out his age based on the premises that Userhet was in position for sixteen years under Ramses II plus another ten for Tutankhamun, four for Ay, fifteen for Horemheb, one for Ramses, thirteen for Sety, a working career of 59 years. Add to this another 15 years before he got his first appointment. This indicates he was approximately 74 years old when he died; which is not implausible. However if Horemheb ruled for 26 years then Userhat died at approximately 85 years old. This age seems to make Egyptologists nervous, as they feel it is too old, and it is unlikely that he lived and worked until such an advanced age.[16] This in itself is not evidence of a short reign, but married to the lack of any evidence of any date above year fourteen it does look compelling. However, as with all archaeological evidence it needs to be considered that only a small percentage of material is actually retrieved, so perhaps there is evidence of later dates yet to be discovered. Until this evidence comes to light, it will remain an issue of academic debate.

Without any evidence to strongly indicate otherwise it seems likely that Horemheb died after 15 years of ruling Egypt based on the dates from his tomb, and this is the date adopted here. He was well prepared and as was traditional had constructed a tomb in the Valley of the Kings and a mortuary temple along the desert edge on the west bank. His tomb at Memphis was virtually complete when he came to the throne and was to be the burial place of his two wives, Amenia and Mutnodjmet. It must have been hard for him to abandon this tomb, which took many years to construct and included hand-chosen designs depicting his military life, manoeuvres and high status. He obviously considered keeping it as the images of him throughout the tomb were adjusted to show his changed status (64), but rather than waste the workmanship and effort he utilised the tomb for his wives. Uraeuae were added to the wig of each figure showing he was now a *King*, which some have interpreted as Horemheb's 'stretching of the truth'[17] by claiming he was 'born to the purple'. However as he was a traditional *King*, it would be inappropriate for him to keep this tomb and adapt it to a royal burial. Instead he commissioned a royal tomb in the Valley of the Kings (KV 57). Like most of the tombs in the Valley, it was unfinished, which has provided scholars with further evidence supporting the theory of only fifteen years reign.

KV 57 was discovered on 25 February 1908 and was full to the ceiling with rubble. The tomb was 127.88m in length, and comprised three sloping corridors, a well chamber, a small pillared chamber, with two further sloping corridors leading to an antechamber and then the burial chamber. The burial chamber comprised six pillars

64 Door Jamb from the Memphite tomb of Horemheb (British Museum). *Photograph courtesy of Clare V. Banks*

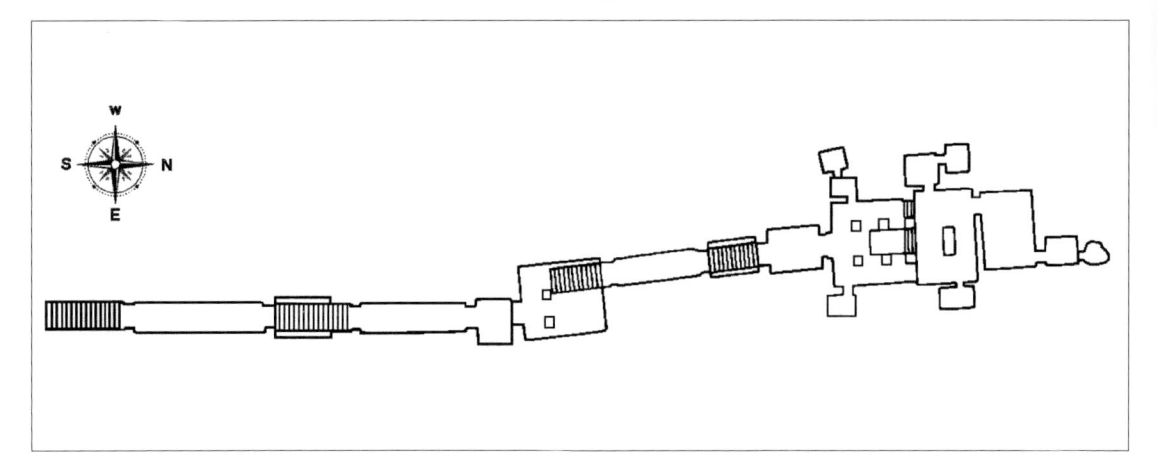

65 Valley of the King's tomb of Horemheb (KV57). Drawing by Brian Billington after Reeves & Wilkinson 1996

together with a series of elaborate storerooms, holding the funerary equipment, leading from the burial chamber.

The well, known as the 'hall of hindering' or 'hall of denial of access' was designed to prevent flood waters from damaging the burial chamber, a deterrent to tomb robbers, and symbolised the underworld realm of the god Sokar.[18] In the well shaft a false wall was built as a ploy to disguise the entrance to the burial chamber. All these walls were decorated, but the false wall had been broken through by robbers as was always the case which has led scholars to believe the robbers were the same people who built the tombs. Due to the quality of the rock, combined with centuries of earthquakes and flashfloods, the pillars were badly damaged. The rest of the burial chamber was incomplete. It appears as if the sculptors and workmen were interrupted by the death of the *King* and abandoned the tomb. Each room was filled with limestone chips, tools and lamps, just where the workmen had left them. A real Marie Celeste. The only evidence of the final activity in the tomb is a path in the detritus, cleared to allow the sarcophagus to be dragged through to the burial chamber during the royal funeral (*colour plate 17*).

Although following tradition in the sense that Horemheb returned to the Valley of the Kings and built the first purpose built royal tomb for four reigns, the tomb itself comprised a number of innovations. It was the first tomb in the Valley to have carved relief rather than painted murals. Sadly, this carved relief was not completed, but every aspect of the process is represented providing a record of the process of decorating a royal tomb. Once the walls were carved from the living limestone smoothed by the stonemasons, and plastered with gypsum, grid squares were painted on each wall; this was done by dipping string in red paint and flicking it quickly onto the wall leaving a red line. The outlines of the illustrations were then sketched in red ink, probably using a pattern book and the grid squares ensured the proportions were accurate. The master painter corrected these outline drawings with black ink, and the corrections are visible in some areas. Once the master painter was pleased with the outlines, the preliminary carving began starting with the outline and lastly the finer details. The final part of the process was to paint these reliefs in bright colours (*colour plates 18 & 19*).

Decoration in the tomb only began in the well shaft, the ante-chamber and the burial chamber. In the completed areas the background colour is blue-grey with polychrome hieroglyphs in raised relief. The artwork presented in the tomb was a transitional style between Amarna and traditional art; picking out the softness of the Amarna body shape with the inflexibility of the traditional poses. The figures of Horemheb and the gods have paunchy stomachs and slightly short legs, but with a much more formal style than the Amarna art. In many places, especially in the burial chamber, the extent of the decoration is grids and outline drawings; none of which were carved or painted. From the available decoration in the tomb, it is clear it was designed to be unusual, as it was the first tomb in the Valley to use the Book of Gates, rendered on the south wall of the burial chamber. These funerary texts, like most others, describe the nocturnal journey of the sun-god Ra, through a series of gateways and caverns. This was to become a popular alternative to the Book of the Amduat. Like most of the funerary texts used in tombs the entire text is not utilised; instead only the most important elements of each hour. What is interesting is that although KV57 was the first tomb to include the Book of Gates, the master copy from which the artists copied the text was clearly damaged, as when the artists came across a section which was fragmentary or difficult to read they simply wrote on the wall gm – 'found empty'. This does suggest that regardless of the very low literacy levels in Egypt, the artists working on this tomb were literate; or at least literate enough to improvise on their hieroglyphs when needed.

Excavation of the tomb has proved Horemheb was buried with all the pomp and splendour that tradition dictated, with funerary goods to match if not surpass those of Tutankhamun. However the tomb robbers and flash floods over the centuries have damaged and depleted the funerary assemblage leaving only remnants behind.

Although the body of Horemheb has not been discovered evidence shows he was mummified to the highest possible standard before being interred in the tomb. In the tomb there were four miniature lion-headed embalming tables possibly used for the embalming of the internal organs (66). These were also broken although this may have been for ritualistic purposes to prevent any harm coming to the organs in the afterlife. The fragmentary remains of his alabaster canopic equipment were discovered which originally contained the mummified viscera of the *King (colour plate 20)*. The box and jars were built as a single unit rather than as a chest with removable jars. The corners of the box were decorated with four goddesses, each with winged arms, spread around the edge of the box pointing downwards. The lids of the four compartments bore the face of Horemheb in the nemes headdress. The canopic equipment was smashed by the robbers in their haste to strip the tomb of its riches.

Embalmed intestines were discovered moulded into the shape of a small mummy placed into miniature canopic jars. However as more than one body was discovered in the tomb, who these belong to is unknown, and only by extracting DNA from the intestines and the bones in the tomb can we hope to find a match between a body and the organs. Further evidence of Horemheb's burial in the tomb are two fragments of clay birth-bricks, which were placed here at the funeral to aid in rebirth. One of the bricks is surmounted by a jackal, and was originally placed in the east end of the tomb, and the other had a ritual inscription in white paint and an image of a *djed* pillar, closely associated with the back-bone of Osiris and re-birth and was originally placed in the west end of the tomb.

Horemheb was probably buried in a series of wooden coffins, and fragments of cedar and acacia from these were discovered. This wood was imported from Byblos and indicates this trade route was re-established and maintained throughout his reign. The fragment types indicate the chests were cedar, with acacia tenons to keep the lid in place. They were inscribed with the cartouche of Horemheb, and some fragments are thought to perhaps belong to a sledge of the type used to drag the sarcophagus to the tomb during the funeral.

The wooden coffins were placed inside a red granite sarcophagus; the lid of which was carelessly pushed aside by the ancient robbers, which shattered it, in an attempt

66 Fragment of embalming table (British Museum). *Photograph courtesy of Brian Billington*

to get to the mummy inside. The lid was un-decorated but the chest was elaborately carved and the robbers caused little damage to this when removing the lid. The chest was decorated along the top edge with the palace façade cornicing which had been used since the Old Kingdom, and a design utilised in the burial chamber of his Memphite tomb. The corners of the sarcophagus were adorned with four goddesses, spreading their arms around them protecting the *King* when he was at his most vulnerable. Isis and Neith stood at the north end and Nepthys and Selket at the south.

When the rubble within the sarcophagus was excavated a skull and some loose bones lay within, although they are not believed to belong to the *King*. Also discovered were the remains of four other bodies, claimed to be members of his family. However this seems rather dismissive as we do not know anything about his family other than his two wives who were buried at Saqqara, so the identity of these individuals is ambiguous. If they are genuinely his family it would be interesting to investigate them further to learn more about Horemheb and his past. Some scholars believe the body of Ay was brought here from the Western Valley to protect it, but as this tomb itself was not secure this seems unlikely. When the skeletal remains were studied it was discovered there were the remains of two women in the antechamber, and in the burial chamber were the skulls of two women and one man scattered upon the floor. These bones have never been properly examined and the location now is uncertain.[19] Fragments of a limestone canopic set have also been found and are thought to be connected to one of these unknown individuals. One of them bears the hieratic name of Sainiwi, which is thought perhaps to be a foreign name. Who these individuals are is unknown, but it is generally accepted that Horemheb's body was removed in antiquity. Graffiti in Horemheb's Valley tomb states his body was taken to the nearby tomb of Twoseret and Setnakht (KV14) for restoration during the twenty-first dynasty (c.1069 BCE) when the royal mummy caches were created. Some scholars have questioned whether the body was moved and then subsequently lost.

The royal coffin in the Cairo Museum,[20] which contained the mummy of Ramses II, bears a hieroglyphic inscription of Herihor and Siamun regarding the removal of Ramses from his original tomb (*colour plate 21*). The coffin however was clearly not made for him, and Porter and Moss[21] state it was originally made for Horemheb but was unfinished; the gesso and gold leaf not applied rather than removed by robbers.[22] The other argument for it not belonging to Ramses II, other than for stylistic reasons, is that he ruled for 67 years and in this period it was more than possible for him to complete his coffin. It is therefore likely to belong to someone else who did not rule as long. This is where the problems occur as it could either stylistically belong to Ramses I who ruled for a period of approximately eighteen months, or Horemheb, ruling for fifteen years, and who did not complete his tomb. As the coffin was not complete, it was ignored by the robbers when they ransacked the tomb. Perhaps therefore the coffin that people accredit to Ramses II actually belongs to the 'forgotten pharoah,' Horemheb. If this is the case then it can be assumed Horemheb's body may have been missing or destroyed when the cache was created; rendering his coffin 'spare'.

Although the funerary goods are in a damaged condition it is obvious Horemheb had numerous objects of a very high quality bearing remarkable similarity to those discovered in the tomb of Tutankhamun. There were two large striding statues of the

67 Wooden deity statues. Valley of the Kings (British Museum). *Photograph courtesy of Brian Billington*

King, identical to those guarding the burial chamber of KV62. Horemheb's were made of sycamore wood, originally standing 2.2m high, with the skin of the *King* painted black, representative of Nile silt and fertility, with a gilded headdress, jewellery and kilt. The gold was stripped from the statues, and the limbs removed or damaged, but there is still enough to give an indication of how they looked. The objects discovered in the tomb reflect Horemheb's reign, in the sense they represented the diversity of his personal pantheon, whilst emphasising the traditional funerary practices and beliefs. There were numerous statuettes of deities, each made of cedar wood imported from Byblos, covered in bitumen with the details picked out in yellow paint within the burial chamber (67). Each statuette was small, standing between 50-100cm, and in themselves unusual, as the deities are not easily identified. One example comprises a turtle-headed deity which was sometimes viewed as hostile, and an enemy of Ra, but conversely was also seen as a divine protector which is probably the role intended in this example (68). However their presence emphasises the diversity of the pantheon of gods, and the colours used show their association with rebirth, as the black bitumen represents black Nile silt, and therefore fertility, and the yellow represents gold, a symbol not only of the sun, but also of eternity as it is the only metal which does not tarnish over time.

More traditional gods are also represented in the tomb, many of them duplicates of those found in Tutankhamun's, including a striding figure of Horus as a man with a falcon's head, Anubis squatting down, also as human with a jackal's head, and a panther walking with his tail down. Upon the back of the panther are two holes where a statue of the *King* once stood, as in the complete object in KV62. There were two statues of hawks, in reverence of Horus, the god most closely associated with kingship and one who was prominent throughout the life of Horemheb, and a full sized Hathor cow, although now in fragments, which originally was painted black and inlaid with blue faience plaques in imitation of cow hide. Hathor was a mother goddess, often presented as the mother of the *King*, and there are common images of the *King* suckling from the breast of Hathor, or from the udders of the Hathor cow. Two reclining jackals

68 Turtle-Headed Diety. KV57 Valley of the Kings. *Photograph courtesy of Brian Billington*

were also part of the funerary assemblage, which originally had inlaid eyes, although these have since been removed, and evidence shows they wore collars of gilded stucco, and one surviving claw indicates these were crafted from copper. Both of these figures were similar to the infamous figure of Anubis guarding the treasury in Tutankhamun's tomb. Wildlife is also presented in the tomb, perhaps providing ample hunting fodder for Horemheb in the afterlife, not only as a pastime but also as a means of reinforcing kingship ideologies and the victory of order over chaos. A particularly unusual item was the model of a swan, with a curved neck and no feet, as they were rare in Egypt it was a delicacy for Horemheb to enjoy. Kingship is emphasised in a number of ways including two hippopotami heads which have sadly come away from their bodies and were the embodiment of Seth, the god of chaos. The *King* would maintain royal ideologies by hunting hippopotami to show domination over chaos.

The traditional funerary beliefs and rituals restored by Tutankhamun are visible throughout Horemheb's tomb and this is reinforced in his funerary goods. One such item is the Osiris bed comprising a tray in the shape of Osiris, filled with Nile silt (*colour plate 22*). At the funeral the soil was planted with grain and its growth represented the rebirth of the *King*. The lid of the bed bore details of Osiris, carved and highlighted with red and black wood. This association between Osiris and agriculture is also represented in eight models of irrigated fields, comprising troughs of un-burnt clay, and there is evidence water was poured into the troughs, representing the inundation and was probably carried out at the funeral. This replication of the inundation of the Nile represented fertility and rebirth and the cycle of life and death with water being the key element. Using this particular imagery to show this cycle is a reference to Osiris as the god of agriculture, who, when ruling Egypt taught the Egyptians, amongst other things, how to irrigate the land. Most kings wanted to associate themselves with this element of kingship in life and in death and can often be seen in temple imagery with a hoe in hand cutting irrigation canals.

The Osiris cult was further represented by model boats designed for the traditional pilgrimage to Abydos, the burial place of Osiris. Every Egyptian hoped to be able to make this journey in life, and if they were prevented from doing so the model boat enabled them to travel there in the afterlife.

Like the tomb of Tutankhamun, furniture and household goods were included in the funerary assemblage, made of similar materials, although Horemheb's was in a poor state of preservation. However we are able to identify the remains of a hippo headed couch representative of the goddess of birth, Taweret, who is represented as a pregnant hippo, which aided the *King* in re-birth, and was identical to one of Tutankhamun's. This was accompanied by a minimally decorated acacia head rest, constructed in three pieces held together by wooden pegs and tenons, the heads of which are covered in wooden buttons inlaid with ivory. The furniture also included fixed and folding chairs, the former for palace living and the latter for military manoeuvres and expeditions and such chairs are represented in the Memphite tomb of Horemheb and were possibly used by Horemheb on his military campaigns.

The similarity between Horemheb's funerary goods and those of Tutankhamun is remarkable, and it needs to be considered how royal funerary assemblages were constructed. As we understand it many objects were donated by courtiers, family and officials, as well as many personal items used in life. The rest of the objects, which could be said to be primarily ritualistic, appear to have been acquired from a central royal store which goes someway to explaining the similarities between Horemheb's and Tutankhamun's funerary goods, and clarifies why many of Tutankhamun's goods were not made for him personally.

The tomb itself only formed part of the funerary cult of the *King*, and the main rituals were not to be carried out here but at his mortuary temple on the west bank of the Nile.

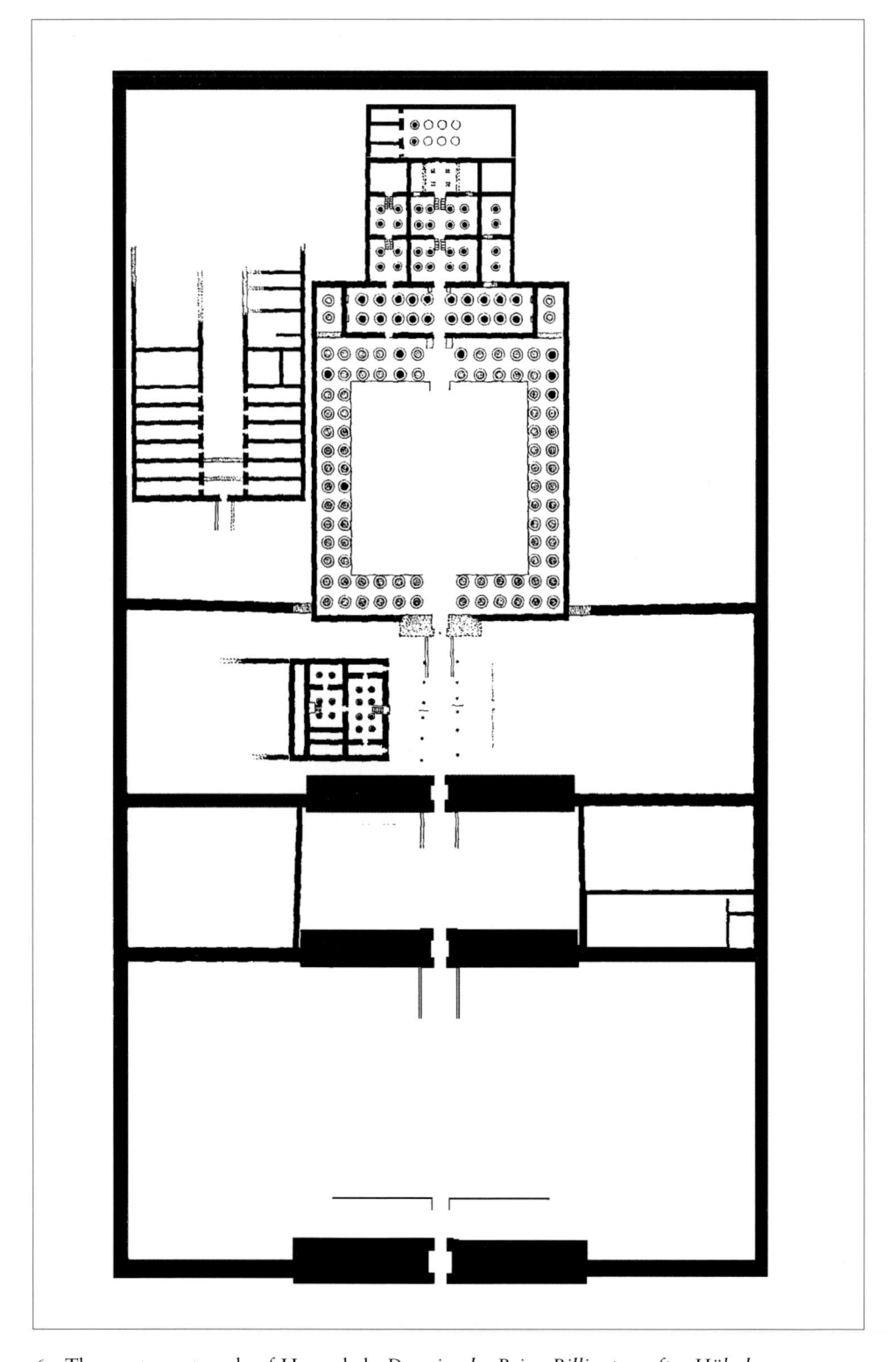

69 The mortuary temple of Horemheb. *Drawing by Brian Billington after Hölscher 1939*

However, rather than building his own temple from scratch, Horemheb usurped that of Ay, who had himself usurped it from Tutankhamun (69). Horemheb however, enlarged the temple substantially, as was fitting a *King* of his calibre and reign length. This was situated north of the later temple of Ramses III at Medinet Habu, and it is clear that when this was built the enclosure wall was offset to avoid the temple of Horemheb. When complete the temple was large, spanning a distance of 258m long by 145m wide. He added an enclosure wall around the site constructed of mud-bricks of which, sadly, nothing remains. He also added two further pylons to the two already on the site, the first one the largest with dimensions of 60m long, only five metres shorter than the current pylon at Medinet Habu, and the second and third each decreasing in size. These pylons were built of mud-brick, and had originally been constructed by Ay; some of the bricks still retain his cartouche. Very little remains of the temple, due to being used as a quarry in later times, but from the statue fragments and isolated inscriptions, it is clear this was an impressive temple, which originally was elaborately decorated. Fragmentary remains indicate Horemheb replaced Ay's cartouches with his own, taking possession of the temple. The artwork in the temple commissioned by Horemheb has been considered of inferior quality to that of Ay, and he did not lay foundation deposits here and this therefore indicates less time and care was given by Horemheb with the construction of this temple.[23] He was clearly focusing his efforts elsewhere.

Horemheb removed one of the pylons of Ay, replacing it with a stone gateway which led to a columned colonnade of 54.4m by 59m, with columns along at least three of the four sides which totally absorbed Ay's hypostyle hall which was on the site. In this court, the cartouches are originals indicating this was not an area built by Ay and usurped by Horemheb but built solely by him. It seems the column bases from this court may have been incorporated into the temple of Khonsu at Karnak during the reign of Herihor (1080-1074 BCE). He also added some substantial storerooms to the west of the site, using bricks of Ay for the foundations, and it is thought there were matching stores on the north of the site although these have not been discovered. Many clay jar stoppers marked with the name of Horemheb indicate these were used to store wine. The stores were probably vaulted, and resembled those on the site of the Rammesseum built by Ramses II. There was possibly also a quay and canal leading up to the entrance of the temple.

Of all the statuary and monumental architecture which originally stood here, only four colossal statues, two standing and two seated, remain. The standing statues originally stood 3.5m high, 5.35m including the pedestal, made from red quartzite from the quarries at Gebel el Silsila, and originally stood in the hypostyle hall of Ay, to the left of the western doorway.[24] The southern statue is now in Cairo (*colour plate 23*) (J 59869 and J 60134) and the northern statue is in the Oriental Institute of the University of Chicago (14088). Certain details of these statues were picked out in paint; including the *nemes* headdress painted yellow and blue surmounted by a blue and red uraeus, painted black and white eyes. The colours were preserved in the 1930s using celluloid dissolved in amyl acetate. It is thought these statues bear the features of Tutankhamun and originally were commissioned by him and were later usurped by Horemheb. The limestone seated figures would have been in front of the entrance to Horemheb's open colonnaded courtyard. Numerous fragments of these statues have been discovered and a few of them are in Cairo (632) and Berlin (1479). They were originally 5.2m high and were made for Ay, but Horemheb carved out Ay's cartouches replacing them with his own. Both statues wore a double crown and on the Cairo statue there is an image of a queen, originally Tiy, the wife of Ay. Other statue fragments have been discovered at the temple including a painted limestone statue of a female, a royal limestone statue wearing the nemes headdress, a life size limestone statue of Amun, and a painted quartzite statue of a *King*, although only fragments of the head have survived.

70 Priestly Ramesside family worshipping the deified Horemheb, Saqqara. Drawing by the author after Martin 1991

The cult of Horemheb's ka or spirit was maintained for some time after his death, and evidence suggests it continued throughout the short reign of Ramses I at least, at the site of the mortuary temple. From Ramses I's reign a number of wine jars were discovered in the temple magazines, labelled 'Wine for the temple of Horemheb.' The maintenance of the mortuary cult of Horemheb was carried out elsewhere, by the Rammesside family in commemoration of the opportunity Horemheb gave them when he made Ramses I *King*. During the reign of Ramses II, Horemheb was revered further at his Memphite tomb, and Ramses II erected two plinths decorated with figures of Anubis acting as guardians to the statue room. The Offering Room in the west end of the tomb was the focus of the mortuary cult, which was a small square room with a limestone ceiling with a mud-brick pyramid surmounting it, capped with a granite or limestone benben stone.[25] As Horemheb was not buried in this tomb the mortuary rituals were for his wives, Amenia and Mutnodjmet, and then for the ka of the deified King Horemheb.

The mortuary rituals were carried out by a series of funerary priests (*70*). The names of these priests were written upon the Anubis plinths erected by Ramses II and beneath images of offering bearers. One of these priests was called Pehefnefer[26] whose role would be to make offerings of food and wine to the ka of the deceased. How long the cult was carried out at the site is uncertain but evidence from Medinet Habu during the reign of Rameses III shows it was still functioning at this time:

> Year 27 (*Ramses III*) the workers of the necropolis had received no provender of grain during the twenty days of the month. Then went the scribe Amennakht to the temple of Horemheb in the estate of Amun and gave to them 46 sacks of grain[27]

This indicates that during the reign of Ramses III the temple stores at least were still functioning and the priests here were responsible for paying the rations of the workers at Deir el Medina. The Ramesside family not only maintained the funerary cult of Horemheb, but they also made additions, and repairs to his building works. These acts were traditionally carried out by a new *King* for their father, and reflected the idea that they viewed Horemheb as the founding father of their dynasty.

CHAPTER 8
AFTERMATH

The death of Horemheb in 1306 BCE saw the throne pass to the family of Prameses (Ramses I) in the absence of any children of his own. There is little information regarding the succession but it was a smooth transition. Horemheb named Ramses as his heir long before his death and he rose in status and power during these years. It is believed that in the Memphite tomb of Horemheb, there is an image of Prameses being honoured by Tutankhamun with shebyu collars, indicating he was a close colleague of Horemheb's for many years (71). We are able to trace Prameses' career through the military, and it is a similar story to that of Horemheb. Prameses was a career army officer and was the son of Sety, a *Troop Commander*; it was traditional during this period for such professions to be hereditary, and therefore this career was mapped out for Prameses should Horemheb not have honoured him with the titles he did. He started his military career as a stable hand and soldier, being promoted to *Master of the Horse*, *Troop Commander* and *Commander of the Fortress at Sile*, a stronghold between the Egyptian Delta and Syro-Palestine. This shows amongst other things that Horemheb had reinforced the borders of Egypt, and the trade routes between these areas as a means of securing Egypt from potential attack. This was the route the Hittites would take should they decide to invade Egypt. This area was also greatly utilised by Horemheb with the maintenance of his Edict, as many of the corrupt officials were mutilated and sent to Sile for hard labour.

Once he was noticed by Horemheb, Prameses was given the title of *King's Envoy*, *General* and the title of *Vizier*; one of two who held the post.[1] As many of his titles and affiliations seem to be connected with the north it can be assumed he was the northern *vizier*, with another man acting as *Vizier* for the south. Even though Horemheb trusted him, he did not trust anyone enough to give them the power of the vizierate over all of Egypt. Ramses also held the religious title *Overseer of Priests* of Upper and Lower Egypt. This was a supervisory role, and put him not only in control of the military, half the administration for the country but also in control of the priesthood.[2] Clearly a man greatly trusted by Horemheb. The only main difference between the two men's life journeys was that Prameses was married to a woman called Sitre,[3] and already had a family and it is generally accepted he was well into his 50s when he came to the throne. There is a little confusion surrounding the wife of Prameses as in the Year 400 Stela from Tanis, Sety I's mother is named as Tia and not Sitre and she does not always carry the title *King's Mother*, as one would expect. However it is believed perhaps she was Tia known as Sitre, and this is reinforced by the name of one of Ramses II's daughters who was named Tia-Sitre. When Sitre died she was given the first tomb in the Valley of the Queens (QV38) rather than being buried in the tomb of her husband as was traditional.

The coronation was traditional, probably taking place at Memphis, and ending with the presentation to the new *King* with his fivefold titulary (72):

Horus King, Mighty Bull, Flourishing in Kingship, He of the Two Ladies, who arises in kingship like Atum, Golden Horus who establishes Maat throughout the land.

71 Ramses I as a *General* receiving shebyu collars, Saqqara. *Drawing by the author after Martin 1991*

72 Cartouches of Ramses I

King of Upper and Lower Egypt, Lord of the Two Lands, Menpehetyra, Son of Ra Ramses.[4]

These names went some way to describing the sort of *King* Ramses hoped to be. He emphasised his role as restorer and maintainer of Maat, in the footsteps of his predecessor Horemheb, as well as acknowledging his humble origins. By using the title *Arises in Kingship like Atum* suggests that, like the creator god Atum, he came from nothing; self-creating and rising like the sun into this new role. The name also reflects those of Ahmose from the start of the eighteenth dynasty; Ahmose's prenomen was Nebpehetyre (*Lord of the Strength of Ra*) and Ramses was Menpehetyre (*Established is the Strength of Ra*), which some have taken to show he believed he was the start of the new dynasty bringing Egypt out of the chaos of the Amarna period.

The reign of Ramses I was a short one, of only two years at the most, although it has been suggested there may have been a co-regency between Horemheb and Ramses shortening his sole rule further. The co-regency theory is based on a fragment of a pink granite obelisk commissioned by Horemheb, currently in Edinburgh. It is thought it may have originally stood in Bubastis, but had been cut, polished and reused as a weight. The fragment bore the cartouches of Horemheb on two faces, and the cartouche of Ramses I has survived on the third. As Ramses' Horus name, Two Ladies (*nebty*) name and the start of his King of Upper and Lower Egypt (*nsw bity*) name were not added at a later late it is thought they were carved at the same time as the Horemheb inscription. However, as the *nebty* name of Ramses on this obelisk, *Repeating Years Like Atum*, is different from his traditional name *Arising as King like Atum*, it indicates this was an early point in his kingship as it is unlikely that in 18 months of rule he would change his name twice.[5] Whereas changing his name as he ascends to the throne as sole ruler is acceptable. Although there is no other evidence supporting a co-regency it does seem quite probable especially as Horemheb had no heirs of his own. If this is the case then it is clear Horemheb should be placed at the start of the nineteenth dynasty rather than the end of the eighteenth dynasty. Ramses himself when on the throne, named his son Sety as co-regent meaning he probably only ruled alone for a few months, even though his regnal years begin at the start of his reign as sole *King*. Whether there was a co-regency or not, it was clear Horemheb, in his later years on the throne, took the advice of his *Commander of the Northern Troops*, *Brigade Commander of Tjaru* and then later *Vizier*, very seriously,[6] and could explain some of the later building works at Qantir, in the Delta, the origins of the Ramesside family.

During such a short reign, Ramses did not have much opportunity to make his mark on the kingship of Egypt. However, there is evidence of small military campaigns including a small raid on the Syro-Palestinian region in the later months, assisted and possibly led by Ramses' son Sety, as a means of reasserting the might of the new pharaoh.[7] At the beginning of any reign, and especially if there was a family change or any inconsistency in the succession, there were small uprisings of the Egyptian territories as a means to test the mettle of the new *King*. These were easily dealt with. Another such raid may have been a military campaign to Nubia recorded on a stela in Wadi Halfa. It is doubtful the army were led by the elderly *King*, as it is thought he was resident in Memphis at the time, but his son Sety, (soon to be Sety I) is mentioned on the stela, perhaps leading the offensive:

Year 2, second month of the second season, 20th day … Lo, His Majesty was in the city of Memphis performing the ceremonies of his father, Amen Ra, Ptah South of his Wall. Lord of the Life-of-the-Two-Lands and all the gods of Egypt according as they gave him might and victory over all lands, united with one heart in praising your ka. All lands, all countries, the Nine Bows are overthrown ... His Majesty, the King of Upper and Lower Egypt, Menpehtire, Ramses I, given life, commanded to establish divine offerings for his father Min-Amun, residing in Buhen the first of his establishment in his temple. Loaves, 100 loaves, 4 jars of beers, 10 bundles of vegetables. Likewise this temple was filled with prophets, ritual priests, and wab priests; his storehouse was filled with male and female servants, of the captivity of His Majesty, the King of Upper and Lower Egypt, Menpehtire Ramses I, given life like Ra, forever and ever. His Majesty was watchful, he was not slothful in seeking excellent things to do them for his father Min Amun, residing in Buhen, making for him a temple like the horizon of heaven, wherein Ra rises. (*The two names of Sety conclude the inscription*).[8]

Whether this was an offensive seems unclear, as the text seems to refer to a religious expedition to Buhen to make offerings to the god Min-Amun. Reference to battles is limited to the generalisation '*all lands, all countries, the nine bows are overthrown*' indicating this is propaganda regarding the ideology of kingship rather than a battle or uprising between the Nubians and the Egyptian *King*. This stela does however emphasise the religious beliefs of Ramses I were traditional and varied, here worshipping a localised form of Min-Amun. The Ramesside family, whilst honouring Amun at Karnak, were not as dedicated to him and the priesthood as Tutankhamun was and indeed as later kings were to be.[9] Their main devotion as a family was to Ra at Heliopolis, and Ramses II totally rebuilt the temple of Ra at Heliopolis and Seth of Avaris, as can be identified by their family names Ramses and Sety. Evidence suggests Ramses II had his coronation at the temple of Ra at Heliopolis, rather than the temple of Ptah at Memphis. The god Atum, the solar deity who was the first on the mound of creation at Heliopolis is often represented as the ultimate *King*, depicted with royal regalia, showing a logical connection between this site and the coronation. Excavations at Avaris/Qantir in the eastern Delta have shown that this was the capital of Ramses II, Pi-Ramesses and have uncovered a number of temples here. The principal deity of the site was Seth. Seth of Avaris was closely associated with the Canaanite storm god Ba'al, due to the high proportion of Asiatics living in the Eastern Delta, and an association has also been made between this version of Seth and Horus of Hansu, the personal god of Horemheb. Horemheb indeed built a temple dedicated to Seth at Avaris, and it is thought he held a particular interest in the north because of this.[10] Despite this predilection with Seth and the northern Delta, Ramses I started building projects at Karnak dedicated to Amun. As was traditional, Ramses I erased the name of Horemheb from the monumental gateway (pylon two) replacing them with his own.[11] There are also reliefs of Ramses I on the second pylon at Karnak temple dedicated to Amun Ra.[12] This is no reflection of antagonism towards Horemheb on behalf of the new *King*, but rather the means in which to leave one's mark on a monument. Behind this doorway, lay the courtyard laid out by Horemheb for the construction of what was to be the hypostyle hall, and although he was unable to make much progress a cartouche of his remains extant on one of the pillars here.

Ramses I died in 1304 BCE, and was well prepared for it. His son Sety had been appointed the title of *Vizier*, as well as *Commander of the Fortress* at Sile, and a number of religious titles associated with the cult of Seth, including the title of the *High Priest* of Seth. It has been suggested that when Horemheb was filling the temples with personnel from the army, the Ramesside family had already caught his attention, and in fact bestowed this title upon Sety at the time[13] indicating that not only was Ramses I, elderly by the time he came to the throne but that his son Sety was also already advanced in years.

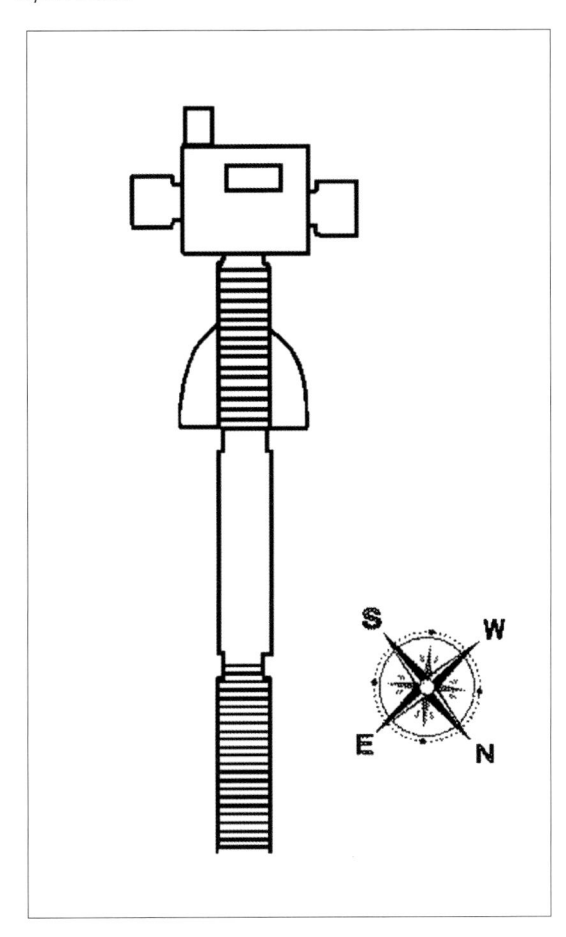

73 Valley of the King's tomb of Ramses I (KV16). Drawing by Brian Billington after Reeves & Wilkinson 1996

Ramses I had started constructing his tomb in the Valley of the Kings tomb (KV16) which was an ambitious project, situated near the tomb of Horemheb. It was unfinished and comprised two stairways linked by a corridor of 9.75m in length, with two unfinished niches carved at the top of the second staircase. His burial chamber was a small room originally (5.18m x 6.4m), intended as an antechamber. During the 70 days after his death whilst his body was mummified, this chamber was plastered and painted, showing Ramses in the presence of the gods. As would be expected Osiris, the god of the underworld dominates the scenes. The decorative style is identical to that of Horemheb in KV57, with blue-grey background and vibrant polychrome images and hieroglyphs. There were two chambers to the east and west of the burial chamber (one 2.4m x 2.1m and the other 3m x 2.1m), which were undecorated.[14]

There were a number of grave goods discovered in the tomb, some of which were similar to those in the tombs of Horemheb and of Tutankhamun, further supporting an idea of a royal store room where funerary assemblages were acquired. These goods included two wooden statues which stood two metres tall (*colour plate 24*), of the type guarding the burial chamber of Tutankhamun, and were probably placed on either side of the sarcophagus. There are traces of gold on these statue fragments showing they were once gilded. There were also a series of small gilded wooden statues of underworld deities, similar to those in the tomb of Horemheb, each bearing the heads of animals. When the tomb was robbed in antiquity, the robbers, in their frustration, had thrown some of these statues against the wall with force, leaving traces of the gold in the plaster on the wall.[15] He was buried in a red quartzite sarcophagus, which was painted with yellow paint, rather than carved, and due to the haste in which this was done there are numerous errors within the texts.[16] The lid of the sarcophagus had been thrown from the coffin by robbers in antiquity, damaging it. The body itself was not in the tomb as it had been removed from the tomb prior to 968 BCE and placed in one of the royal caches, either in the tomb of Amenhotep II (KV35) or the tomb of Queen Inhapi (DB320).[17] However the body was not recovered from either of these caches. In 2003 a mummy which had been in the Museum of Art at Niagara Falls for almost a century was identified as Ramses I. It was identified as a royal mummy of the late eighteenth or early nineteenth dynasty by Peter Lacovara, who purchased the mummy and some blocks from Sety I's tomb for the Michael C. Carlos Museum in Atlanta in 2000.[18] It was returned to Egypt in 2003, and is currently on display in the Luxor Museum (74). However this identification with Ramses I is not accepted by most, as it was based on tenuous evidence. Mummification techniques, a similar profile to Sety I and Ramses II, and the royal arm position, were primarily used for the identification. However both Sety I and Ramses II have their arms crossed left over right, whereas the Niagara mummy is right over left, and the C14 tests indicate the mummy is from the twenty-second dynasty, which is in line with the date of the coffin he was discovered in, with the original owner's names removed to be replaced by those of Ramses. The mummy itself was discovered a decade before the cache containing his coffin, which adds further doubt on his identification. Maspero described a well-built man wrapped in a mat in the Deir el Bahri cache near the coffin of Ramses I, which he believed could be him.[19] This body which is now sadly lost, was blackened in the same manner of the mummy of Sety I, which became this colour due to oxidization after being unwrapped.[20] The only way of identifying whether the Niagara mummy is Ramses I or not would be through DNA testing and comparison with the mummies of Sety I and Ramses II.

The Ramesside family never forgot the opportunity given by Horemheb to Ramses I, and revered him as the founder of their royal house. This reverence is clear, when we examine the tomb of Ramses II's sister Tia which annexes that of Horemheb in the Saqqara necropolis, and one of the burial chambers of Horemheb's tomb uncovered the burial of a daughter of Ramses, Bintanath. He was considered a member of the family, albeit it an honorary one, and his tomb was treated as a family monument, and an important religious site.[21]

Many of Horemheb's policies and practices were continued into the reign of Ramses II, especially in regard to legitimising their right to the throne. The coronation of Ramses II followed Horemheb by having the Festival of Opet as one of the first acts of his reign, showing an emphasis on the worship of Amun and the important of Karnak.[22] Ramses II made a point of showing he was co-regent with Sety I before he became *King*, on monuments after he ascended to the throne including a statue base from the temple of Medamud. Horemheb did the same, emphasising his co-regency on his coronation statue.[23] It suggests that being the crowned prince or named heir did not mean that succession was certain, whereas it could be used after crowning to indicate the throne was always intended for them.

Another tradition from the reign of Horemheb carried on to the reign of Ramses II was the title *Commander in Chief of the Army*. This was held by Horemheb when he was *Deputy King*, and Ramses II associated this title with that of crowned prince. Therefore every crowned prince until the end of the Ramesside period held this title, regardless of their age and ability suggesting in many instances it was honorary.[24]

Despite the numerous pieces of evidence supporting Horemheb as the founder of what is now known as the nineteenth dynasty, many modern scholars refuse to acknowledge it, insisting on following Manetho, writing in the third century BCE

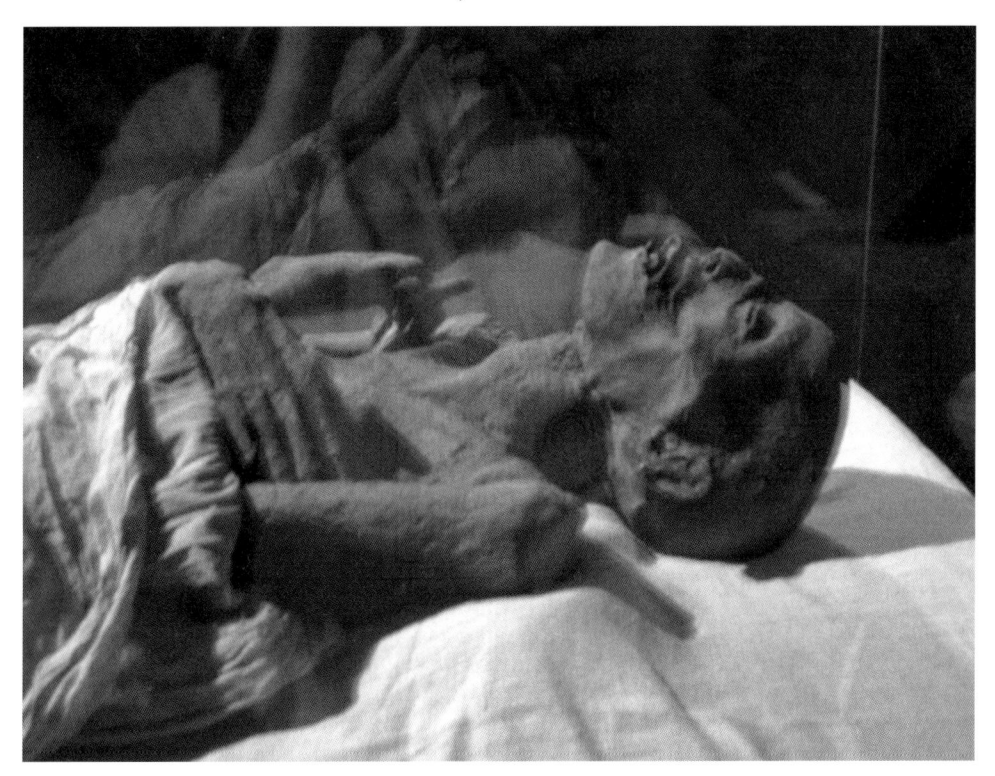

74 Mummy of Ramses I (?) (Luxor Museum). *Photograph by the author*

who places him at the end of the eighteenth dynasty as the final *King* of the Amarna heresy. He associates Horemheb with what is believed to be the decline of the eighteenth dynasty both economically and politically.[25] However the economic and political decline of the period happened during the reign of Akhenaten and during the subsequent kings. During the reign of Horemheb this decline was reversed. The idea of dynasties is not something the ancient Egyptians utilised, and therefore Horemheb was not the end of the eighteenth dynasty to the Egyptians he was the *King* who brought Egypt back to the glory years of Amenhotep III, so a prosperous Egypt was passed on to his successor.

However, as we currently use the dynasty system, it is considered more sensible to start the nineteenth dynasty with the Ramesside family, which would have horrified the Ramessides, who saw Horemheb as the founder of their family of kings. An ostraca from the Valley of the Kings[26] listing the succession of kings from Ahmose through to Ramses II, omits Hatshepsut, Akhenaten, Smenkhkare, Tutankhamun and Ay. At the bottom of the list, the cartouches of Ahmose and Horemheb are placed[27] as if they are linked. The only connection was they both started great royal houses after a turbulent time; Ahmose of the eighteenth dynasty after the Hyksos rulers and Horemheb of the nineteenth after the Amarna period. Even in the Abydos King list created by Sety I, although the Amarna kings are omitted, Horemheb is present following directly after Amenhotep III (*colour plate 25*).[28] These king lists were designed to show a direct lineage between the current *King* (in this instance Sety I), the preceding kings and ultimately the gods. Therefore Horemheb's presence on this list shows he was considered part of the royal lineage, and therefore a legitimate *King* who ruled under the laws of Maat.

It was not only the royal family who revered Horemheb but also the ordinary people. He was deified and worshipped by those residing at the workman village of Deir el Medina, the wider area of Thebes and also in his Saqqara tomb. A stela belonging to the scribe Ramose, from Deir el Medina, depicts Ramses II at the top, alongside Sety I and Horemheb, with the deceased Ramose worshipping the cartouches of Ramses II. The tomb of two brothers Penbuy and Kasa, also from Deir el Medina under Ramses II contains a niche shrine which shows Penbuy and his brother Penshenabu standing before Amenhotep I, Ahmose Nefertari, Sety, Rameses I and Horemheb. On another wall Kasa and his son stand before Sety I, Ramses I and Horemheb. It is clear Horemheb was considered a member of the Ramesside family and not the last *King* of the Amarna heresy.[29] The tomb of Roy (TT255), a steward during the time of Horemheb has a double scene of Horemheb and Mutnodjmet standing before the god Osiris (75). This scene is in conjunction with another of Amenhotep I and his mother Ahmose-Nefertari.[30] In these tombs he was consistently worshipped alongside the founder of Deir el Medina, their patron and the current ruling family, which clearly included Horemheb. These people were worshipped as humans but also as gods, deities who could act as intermediaries between the people and the gods and who could help individuals as well as Egypt as a whole.

Therefore surely Horemheb should be placed correctly in the chronology of Egypt as the founder of the nineteenth dynasty as the Egyptians themselves believed rather than following the writings of Manetho, writing 1000 years or so after his death. Once he has been correctly placed within the chronology of Egypt, he should be acknowledged as a *King* in his own right independant of Tutankhamun and the Amarna period. In the preceding pages we have traced his life from birth in a small town on the edge of the Fayum, to occupying the highest position in Egypt: King. We have been able not only to trace his rise to power through his career path, but also more personal details about him as an individual. We know he suffered at the death of both his wives, one whilst trying to produce a much desired heir, but he cared about them enough to furnish them with a burial

75 Scene from the tomb of Roy. *Drawing by the author*

suitable to their status. His religious beliefs developed and changed through his life, and we are able to trace a changing loyalty from Horus of Hansu, his local deity, to Thoth when he became a scribe, adapting both of these to his new royal status. As he befriended Pramses, and became involved in this new Delta circle he began to see the virtues of the god of chaos Seth; a powerful god greatly feared by many kings. These religious changes track his development as an individual from child, to scribe, to soldier to *King*. When we know so much about an individual surely they become more than just a bit part in someone else's story. Here he has been presented in his own story, with Akhenaten, Tutankhamun and Ay forming bit-parts in his life story, and hopefully has gone one step towards bringing the Forgotten Pharaoh back to life.

NOTES

INTRODUCTION

1. Sackler Library, 1 St John Street, Oxford OX1 2LG, United Kingdom
2. Booth 2007
3. Doherty 2004, 6
4. Doherty 2004, 73
5. Mahfouz 2000
6. Montserrat 2000, 162
7. Phillips 1977, 118

CHAPTER 1

1. Wilkinson 2007, 156
2. Aldred 1957, 30
3. Fletcher 2000, 50
4. Tyldesley 2000, 92
5. Fletcher 2000, 146
6. El Mahdy 1999, 170
7. Gardiner 1961, 213
8. Tyldesley 2000, 93
9. Winfield Smith 1976, 23
10. Tyldesley 2000, 95
11. Reeves 2005, 110
12. Dollings 2007, 34
13. Reeves 2005, 103
14. Seele 1955, 172
15. Harris 1973, 16
16. Tyldesley 2000, 132
17. James 1997, 26
18. Luban 1999, my own itallics
19. Huppertz et al 2009
20. James 2003, 25
21. Tyldesley 2003, 176
22. James 2003, 25
23. Tyldesley 2005, 176
24. Samson 1985, 96-7
25. Gardiner 1928, 10
26. Panagiotakopulu 2004, 273
27. Panagiotakopulu 2004, 269-75
28. Tyldesley 2002, 202

CHAPTER 2

1. Clayton 1997, 137
2. Davies, N de Garis, 1907, 15 pl xiii
3. Hari 1964, 30
4. Seele note 50 p.60 of Schulman 1965, 58
5. Baines & Malek 1980, 35
6. Lichtheim 1973, 185
7. Fletcher 2000, 26
8. Janssen & Janssen 1990, 76
9. Lichtheim 1976, 171
10. Lichtheim 1973, 185-6
11. Partridge 2002, 81
12. Martin 1993, 61

CHAPTER 3

1. Winfield Smith 1976, 45
2. Klemm & Klemm 2001, 637
3. Martin 1993, 83
4. Winfield Smith 1976, 29
5. Baines & Malek 1980, 74
6. Kamil 1993, 135
7. Trigger et al 1994, 123
8. Schulman 1965a, 59
9. Baines & Malek 1980, 165
10. Klemm & Klemm 2001, 640
11. Wilkinson 2000, 188
12. Tyldesley 2000, 94
13. Panagiotakopulu & Buckland 1999, 908
14. Martin 1993, 50
15. Spencer 1989, 15-16
16. Talatat blocks were introduced by Akhenaten and comprised a block of one hands length wide, by one long and one high. The name comes from the Arabic for three
17. Martin 1993, 53
18. Spalinger 2005, 179
19. Gardiner 1961, 244
20. Martin 1993, 78-80
21. Van Dijk 1996, 38
22. Johnson 1992, 7
23. Martin 1993, 62
24. Martin 1993, 59
25. Schulman 1965a, 56
26. Schulman 1965a, 57
27. Van Dijk 1996, 39
28. Van Dijk 1996, 36
29. Martin 1978, 16
30. Martin 1992, 45
31. Martin 1976, 5-13
32. Martin 1978, 7

33 Martin 1978, 16
34 Martin 1978, 8
35 Martin 1979, 13
36 Schulman 1965a, 58
37 Van Dijk 1996, 35

CHAPTER 4

1 Van Dijk 1996, 36
2 Seele 1955, 169
3 Seele 1955, 171-2
4 Van Dijk 1996, 32
5 Seele 1955, 171
6 Seele 1955,170
7 Gardiner 1947, no 127
8 Aldred 1957, 35- 37
9 Seele 1955, 176
10 Schaden 1977, 154-5
11 Van Dijk 1996, 33
12 Schulman 1965a, 61-2
13 Schulman 1965a, 63, Van Dijk 1996, 33
14 Schulman 1965a, 64
15 Van Dijk 1996, 33
16 Schulman 1965a, 63
17 Reisner 1920, 84
18 Schulman 1965a, 64
19 Schaden 1977
20 Dodson & Hilton 2004, 151
21 Schulman 1965, 125
22 Brier 1999, 181
23 Van Dijk 1996, 40
24 Gardiner 1953, 14
25 Shulman 1965, 65
26 Seele 1955, 180
27 Dodson 2000, 114
28 Schaden 1977, 195
29 Schaden 1977, 143
30 Bryce 1990, 105
31 Van Dijk 1996, 40
32 Reeves 1999, 175
33 Brier 1999, 179
34 Bryce 1990 105
35 Reeves 1999, 176
36 KUBXIX20
37 Murnane1990, 26-34
38 Bryce 1990, 99
39 Van Dijk 1996, 38
40 Brier 1999, 176
41 Redford 1973, 14
42 Brier 1999, 181
43 Bryce 1990, 100

44 Gardiner 1961, 241
45 Van Dijk 1996, 41
46 Martin 1993, 48
47 Schaden 1977, 276
48 Schaden 1977, 255
49 Schaden 1977, 218-9
50 Schaden 1977, 258
51 Hölscher 1932, 50
52 Hölscher 1939, 75
53 Hölscher 1934, 114
54 Schaden 1977, 148
55 Martin 1993, 192
56 Gardiner 1953, 14
57 Martin 1993, 94
58 Martin 1993, 84
59 Dodson 2000, 114
60 Schaden 1977, 281
61 Tyldesley 2000, 105

CHAPTER 5

1 Schaden 1977, 13
2 Dodson & Hilton 2004, 155
3 Schaden 1977, 12
4 Fletcher 2004, 258
5 Aldred, 1957, 39
6 Dodson & Hilton 2004, 153
7 Breasted 1906, 14-19 line 15-16
8 Van Dijk 1996, 37
9 Van Dijk 1996, 37
10 Aldred 1968, 105-6
11 Dodson & Hilton 2004, 153
12 Martin 1979, 15
13 Lesko 1977, 19
14 Newberry 1925, 4
15 Dodson & Hilton 2004, 156
16 Gardiner 1953, 13
17 Gardiner 1916, 73
18 Redford 1984, 36
19 Gardiner 1953 30
20 Dodson 2000 115
21 Gardiner 1953, 21
22 Gardiner 1953, 15
23 Breasted 1906, 14-19
24 Gardiner 1994, 25
25 Desroche-Noblecourt 1971, 127-30
26 Breasted 1906, 14-19

CHAPTER 6

1. Tyldesley 2000, 30
2. Gardiner 1961, 229
3. Habachi 1979, 35 – this is now in the Staatliche Museum in Berlin
4. Dodson 2005, 77
5. Briers 1995, 219
6. Eyre 2005, 7-8
7. Inscription of Mes
8. Schaden 1977, 280
9. Schaden 1977, 275
10. Schaden 1977, 190-1
11. Cross 2009, 14
12. Van Dijk 1996, 40
13. Dodson & Hilton 2004, 156
14. Tyldesley 2002, 203
15. Translation of the Edict from Pfluger 1946
16. Gardiner 1961, 245
17. Azim 1982, 135 & 143
18. Azim 1982, 95
19. Azim 1982 98-105
20. Wente 1968
21. Tyldesley 2002, 212
22. Winfield Smith 1976, 19-57
23. Tyldesley 2001, 212
24. Klemm & Klemm 2001, 637
25. Dodson & Hilton, 153
26. Wilkinson 2000, 208
27. Forbes 2004, 68
28. Wilkinson 2000, 208
29. Forbes 2004, 74
30. Sidro 2006, 22
31. Arnold 2003, 1
32. Sidro 2006, 23
33. Murray 1931, 236
34. Wilkinson 2000, 228
35. Hari 1964, 371
36. Murray 1931, 236
37. Hari 1964, 373
38. Bietak 1979, 269
39. Bietak 1979, 271
40. Uphill 1984, 191-3
41. Uphill 1984, 201
42. Bietak 2009
43. Pusch 1991
44. Åström 1979, 46
45. Hari 1985, 251
46. Hari 1989, 25
47. Redford 1992, 212
48. Redford 1992, 210

49 Dodson 2000, 117
50 Van Dijk 1996, 41
51 Pfulger 1946, 267
52 Tyldesley 2000, 55
53 Tyldesley 2000, 31
54 Gardiner 1961, 224
55 Tyldesley 2000, 31
56 Trigger et al 1983, 258
57 Thiem 2000, 141
58 Forbes 2004, 75
59 Thiem 2000, 319
60 Breasted 1906, 21-22, Thiem 2000, 321 hieroglyphic text
61 Save Söderbergh in Shulman 1965a, 65
62 Porter & Moss 1964, 569
63 Tyldesley 1996, 145
64 Ray 2001, 50
65 Trigger el al 1983, 270

CHAPTER 7

1 Gardiner 1961, 241
2 Gardiner 1905, 52
3 Harris 1965, 95
4 Hölscher 1939, 107
5 Redford 1973, 6
6 Harris 2007, 28
7 Harris 2007, 27
8 Martin 1988, 119
9 Van Dijk quoted in Arbouw 2008
10 Harris 1965, 97
11 Harris 1965, 98
12 Harris 1965, 98
13 Redford 1973, 7
14 Van Dijk 1995, 29
15 Van Dijk 1995, 32
16 Van Dijk 1995, 34
17 Shulman 1965a 60
18 Reeves & Wilkinson 1997, 25
19 Dodson 2000, 118
20 61020
21 Porter and Moss 1964, 661
22 Aldred 1968, 102
23 Hölscher 1934, 111
24 Hölscher 1939 102
25 Martin 1993, 85
26 Martin 1993, 61
27 Hölscher 1939, 65

CHAPTER 8

1. Dodson & Hilton 2004, 160
2. Dodson 2000, 119
3. Tyldesley 2000, 35
4. Tyldesley 2000, 36
5. Aldred 1968, 101
6. Schulman 1965a, 66
7. Tyldesley 2000, 37
8. Breasted 1906, 35-6
9. Tyldesley 2002, 218
10. Van Dijk 2000, 294
11. Tyldesley 2000, 36
12. Clayton 1996, 140
13. Van Dijk 2000, 295
14. Reeves & Wilkinson 1997, 134-5
15. Clayton 1996, 141
16. Tyldesley 2000, 38
17. Clayton 1996, 141
18. Hawass 2004, 12
19. Bickerstaffe 2009, 100
20. Bickerstaffe 2009, 41
21. Tyldesley 2000, 36
22. Gardiner 1953, 22
23. Van Dijk 2000, 297
24. Van Dijk 2000, 287
25. Tyldesley 2000, 34
26. OCairo 25646
27. Phillips 1977, 116
28. Van Dijk 2000, 295
29. Phillips 1977, 120
30. Dodson & Hilton 2004, 156

FURTHER READING

Aldred C. 1957: *The End of the El-Amarna Period* in Journal of Egyptian Archaeology 43 p.30-41
Aldred C. 1968: *Two Monuments of the Reign of Horemheb* in Journal of Egyptian Archaeology 54 p.100-6
Arbouw E. 2008: *Pottery sherds shatter timeline ancient Egypt* www.uk.rug.nl/archief/jaargang37/32/20b.php
Arnold D. 2003: *The Encyclopaedia of Ancient Egyptian Architecture*. London. IB Tauris
Aström P. 1979: A Faience Sceptre with the cartouche of Horemheb in Karageorghis V. et al (Eds) *Studies presented in memory of Porphyrios Dikaios*. Nicosia, Cyprus: Lions Club of Nicosia (Cosmopolitan)
Azim M. 1982: Découverte de Dépôts de Fondation D'Horemheb au IXe Pylône de Karnak in *Cahiers de Karnak VII; 1978-1982*. Paris. Edtions Reserche sur les civilisations. 93-120
Baines J. and Malek J. 1980: *Ancient Egyptian Atlas*. Oxford. Facts on File
Bickerstaffe D. 2009: *Refugees for Eternity; The Royal Mummies of Thebes. Part four; Identifying the Mummies*. Canopus Press
Bietak M. 1979: *Avaris and Pi-Ramesse: Archaeological exploration in the Eastern Nile Delta*. London. Proceedings of the British Academy
Bietak M. 2009: Perrunefer: the principal New Kingdom naval base in Egyptian Archaeology 34 Spring p.15-17
Booth C. 2007: *The Boy Behind the Mask: The Life and Times of Tutankhamun*. Oxford. Oneworld Publishing
Breasted J.H. 1906: *Ancient Records of Egypt: historical documents from the earliest times to the Persian conquest*. Chicago. Chicago University Press
Brier B. 1994: *Egyptian Mummies; unravelling the secrets of an ancient art*. London. Michael O'Mara Books
Brier B. 1999: *The Murder of Tutankhamen: A 3000-year-old Murder Mystery*. London. Phoenix
Bryce T.R. 1990: The Death of Niphururiya and its Aftermath in Journal of Egyptian Archaeology 76 p.97-105
Clayton P. 1994: *Chronicle of the Pharaohs*. London. Thames and Hudson
Cross S.W. 2009: The Hydrology of the Valley of the Kings, Egypt in The Heritage of Egypt vol 2 No 1 Issue 4 p.5-23
Davies T.M. 2001 (Reprint) *The Tombs of Harmhabi and Touatânkhamanou*. London. Duckworth Egyptology
Davies, N de Garis, 1908: *The Rock Tombs of el-Amarna; Part 5, Smaller tombs and boundary stelae*. London, Egypt Exploration Fund
Desroches-Noblecourt C. 1971 *Tutankhamen: life and death of a pharaoh*. London. Penguin
Dodson A. 2000: *Monarchs of the Nile*. Cairo. American University in Cairo

Dodson A. 2005: Bull Cults in Ikram S. (Ed) 2005: *Divine Creatures; animal mummies in ancient Egypt Cairo*. American University Press in Cairo

Dodson A. and Hilton D. 2004: *The Complete Royal Families of Ancient Egypt*. London. Thames & Hudson

Doherty P. 2004: *An Evil Spirit out of the West*. London. Headline

Dollings W. 2007: Tell el-Amarna 2006-7; South Tombs Cemetery in Journal of Egyptian Archaeology 93 p.11-35

Eaton-Krauss M. 1988: Tutankhamun at Karnak in MDAIK 44 p.1-11

El Mahdy C. 1999: *Tutankhamen: The Life and Death of the Boy-King*. London. Headline

Eyre C. 2002: *The Cannibal Hymn; a cultural and literary study*. Liverpool. Liverpool University Press

Fletcher J. 2000 *Chronicle of a Pharaoh: the intimate life of Amenhotep III*. Oxford. Oxford University Press

Fletcher J. 2004: *The Search for Nefertiti*. London. Hodder and Stoughton

Gardiner A. 1905: *The Inscription of Mes*. Leipzig. J.C. Hinrichs'sche Buchhandlung p.11, inscription p.52

Gardiner A. 1916: Three Engraved Plaques in the Collection of the Lord of Carnarvon', in Journal of Egyptian Archaeology 3: 73-5

Gardiner A. 1928: The Graffito from the tomb of Pere in Journal of Egyptian Archaeology 14 p.10-11

Gardiner A. 1947: *Egyptian Onomastica*. Oxford. Oxford University Press

Gardiner A. 1953: The Coronation of King Haremhab in Journal of Egyptian Archaeology 39 p.13-31

Gardiner A. 1961: *Egypt of the Pharaohs*. Oxford. Oxford University Press

Glanville S.R.K. 1927: Note on the Nature and Date of the 'Papyri' of Nakht, BM 10471 and 10473 in Journal of Egyptian Archaeology 13 p.50-6

Habachi L. 1979: Unknown or Little-known Monuments of Tutankhamun and his Viziers in Ruffle J., Gaballa G.A., and Kitchen K. (Eds) *Glimpses of ancient Egypt: studies in honour of H.W. Fairman* Warminster, Aris & Phillips p.32-41

Hari R. 1964: *Horemheb et La Reine Moutnedjemet; ou la fin d'une dynastie*. Genève. Imprimerie La Sirène

Hari R. 1985: Un monument Cypriote D'Horemheb in Bondi S.F., Pernigotti S., Serra A., Vivian F (Eds) *Studi in onore di Edda Bresciani*. Pisa. Giardini Editori E Stampatori in Pisa p.249-53

Harris J. 1968, How Long was the Reign of Horemheb in Journal of Egyptian Archaeology 54 p.95-99

Harris J. & Weeks K. 1973, *X-raying the pharaohs*. New York. Scribner

Harris J.R. 2007: Historie-forvrængning in Papyrus 27 (Dec 07) p.24-29

Hawass Z. 2004: King Ramses I returns to his homeland in Horus January March. 9-13 Egyptair in-house magazine

Hölscher U. 1932: *Excavations in Ancient Thebes 1930/1*. Chicago. University of Chicago Press

Hölscher U. 1939: *The Excavation of Medinet Habu Vol II; The temples of the eighteenth dynasty*. Chicago. University of Chicago Press

Huppertz et al 2009: Nondestructive Insights into Composition of the Sculpture of Egyptian Queen Nefertiti with CT. in Radiology 251 Number 1 p.233-40

James S. 2003: Duelling Nefertitis in KMT Vol 14; No 3 p.22-29

Janssen J. & Janssen R. 1990: *Growing up in Ancient Egypt*. London. Rubicon

Johnson. W.R. 1992: *An Asiatic Battle Scene of Tutankhamun from Thebes: A late Amarna Antecedent of the Ramesside Battle Narrative*. Unpublished PhD Thesis. University of Chicago p.12

Kamil J. 1993: *Aswan and Abu Simbel; History and Guide.* Cairo. American Univeity Press in Cairo

Kitchen K.A. 1987: The Basics of Egyptian Chronology in Relation to the Bronze Age in Aström P. (Ed) *High, middle or low?: acts of an international colloquium on absolute chronology held at the University of Gothenburg, 20th-22nd August 1987.* Gothenburg: P. Åströms Forlag p.37-55

Klemm D.D. and Klemm R. 2001: The Building stones of ancient Egypt – a gift of its geology in African Earth Sciences 33 p.631-642

Lesko L. 1977: *King Tut's wine cellar.* Berkeley. B.C. Scribe Publications

Lichtheim M. 1973: *Ancient Egyptian Literature. Vol. 1; The Old and Middle Kingdom.* Berkeley. University of California Press. 185

Lichtheim M. 1976: *Ancient Egyptian Literature. Vol. II; The New Kingdom.* Berkeley. University of California Press p.171

Luban M. 1999: *Do we have the mummy of Nefertiti?* www.geocities.com/Athens/Crete/3102/do_we_have_.htm

Mahfouz N. 2000: *Dweller in Truth.* Bantam Doubleday Dell Publishing Group

Martin G. 1976: Excavations at the Memphite Tomb of Horemheb, 1975; Prelimnary Report in Journal of Egyptian Archaeology 62 p.5-13

Martin G. 1978: Excavations at the Memphite Tomb of Horemheb, 1977: Preliminary Report in Journal of Egyptian Archaeology 64 p.5-16

Martin G. 1978a: The Tomb of Horemheb; Commander in chief to Tutankhamun in Archaeology 31 No 4 p.14-23

Martin G. 1982: Tutankhamun's Commander-in-Chief and his Memphite Tomb in Popular Archaeology 3 No 9 p.27-30

Martin G. 1988: Three Objects of New Kingdom Date from the Memphite Area and Sidmant in Baines J., James T.G.H., Leahy A., Shore A.F. (eds) *Pyramid Studies and Other Essays Presented to I.E.S. Edwards.* London. Egypt Exploration Society Ocasional Pulication 7 p.114-20

Martin G. 1993: *The Hidden Tombs of Memphis.* London. Thames and Hudson

Montserrat D. 2000: *Akhenaten; History, fantasy and ancient Egypt.* London. Routledge

Murray M. 1931: *Egyptian Temples.* London. Sampson Low, Marston and co. Ltd

Murnane W.J. 1990: *The Road to Kadesh.* Chicago. Oriental Institute of the University of Chicago

Nelson H. & Hölscher U. 1934: *Work in Western Thebes 1931-4.* Chicago. University of Chicago Press

Newberry P. 1925: A Duplicate Text of Horemheb's Coronation Inscription in Ancient Egypt X p.4

Panagiotakopulu E. 2004: Pharaonic Egypt and the origins of plague in Journal of Biogeopgraphy 31 p.269-75

Panagiotakpoulu E. & Buckland P.C. 1999: Climex lectularius L., the common bed bug from Pharaonic Egypt in Antiquity 73 p.908-911

Panagiotakpoulu E. 2001: Fleas from Pharaonic Amarna in Antiquity 75 p.499-500

Panagiotakpoulu E. 2004: Pharaonic Egypt and the origins of plague in Journal of Biogeography 31 p.269-275

Partridge R. 2002: *Fighting Pharaohs.* Manchester. Peartree Publishing.

Pfluger K. 1946: The Edict of King Haremheb, in JNES 5 p.260-68

Phillips A.K. 1977: Horemheb, Founder of the XIXth dynasty; O.Cairo 25646 reconsidered in Orientalia 46 p.116-121

Porter B. & Moss R. 1951; *Topographical Bibliography VII. Nubia the deserts and outside Egypt.* Oxford. Clarendon Press

Porter B. & Moss R. 1964; *Topographical Bibliography I. The Theban Necropolis Part 2; Royal Tombs and Smaller Cemeteries.* Oxford Clarendon Press

Pusch E.1991: Recent work at Piramesse in Bleiberg E. and Freed R. (Eds) *Fragments of a Shattered Visage; the proceedings of the international Symposium of Ramesses the Great*. Memphis. Memphis State University p.199-213

Redford D. 1973: A new dated inscription from the reign of Horemheb, in Journal of the Society for the Study of Egyptian Antiquities 4 (1973), pp.6-23

Redford D. 1984: *Akhenaten, the heretic king*. Princeton. Princeton University Press

Redford D.B. 1992: *Egypt, Canaan and Israel in Ancient Times*. Cairo. American University in Cairo Press

Reeves N. 2005: *Akhenaten; Egypt's false Pharaoh*. London. Thames and Hudson

Reeves N. & Wilkinson R.H. 1997: *The Complete Valley of the Kings*. London Thames and Hudson

Reisner G. 1920: The Viceroys of Ethiopia in Journal of Egyptian Archaeology 6 pp.73-88

Samson J. 1985: *Nefertiti and Cleopatra*. Queen-Monarchs of Ancient Egypt. London. The Rubicon Press

Schaden O. 1977: *The God's Father Ay*. London. University Microfilms International.

Schulman A.R. 1965: Excursus on the 'Military Officer' Nakhtmin in JARCE III p.124-126

Schulman A.R. 1965a: The Berlin 'Trauerrelief' (No. 12411) and some officials of Tutankhamun and Ay in JARCE IV p.55-68

Seele K.C. 1955: King Ay and the close of the Amarna Age in JNES 14 p.168-180

Sidro M. 2006: *Der Felstempel von Abu'Oda; Eine architektonische und ikonographische Untersuchung*. Hamberg. Verlag, Dr

Spalinger A.J. 2005: *War in ancient Egypt; the New Kingdom*. Oxford. Blackwell

Spencer A.J. 1989: *Excavations at El-Ashmunein II: The Temple Area*. London. British Museum Press

Thiem A-C. 2000: *Speos von Gebel es-Silsileh: Analyse der architektonischen und ikonographischen Konzeption im Rahmen des politischen und legitimatorischen Programmes der Nachamarnazeit*. Wiesbaden: Harrassowitz in Kommission

Trigger et al. 1994: *Ancient Egypt: a social history*. Cambridge. Cambridge University Press

Tyldesley J. 1996: *Hatchepsut: the female pharaoh*. London. Penguin

Tyldesley J. 2000: *Judgement of the Pharaoh*. London. Penguin

Tyldesley J. 2000a: *The Private Lives of the Pharaohs*. London. Channel Four Books

Tyldesley J. 2002: *Egypt's Golden Empire*. London. Review

Tyldesley J. 2005: *Nefertiti; unlocking the mystery surrounding Egypt's most famous and beautiful queen*. London. Penguin

Uphill E.P. 1984: *The Temples of Per Ramesses*. Wiltshire. Aris and Phillips Ltd

Van Dijk J. 1996: Horemheb and the Struggle for the Throne of Tutankhamun in BACE 7 p.29-42

Van Dijk J. 2008: Abstract – New evidence on the length of the reign of Horemheb

Wente E. 1968, Review of Hari 'Horemheb et la reine Moutnedjemet ou la fin d'une dynastie in Journal of American Oriental Society Vol 88

Wilkinson R. 2000: *The Complete Temples of Ancient Egypt*. London. Thames and Hudson p.228

Wilkinson T. 2007: *Lives of the Ancient Egyptians*. London. Thames and Hudson

Winfield Smith R. 1976: Interpretation and Discoveries in *The Akhenaten Temple Project Vol I*. Warminster. Aris and Phillips p.19-57

INDEX

Abahuda 111, 113
Africanus 17
Ahmose I 19, 20, 127, 141, 145
Ahmose-Nefertari 146
Akhenaten 15-17, 19-24, 26-30, 32, 33, 45, 47, 48, 49, 50, 51, 63, 64, 65, 67, 73, 75, 80, 83-87, 94-97, 99, 104, 106, 111, 120-124, 145, 147
Akhenaten Temple Project 99
Akhmin 67, 79
Amarna Letters 19, 23, 73
Amenhotep I 146
Amenhotep II 92, 104, 105, 115, 144, 27, 39
Amenhotep III 19, 20-24, 29, 30, 32, 33, 46, 63, 65-67, 73, 76, 79, 80, 87, 90, 94, 96, 104, 105, 115, 144
Amenia 128, 138, 41, 42, 44, 60, 83, 97, 88
Amka 71, 73, 74
Ankhesenamun 34, 65, 69, 70, 71, 74, 75, 79, 84, 85, 98, 106, 121
Apis Bull 96, 271
Aswan Dam 111
Aten 15, 20, 21, 23, 24, 26, 29, 30, 31, 32, 33, 45, 47, 50, 64, 80, 83, 94, 95, 96, 97, 104, 109
Atum 20, 21, 93, 109, 139, 141, 142
Avaris 19, 20, 142
Babylon 21, 22
Bek 45
Bintanath 144
Boundary Stela 24, 25, 46
Buhen 114, 142
Cannibal Hymn 96
Canopic Jar 88, 96, 131
Christie, Agatha 16
Coffin 27, 60, 83, 87, 131, 133, 144
Co-regent 20, 22, 23, 27, 29, 67, 141, 144
Coronation Stela 91
CT Scan 28, 31
Cyprus 115, 116
Dahamunzu 71, 73, 74
Djoser 59
Doherty, Paul 16
Edict 98, 116, 118, 119, 120, 139

El Ashmunein 49
Flood 50, 79, 99, 137
Foundation Deposit 50, 79, 99, 137
Gebel Adda 111
Gebel Ahmar 45-46
Gebel el Silsileh 45, 46, 49, 105, 109, 111, 112, 121, 137
Golden Flies 37
Hansu 33, 34, 38, 82, 91, 96, 142, 147
Harem 21, 34, 65, 91, 118
Hatshepsut 19, 20, 92, 106, 109, 123, 145
Hatti 70, 73, 74, 75, 122
Hattusha 30, 75
Heliopolis 20, 51, 58, 96, 142
Herakleopolis 33, 34
Hittite 23, 30, 48, 49, 69, 70, 71, 73, 74, 75, 76, 79, 83, 84, 120, 122
Hyksos 19, 20, 75, 144, 145
Hypostyle Hall 79, 98, 99, 101, 104, 137, 142
it ntr 65, 66
Kadashman-Edil 22
Kadesh 20, 73
Karnak 19, 21, 22, 23, 26, 34, 45, 50, 55, 80, 82, 85, 91, 92, 94, 95, 97, 98, 100, 101, 102, 103, 104, 105, 106, 109, 114, 116, 121, 125, 137, 142, 144
Kiya 28, 30, 65, 67
Kush 22, 68, 69, 121
Luxor 21, 22, 38, 39, 40, 42, 77, 79, 80, 81, 91, 92, 93, 104, 105, 106, 107, 114, 115, 144, 145
Maat 50, 52, 71, 76, 83, 98, 119, 120, 139, 141, 145
Mahfouz, Naguib 16
Mai 45, 46
Manetho 16, 76, 124, 144, 146,
Megiddo 20
Memphis 20, 24, 31, 34, 37, 38, 45, 58, 59, 69, 76, 88, 90, 91, 96, 105, 115, 127, 128, 139, 141, 142
Memphite tomb 44, 50, 51, 52, 55, 57, 59, 60, 61, 68, 76, 83, 87, 129, 132, 135, 138, 139,
Merenptah 17
Mes 124, 125

Mitanni 21, 73
Mortuary Temple 22, 53, 54, 79, 80, 105
Mummy 28, 131, 132, 133, 144, 145
Museum of Art Niagara Falls 144
Musilli 73
Mutnodjmet 79, 83, 85, 86, 87, 88, 89, 90, 97, 98, 106, 238, 248, 246
Nakhtmin 58, 67, 68
Nefertiti 15, 24, 26, 27, 28, 29, 30, 50, 65, 71, 84, 85, 86, 87, 90, 99, 104
Nibhuruiya 73
Nubia 37, 45, 53, 65, 67, 68, 69, 80, 94, 111, 113, 142
Opet Festival 80, 81, 85, 90, 105, 106, 107, 144
Oracle 22, 82, 85,
Osiris Bed 135
Paatenemheb 32, 33, 59
Paster Stela 29, 68
Perunefer 115
Plague 30, 70, 74, 75, 83
Pramesses 114, 124, 139
Ptahemhat-Ty 82
Punt 122, 123
Pylon 22, 23, 50, 59, 60, 79, 88, 99, 100, 102, 103, 104, 105, 114, 116, 121, 122, 137, 142
Qantir 114, 115, 141, 142,
Ramose 44, 46, 146
Ramses I 17, 18, 44, 96, 98, 101, 114, 133, 138, 139, 140, 141, 142, 143, 144, 145, 146
Ramses II 15, 17, 18, 34, 50, 63, 75, 98, 99, 101, 104, 106, 111, 124, 127, 133, 137, 138, 139, 142, 144, 145, 146
Ramses III 20, 111, 123, 127, 128, 137, 138
Redford's Bowl 125, 127
Red-ware vessels 83
Restoration Stela 51, 98
Royal Cache
  DB320 144
Rpat 57, 58, 60, 63, 67, 75, 82
Sarcophagus 60, 130, 131, 132, 143, 144
Satire of the Trades 34, 36
Sementawy 43, 44, 52
Seqenenre Tao 19, 75
Seth 82, 83, 113, 114, 135, 142, 147
Sety I 75, 98, 99, 101, 104, 114, 115, 118,
Shabti 89, 128
Sharuhen 20
shebyu collars 37, 46, 55, 65, 120, 139, 140
Sile 20, 34, 117, 118, 139, 142
Sitre 139
Smenkhkare 16, 17, 27, 28, 29, 30, 65, 67, 96, 97, 124, 145
Speos 111
Sphinx (Giza) 21, 128

Sphinx Avenue 80, 105
Suppiluliumas 23, 71, 73, 83
Syria 20, 21, 26, 73, 98, 122
Talatat 45, 52, 53, 55, 99, 103, 104
Tax 118, 119
Tell el Amarna 24, 26
Temple 19, 20, 22, 23, 26, 27, 29, 34, 35, 45, 46, 50, 53, 54, 59, 60, 65, 66, 67, 79, 80, 81, 83, 88, 91, 94, 95, 96, 97, 98, 99, 104, 105, 106, 107, 108, 109, 111, 113, 114, 118, 121, 122, 125, 128, 135, 136, 137, 138, 142, 144
Temple-tomb 59, 60
Theban Tombs 29, 125
TT139 29
TT19 96
TT50 125
Thebes 19, 22, 24, 29, 31, 38, 45, 46, 53, 55, 63, 66, 75, 80, 91, 95, 96, 97, 105, 106, 121, 146
Thutmosis II 20
Thutmosis III 19, 20, 24, 39, 105, 106, 108, 109, 123
Tia-Sitre 139
Tiy 65, 66, 67, 79, 84, 85, 137
Tiye 20, 23, 27, 30, 63, 65, 66, 67, 87, 90
~~Tiye~~
Trauerrelief 58, 69, 82
Tutankhamun 15-32, 37, 44-60, 62-71. 73-76, 79, 80-87, 95-99, 106, 107, 108, 115, 116, 124, 125, 128, 131, 133, 135, 137, 139, 142, 143, 145, 146, 147
Ugarit 115, 116
Uluburun Shipwreck 116
Uronaroti 37
Valley of the Kings 64, 83, 87, 97, 109, 122, 125, 126, 128, 130, 133, 134, 143
  KV55 27, 97
  KV62 58, 97, 98, 134
  KV57 122, 128, 130, 131, 134, 143
  KV35 27, 144
  KV16 143
  KV14 133
Valley of the Queens 139
  QV38 139
Viceroy 65, 68, 69
Wadi Halfa 141
Wawat 69, 121
Wet-nurse 65, 85
Window of Appearances 65, 76, 120
Wine 87, 88, 115, 116, 126, 127
Zennanza 69, 70, 71, 73, 74, 75